LOOKING BACK AT WHITE BEAR LAKE

LOOKING BACK AT WHITE BEAR LAKE
A Pictorial History of the White Bear Lake Area

Cynthia E. Vadnais

"All historical thinking involves tinkering with the lenses that shine the light of other days into our lives."

Richard F. Snow

Looking Back at White Bear Lake – A Pictorial History of the White Bear Lake Area

© 2004 by Cynthia E. Vadnais
White Bear Stereoptics Co.

All rights reserved. No part of this book may be used or reproduced in any form without written permission. This includes any electronic or mechanical means, including, but not limited to, photocopying or any information storage and retrieval system.
For information, write: Cynthia E. Vadnais, 1862 N. 22nd St., Laramie, WY 82072.

Published 2004.
First Edition.

Printed by Sentinel Printing Company, Inc.

Chief editor: Kathy Evertz
Consulting editors: Saralyn Laughlin, Steve Costin, and Jeanette Reisenburg.
Historical editor: Sara Markoe Hanson.

Cover photo: Circa 1870 Lake Superior and Mississippi Railroad Depot at White Bear Lake.
Source: Cynthia Vadnais

Printed in the United States of America.

ISBN: 0-9755443-0-6

To my husband, Steve,

My family,

My friends,

and

All the people of White Bear Lake

Contents

Foreword IX
Preface XI
Introduction XIII
Indian Legends 1
John Carbutt and Company 5
Indian Mound Versus Progress 9
Manitou Island 15
Summer Resorts and Hotels 23
Cottage Park Clubhouse 51
Dolce Far Niente 57
The Red Chalet 65
Mr. Wilkinson's Cottage 69
Trains to Automobiles 71
Truman Ward Ingersoll 85
White Bear Yacht Club 91
Boat Builders 101
Ramaley's Lake Shore Pavilion 109
Lake Steamers and Naphtha Launches 115
Wildwood Park 121
St. Paul Automobile Club 139
The Plantation 145
Sir Aubrey John Paul and Lady Laura Paul 151
Early Community Churches 153
Schools 171
Looking Down Railroad (Washington) Avenue 187
Looking Down Third Street 215
U. S. Post Office 243
Looking Down Fourth Street 249
Looking Down Banning Avenue 283
Looking Down Clark Avenue 295
White Bear Fire Department 305
White Bear Lake Public Library 313
Parks, Players, Pike and Plays: Pleasant Pastimes 317
Bald Eagle Lake Area 335
Mahtomedi Area 341
Stormy Weather 357
Bibliography 361
Index 365

FOREWORD

My connection to the history of this area began when I was very young. Growing up in a home that once sheltered the first postmaster of White Bear Lake, I was able to envision the Indians who much earlier had traveled the paths on the crest of the lake's bank as I myself meandered down Lake Avenue to a Sunday tour of the Fillebrown House. Countless trips to the dime store and "the" bank uptown conjure images of what these places once housed or where their predecessors and counterparts were located. My mother and father's stories brought me to know buildings by the merchants they would have housed in the 1940s, '50s and '60s like Greengard's and Kohler's Romance Parlors.

My own childhood was not that far in the past, but it was full of references to White Bear's early days. My ancestors came to White Bear Lake for the first time before the State of Minnesota or White Bear Township was organized in 1858. They were attracted to this area by the lakes the same way families are still 150 years later.

In our house, stories of my ancestors and the other families of this area were common. It was almost as though these people were still living nearby. I never knew many of the individuals, but I certainly knew about them. These stories live on in my memory, but they may often be just that — stories without verification.

I routinely tell people that historical research is "hit or miss." One may uncover a gold mine of information or one may search indefinitely for such facts that seemingly should be there but do not exist. To be a responsible historian there must be a respect for accuracy. Often, this drive not just to tell a story, but to corroborate it with primary source materials can delay or defeat a project. Fortunately, for the people of White Bear Lake that is not the case here. With a healthy dose of painstaking research, this volume strives to be as accurate as the sources allow.

The historical record of the people and the built environment around White Bear Lake is no different than many other communities. Much is represented and some is not. What is rather unusual is the quantity of images and information that has survived. As a whole, the people of this area recognize our strong heritage and place a high value on that connection to the past. As a local historical society and as a community we should be thankful for that gift to us and carry on that legacy for the future. Our history is brought alive in the pages that follow through images and the surviving narrative. Without first acknowledging the past how can we clearly see the future? This community has a grand future.

Sara Markoe Hanson
Executive Director
White Bear Lake Area Historical Society

PREFACE

A number of years ago, my husband, J. Steve Costin, and I started collecting stereoviews, an early photographic format. I found that there were many interesting images of White Bear that I had no idea existed. My interest was sparked, and I started seeking out stereoviews, along with other images and information, pertaining to White Bear Lake.

As my White Bear Lake collection grew, my thoughts turned to deciding what I would eventually do with all that I had amassed. Rather than keep these rich resources to myself, I decided to create a pictorial history of the area so the photographs could be enjoyed by all.

I never understood why a pictorial history of the area had not been done before until I started working on it and realized that without the technology we have today, this would have been an almost insurmountable task. Even with the technology, the project was often daunting.

Although I've not lived in White Bear Lake for more than twenty years, much of my family is there, and I'm fortunate to be able to spend a number of months each year enjoying the place where I grew up. As I researched information for the book and continued to gather more images, I found that, even though most of the history comes before my birth, I felt so much closer to the town I left in 1982. Creating this book has drawn me nearer to, and made me more appreciative of, the unique location called White Bear Lake. No matter where I live, in my heart it will always be my home. Maybe I'm biased, but none compare.

It is possible there are historical errors in this book due to contradictions among my sources. I have tried to be as accurate as circumstances allow, given the fact that much of my source material pre-dates the oldest residents of White Bear Lake. If you find any inaccuracies in my book, I will gladly correct them in any subsequent printing.

I would like to thank the following people and organizations who so graciously gave me permission to use their photographic images. Without their generosity, this book would not have been possible:

Julie Ahlman	Bob Thein
Ray Asmus	Beverly (Wallerick) Vadnais
Willard Bibeau	Jack Vadnais
Lorraine Billingsley	Richard Vadnais
Bill Dillon	Robert Vadnais Family
Dick Hanson	Lawrence R. Whitaker Family
Independent School District 832	White Bear Lake Area Historical Society
Ruth Mattlin	*White Bear Press*, Gene Johnson
St. John in the Wilderness Episcopal Church	Tom and Leona Whitrock

My enthusiasm for the history of White Bear Lake does not end with this book. I welcome dialogue with anyone else who shares this passion. Write me at 1862 N. 22nd St., Laramie, WY 82072 or email me at cosvad@earthlink.net.

Cynthia E. Vadnais

INTRODUCTION
Written by J. Steve Costin

    This book is the product of an intense love for a small, Minnesota resort town, and a generation whose world view was shaped by the pages of *Life* and *Look* magazines. Each picture was indeed worth a thousand words. We could ponder, at leisure, the joy, fear, desperation, hopes, love, and hate in the faces, frozen forever, in the blink of the camera's shutter. On the surface, this volume is an assemblage of illustrations, with text used to define, explain, and add a bit of human perspective. But with a little historical imagination, one can slip from a visual history of the White Bear Lake area into the history of photography, or how a small town reflected the ebb and flow of American history, or how the great American drama is played out by hundreds of our ancestors.

    The oldest images of the White Bear Lake area are stereoviews, one of the earliest mass media. Beginning in the 1850s, enterprising photographers would haul hundreds of pounds of equipment to exotic locations and once-in-a-lifetime events. They would photograph, then develop and sell, hundreds, or even thousands, of three-dimensional copies all over the world. Looking at the pair of photos through a stereoscope was almost like being there. As manufacturing efficiency allowed ever cheaper stereoviews, most middle-class families could stare, awestruck, at disasters, wars, exotic people, and homely expressions of American ideals, all in the comfort of their parlors.

    The postcard severely wounded the popularity of the stereoview. It was much cheaper for the local photographer to produce than its older cousin, either in mass quantity or in small numbers. One could stick a penny stamp on it, along with a note on the back, and drop it in a mailbox.

    In 1888 George Eastman introduced his box camera. "You push the button, we'll do the rest." The democratization of photography had started. Its legacy is hundreds of millions of snapshots fading in attics and basements, unidentified and unlamented. Those that are identifiable present an intimate view of what was important to the many participants of history.

    From John Carbutt's visit in 1866 through Truman Ward Ingersoll's comic scenes, White Bear Lake was well surveyed stereographically. They chronicle a budding resort town. These are the "official stereographs," designed to increase trade for the railroads, hotels, and lake steamers. The people in these three-dimensional pairs represent Summit Avenue kicking off its Victorian shoes. Gone are the top hats, bowlers, starched collars, voluminous silk dresses, and multiple petticoats. These folks had escaped the bonds of St. Paul society, an all encompassing code that buttoned-up behavior tighter than the whalebone corset that was a symbol of the era.

    The half-stereoview of the Getty family, on page 227, is the "unofficial" art of stereo photography. A fairly well-to-do family, in this case a nascent merchant baron, would hire a photographer to take the family portrait. Exposures would require so much light that the entire family would sit out in front of their house. The image invites the viewer into their lives, but the mysteries remain. Does the arrangement represent a family dynamic? Wife number two is in the foreground while poor sister Ida is relegated to the background.

As the Gilded Age drew to a close, the wealthy built cottages and moved their households to the lake for the summer. A less prosperous class of managers, shopkeepers, teachers and young professionals filled the hotels, and a whole new class of clerks, tellers, mechanics, and skilled laborers, who had enough money and leisure time, crowded trains and streetcars for day trips away from the smoky, sweltering city. They filled Ramaley's Pavilion and Wildwood Amusement Park. The era of mass transit had begun, and it required a new, cheap mass medium to display it. Daytrippers began to buy cheap postcards by the tens of thousands, and they brought the ubiquitous Kodak camera. As newspapers began publishing photos, a new immediacy was added. Every event deemed newsworthy would be covered by an "expert." From a parade of manure spreaders in 1914, the *White Bear Press* documented events, momentous and mundane. But it is the lowly snapshot, the moments captured by a box camera, that breathes life into this collection. These are the folks who poured their souls into creating a vibrant community surrounding a lake in the suburbs of St. Paul.

The township of White Bear Lake was surveyed in 1847. By 1851 a petition was presented for a road between St. Paul and White Bear Lake. According to a retrospective in the *White Bear Press,* it wasn't until 1858 that $30 was appropriated to survey a road.

When Minnesota entered the Union in 1858 the township was organized (thirty-six square miles), with twenty-seven votes cast. The township already had the Barnum Hotel (1854), the Murray House (1857), a schoolhouse (1857), the Aubrey's home, and a number of log cabins belonging to the early settlers of the area. White Bear township had grown to 267 by 1860.

The end of the Civil War had brought long-lasting effects to Minnesota. "King Corn" had replaced "King Cotton," and war had pushed America squarely into the industrial age. Rails pushed north from St. Paul to Duluth to ship flour via the Great Lakes, and to bring lumber back to the Twin Cities. The railroad passed through White Bear in 1868. In 1874 a roundhouse was built to accommodate expanding rail service. The railroad assured the success of the lake area. It provided efficient transportation from St. Paul for the resorts in the summer months, and it provided a fairly well-paid workforce to help keep the economy rolling year round. Lumber mills had access to the Twin Cities; ice companies could harvest all winter to provide for refrigerator cars; boatmakers had a wider reach for their clientele; and carpenters, plasterers and bricklayers built cottages, hotels, and shops.

Between 1875 and 1880 the township's population climbed from 647 to 1,135 (435 in the village of White Bear). Assessed property values grew from $62,361 to $265,962 between 1860 and 1880.

By 1890, White Bear was boasting "5 hotels, 5 saloons, 3 depots, 2 bakeries, 1 physician, 1 attorney, 5 churches, 1 ice dealer, public library, graded streets, 1 drug store, good sidewalks, 2 real estate and insurance agencies, electric lights, 2 boat builders, 2 graded schools, 3 markets, 2 lumber yards, 1 livery stable, 3 secret societies, 1 hardware store, and 2 dry goods stores," according to A. H. S. Perkins in his book, *All About White Bear Lake*. All this was maintained by 1,500 residents.

Historian Frederick Lewis Allen evokes a crystalline image of resort towns at their peak:

> It was still the heyday of the big summer-resort hotel, to which well-to-do vacationists would come for a short stay, ranging usually from a week to a month: the shingled hotel with towers and turrets and whipping flags, with wide piazzas and interminable carpeted corridors, and with a vast dining room in which were served huge meals on the American plan, with a menu which took one from celery and olives through soup and fish and a roast to

ice cream, cake, and nuts and almonds, with sherbet as a cooling encouragement in mid-meal.

For those who could not afford such grandeur, there were boardinghouses innumerable, with schoolteachers rocking on the porch and a group of croquet players on the lawn; and, here and there along the seashore or the lakeside, crowded colonies of tiny shingled shacks, each labeled clearly with it sentimental or jocose name – "Bide-a-Wee Cottage," "Doocum Inn," or the like. But the overwhelming majority of Americans outside the upper income brackets stayed at home, through the full heat of summer. And being carriageless, they had to satisfy their holiday dreams by taking a special reduced-rate railroad tour by day-coach to Niagara Falls or Atlantic City; or, more likely, an occasional trip out of town in an open trolley car to the Trolley Park, an amusement park at the end of the line.

…For the small minority who were lucky enough to have a summer cottage to go to, the ritual of departure was complex. First, the city house would be put through a thorough cleaning and dismantling, a process that lasted for days. On Departure-Day-Minus-One the expressman called for the trunks, which were many; it would have astonished a family of the 1900 era to be told that in later years vacationists would manage for weeks with nothing but suitcases. On the fateful morning the family would grasp bags, overcoats, umbrellas, and such other possible incumbrances as fishing tackle, golf clubs, dog, cat, and caged canary, and proceed to the station in one or more horse-drawn cabs. Then came the long journey–either by Pullman car, incredibly grand with its elaborate paneling of the Chester A. Arthur vintage, or by open-platform daycoach, very cindery. Arrived in the neighborhood of Elysium, the family would dismount on the sunbaked board platform, assemble its belongings, and proceed in a big three-seater wagon (for the family and personal equipment) followed by an even larger wagon (for the trunks)…

On summer evenings, along the tree-lined streets of innumerable American towns, families sitting on their front porches would watch the fine carriages of the town as they drove past for a proud evening's jaunt, and the cognoscenti would wait eagerly for a glimpse of the banker's trotting pair or the sporting lawyer's 2:40 pacer. And one of the magnificent sights of urban life was that of a fire engine, pulled by three galloping horses, careening down a city street with its bell clanging.

Most of the year-round residents who serviced the elite lived on the other side of the tracks. They were the railroaders, saloonkeepers, cooks, housekeepers, carpenters, draymen, and blacksmiths, who toiled ten to twelve hours a day, six days a week. If they were lucky, they made about twenty-two cents an hour. The ambitious ones would start a business of their own while maintaining this grueling pace. This was the era of Horatio Alger; with ambition; pluck, and a little luck, each man could make a fortune. After all, "business was the business of America."

In 1900 there were fewer than fourteen-thousand automobiles in the entire country. Yet, we were on the verge of a revolution so profound, so ongoing, that one can't fully comprehend the effect that the car had on American culture. The auto industry provided impetus to many industrial giants: rubber tire makers, petroleum companies, headlight producers, glass companies, chemical companies, highway construction, motor hotels, drive-ins, shopping malls, drive-through banks, and golden miles of auto dealerships in every town of consequence. From the flivver on, the family dynamic, courtship patterns, and domestic legislative priorities changed forever. In White Bear Lake the St. Paul Automobile Club began building a bastion against pedestrian vigilantism, while the vehicles were still the toys of the rich. The town photos portray the transformation of blacksmith shops into auto repair and garage facilities, and then into full-fledged dealerships. An enterprising visionary might put in a gasoline pump or two in his front yard or in front of his store. These would grow into full-service, corporately badged fiefdoms competing for the automotive dollar. Then they would evolve once more into twenty gasoline pumps in front of the corner general store. Through photographs, we watch White Bear slowly lose its carriages, then its delivery wagons, its fire fighting carts, and its dray wagons, until there is nary a horse or smithy to be found. The railyards were eventually ripped up to make room for a highway from St. Paul, dooming both streetcars and rail passenger business.

The financial boom of the 1920s and the bust of the 1930s were neither as dazzling nor as dark for much of semi-rural America as it was in the financial and industrial centers. Agricultural prices tumbled as European demand disappeared after World War I, and the warring nations got back to growing their own foodstuffs. In an effort to maintain their income, American farmers grew more, further depressing the market. For a decade, agricultural purchasing power slipped behind that of their urban cousins. That is not to say the urbanites were doing that much better. The economy stuttered when war contracts were cancelled overnight, and nearly four-million veterans were dumped back into the job market. This resulted in the local press complaining about the surge in tramps and petty thefts in the area throughout the early twenties. The industrial output of the twenties nearly doubled, while the workforce barely grew at all. While corporate profits climbed 62 percent between 1923 and 1929, wages increased only 11 percent during the same period. Workers found themselves unable to afford the products they manufactured. Using figures from The Brookings Institution, economist Frederick Lewis Allen estimates almost sixty percent of American families fell below the poverty level. This is not to say Americans didn't spend. There was a dazzling array of choices: refrigerators, electric stoves, radios, vacuum cleaners, and cigarette lighters mass marketed through nickel magazines like the *Saturday Evening Post* and the ever-present radio. By the end of the twenties three-quarters of all radios and automobiles were being sold on the installment plan.

The standard of living achieved by the U.S. in this period was unparalleled in the world. Compared to the turn of the century, we spent more than twice as much on libraries, and three times as much on hospitals. In 1900, one in ten children reached high school; within three decades, 50 percent were attending. Life expectancy increased from forty nine to fifty nine in the same period. The Republicans continued their hold on Washington in 1928, sweeping into office with the slogan "A chicken in every pot, a car in every garage."

The White Bear area missed the convulsions that shook the larger cities from 1930 to 1933. As rail traffic plummeted, the railroads tried to maintain their infrastructure by keeping most employees part-time. As times got worse, everybody worked fewer hours; after all, the Northern Pacific Railroad would need their skills when the good times returned.

In the environs of White Bear one could hunt and fish a little more, as well as garden and raise a few chickens in the backyard. One could barter skills and products with neighbors. Churches provided much of the social cohesion, but family and friends could help keep each other going. Typically, folks would squeeze a penny tighter than they had before. Clothes were mended more, shoes had to last longer, meals had to stretch farther, rabbit replaced pork, and vegetables put up in fall carried a family through the winter. Even if they couldn't afford to go to the Plantation, couples could listen to the dances on the radio for free. Or one could slip into one of the two local movie palaces to escape the week's travails in air-conditioned darkness.

But the area's claim to fame in the twenties and early thirties was its status as a nice, quiet retreat for gangsters to unwind, and occasionally, to ventilate their competitors. The mobster's heyday abruptly ended with the Hamm's kidnapping in 1933.

Prohibition also provided a new cottage industry for enterprising locals, supplying moonshine to the Twin Cities, as well as the lake area speakeasys. The *White Bear Press* reported on one 1929 raid on Otter Lake, "Government agents, this forenoon, discovered within 3 miles of White Bear one of the biggest and most unique stills in this section of the country. The plant is on the Cardinal farm near Otter Lake, in an excavation in a hill in the woods. The excavation is said to be about 60x80 feet and contains 6 large vats of 10,000 gallons each, and two column stills, 30 feet high. The capacity of the plant is about 200 gallons a day. The alcohol distilled was selling at $5 per gallon, making a return of $1,000 per day. The heating was carried on with gasoline which avoided smoke appearing, while the fumes were carried off through a large hollow tree which had been lined with iron and conveniently set in position."

The two lasting monuments to the Great Depression and government effort to end it through massive public works were the Third Street Post Office and Highway 61.

World War II would finally end the Depression, and its aftermath would remap the face of the United States. The end of the war found a nation consumed with pent-up demand for all sorts of products. Soldiers were funneled back into the States and offered a chance to go to college, keeping many of them out of the job market during the switchover from a wartime to a peacetime economy. Finally the Veteran's Administration created the largest housing boom by guaranteeing home loans. Tract housing was born. Urban sprawl seemed limitless. The result is that the Twin Cities are second only to Los Angeles in spreading suburbs. From 1920 to 1950, the population of White Bear township grew steadily from 2,022 to 3,646. By 1957 the population had burgeoned to over thirteen-thousand, with another seven-thousand in the following decade. That meant new schools, new churches, and new and expanded government services. Supermarkets replaced corner stores. Shopping centers threatened downtown White Bear Lake, and they in turn were threatened by giant malls.

Downtown White Bear Lake managed to revitalize itself. As the old staples of American shopping, like Ben Franklin and Coast-to-Coast disappeared, they were replaced by boutiques and tony, upscale shops catering to an affluent bedroom community. Events like the weekly Marketfest now fill the area with shoppers. The city government had an extensive program of urban renewal, providing a uniform look, vaguely railroadesque.

The real strength of a book like this is that it puts a very human face on local history. Just as great-great grandparents were neighbors, generation's later their descendents still share a community. I studied the face of Father Joseph Goiffon, trying to fathom his personal strength and his religious zeal. He lost a leg and part of a foot to frostbite, yet he continued to serve the Catholic Church, whittling a new leg as needed. Fundraiser, architect, laborer: Goiffon built White Bear's Catholic church in two months. As I look at the pictures of the railway workers, I wonder how many would be killed, maimed, and scalded before the next picture was taken. These men worked in one of the most dangerous industries in the country at that time. Johann Johnson arrived from Oslo, Norway to work for Gus Amundson's boatworks. Within seven years Johnson had started his own boat shop. John Otto (Johann) Johnson had seized the brass ring. One of the most intriguing photos is of an early 1900s lumberyard. The Swedes wore light shirts and the French dark ones. It was a pragmatic, typically American solution to keep productivity and communication flowing. You knew at a glance with whom you could talk. Also in the photo is an ambitious young Frenchman, Prosper LeVasseur. LeVasseur would go on to open his own grocery store, enlarging it through the years and passing it on to his sons. It was a pattern repeated with children succeeding their parents in businesses that struggled and grew to substantial success. Family names like Amundson, Auger, Getty, Hanson, Jensen, Johnson, Kohler, Mackenhausen, Parenteau, and Vadnais defined family business.

I have spent so much time going over the photos that as I travel around the lake, I am sure I see your grandparents reflected in your eyes. And I see their dreams fulfilled in your successes.

Indian Legends

There is not much written history about the White Bear Lake area prior to 1851. The closest roads were no nearer than Little Canada and the lake was virtually unknown to whites. The only human inhabits were the American Indians. The Sioux (Dakota) and the Chippewa tribes probably used the areas surrounding the lake. Many legends have surfaced over the years about how White Bear Lake and Manitou Island got their names. Two of the more popular legends are given here. The first gives the lake its name and the second gives the island its name.

In 1883, Mark Twain's *Life on the Mississippi* was published. In it he writes of the legend of White-bear Lake.

Courtesy of the White Bear Press

Every spring, for perhaps a century, or as long as there has been a nation of red men, an island in the middle of White-bear Lake has been visited by a band of Indians for the purpose of making maple sugar.

Tradition says that many springs ago, while upon this island, a young warrior loved and wooed the daughter of his chief, and it is said, also, the maiden loved the warrior. He had again and again been refused her hand by her parents, the old chief alleging that he was no brave, and his old consort called him a woman!

The sun had again set upon the "sugar-bush," and the bright moon rose high in the bright blue heavens, when the young warrior took down his flute and went out alone, once more to sing the story of his love, the mild breeze gently moved the two gay feathers in his head-dress, and as he mounted on the trunk of a leaning tree, the damp snow fell from his feet heavily. As he raised his flute to his lips, his blanket slipped from his well-formed shoulders, and lay partly on the snow beneath. He began his weird, wild love-song, but soon felt that he was cold, and as he reached back for his blanket, some unseen hand laid it gently on his shoulders; it was the hand of his love, his guardian angel. She took her place beside him, and for the present they were happy; for the Indian has a heart to love, and in this pride he is as noble as in his own freedom, which makes him the child of the forest. As the legend runs, a large white-bear, thinking, perhaps, that polar snows and dismal winter weather extended everywhere, took up his journey southward. He at length approached the northern shore of the lake which now bears his name, walked down the bank and made his way noiselessly through the deep heavy snow toward the island. It was the same spring ensuing that the lovers met. They had left their first retreat, and were now seated among the branches of a large elm which hung far over the lake. (The same tree is still standing, and excites universal curiosity and interest.) For fear of being detected, they talked almost in a whisper, and now, that they might get back to camp in good time and thereby avoid suspicion, they were just rising to return, when the maiden uttered a shriek which was heard at the camp, and bounding toward the young brave, she caught his blanket, but missed the direction of her foot and fell, bearing the blanket with her into the great arms of the ferocious monster. Instantly every man, woman, and child of the band were upon the bank, but all unarmed. Cries and wailings went up from every mouth. What was to be done? In the meantime this white and savage beast held the breathless maiden in his huge grasp, and fondled with his precious prey as if he were used to scenes like this.

One deafening yell from the lover warrior is heard above the cries of hundreds of his tribe, and dashing away to his wigwam he grasps his faithful knife, returns almost at a single bound to the scene of fear and fright, rushes out along the leaning tree to the spot where his treasure fell, and springing with the fury of a mad panther, pounced upon his prey.

The animal turned, and with one stroke of his huge paw brought the lovers heart to heart, but the next moment the warrior, with one plunge of the blade of his knife, opened the crimson sluices of death, and the dying bear relaxed his hold.

That night there was no more sleep for the band or the lovers, and as the young and the old danced about the carcass of the dead monster, the gallant warrior was presented with another plume, and ere another moon had set he had a living treasure added to his heart. Their children for many years played upon the skin of the white-bear—from which the lake derives its name—and the maiden and the brave remembered long the fearful scene and rescue that made them one, for Kis-se-me-pa and Ka-go-ka could never forget their fearful encounter with the huge monster that came so near sending them to the happy hunting-ground.

Courtesy of the White Bear Press

Indian Legends of Minnesota, by Mrs. Carl T. Thayer, contains a different legend of White Bear Lake. The legend was submitted by Helen Stickley:

It was at the close of a warm summer day, in the Land of the Dakotas. As the blazing sun slowly sank to the western horizon, the squaws set about the preparation of the evening meal, around the camp fire. Suddenly the barking of dogs heralded the return of the hunting party. The shouts of the children added to the din and soon all was confusion in the camp. It was a great homecoming, for the hunt had been successful and the party was laden with buffalo and antelope. Chief Eagle Eye, riding at the head of his band, dismounted before the door of his wigwam, where he saw his lovely daughter, Naugawese, industriously grinding rice. She barely glanced at him, though the light in her dark wistful eyes betrayed the adoring love she felt for her father.

Now about this time Chingachouk, a Chippewa scout, was stealthily approaching the Camp of the Dakotas. Chingachouk was the son of a Chippewa Chieftain. He was a noble warrior, tall, strong, fleet of feet and the best archer of his band. He was trained in the cunning of woodcraft. While yet a youth he had successfully withstood all the tests for fortitude devised by his people. Long periods of fasting he had patiently endured as was the custom of his tribe. Every temptation of thirst and of hunger he had resisted. The test of fire and the test of water-all had fallen before his strong clean body, the courage of his soul. Many times his wisdom and his courage had made him the deliverer of his people. His knowledge of the woods and country had saved them from famine while his experience, as a scout, had made it possible for him to warn them against invading enemy.

The maiden Naugawese was at the spring in the glen drawing water for the evening meal; a twig snapped in the bush close by. Startled, she jumped, poised like a frightened fawn. But she saw nothing, so reassured, she started along the shady trail which led back to the camp. Suddenly there appeared in the path before her the lithe form of a young brave. It was Chingachouk, the Chippewa scout. Silently he gazed at her, fascinated by her beauty. Finally, gathering courage, she advanced to pass him, when he seized her in his arms, stifling her cries with his hand. He would bear her away with him. But some feeling, he know not what, made him release her. Like a deer, she sped toward the camp, but before she reached her father's wigwam, she slowed to a walk, her fright turned to wonder. "Who was the handsome warrior and whence came he?" That night and for many thereafter, Naugawese dreamed of him. She saw him in the smoke of a fire and he beckoned to her.

Less than a moon later, Eagle Eye called a council of his people. The Braves and the warriors responded to the beat of the tom tom. Soon many were gathered around the Council Fire. In the extreme outer circle hovered the women and children. Then their Chieftain, Eagle Eye, so magnificent in war paint and feathers, disclosed to them his plan for an immediate attack upon their enemy, the Chippewa. With shout and ceremonious dance the braves and warriors enthusiastically agreed to the proposal of their chief for an advance upon their foes before dawn. But one poor Dakotah maiden felt only grief and despair.

In the meantime Chingachouk, the Chippewa scout, was seated at the foot of a great oak in the forest. The solitude of the place quieted the tumult in his breast, while the swaying branches whispered to him of peace-peace. Peace, fight no more, teach your people peace. The crunching of leaves betrayed the coming of hurrying feet. Swiftly approaching was Naugawese, who came this time without hesitation or fear. Gaspingly she told him of the proposed attack upon the Chippewa, before dawn. Then Chingachouk and Naugawese went away together to the camp of his people. Later that night, they returned and with them was a band of Chippewa braves. As they approached the sentry of the Dacotahs, Chingachouk advanced alone and gave the sign of friendship. After a parley, the entire band was admitted to the Council of Eagle Eye, who gravely listened while Chingachouk eloquently pleaded for a truce between the two nations. Peace between the Chippewa and the Sioux. Then came prolonged silence after which with much deliberation, they solemnly discussed the proposal. At length Eagle Eye said that only on one condition would he smoke the Pipe of Peace with his enemy and consent to the marriage of his daughter with a Chippewa brave. "Chingachouk must first prove himself worthy of the maiden by some deed."

It was late in the next moon, late in the afternoon of a beautiful August day that a light birch bark canoe drew up to the shore of a thickly wooded island. A stalwart young Indian brave stepped from the boat as it touched the sand. It was Chingachouk. He had come to keep a tryst with the lovely Naugawese. Swiftly he bounded along the path. One more turn and he would see her. He made the bend but the sight struck horror to his heart-for a huge white bear was poised ready to seize his Naugawese. Chingachouk grasped his hunting knife, immediately attacking the beast, whose claws had already torn the shawl from his loved one's shoulders. Naugawese, stunned only for a moment, fled in terror to the village of her people and almost the entire band returned with her to the scene of that terrible conflict between man and beast. At last, through the gathering dusk, Chingachouk, torn and bleeding, was seen to sink his knife in the breast of the beast, then both fell and lay motionless on the crimson sod. Little clouds of mist arose through the dusky air. They seemed to take the forms of Chingachouk and the bear, which slowly floated upward and were lost from sight. The silence was broken by Eagle Eye, who said, "Chingachouk, you've won the test, Naugawese is yours." But only the whispering breeze was heard, as the spirit of the young brave and the great white bear sped on their way to the Happy Hunting Ground. And always thereafter this lovely but tragic spot was known as Manitou, or Spirit Island. It lies in the lake called White Bear.

Each legend portrays a white bear as a mythical creature. However, there is scientific evidence that could support the reality of a white bear. The glacier bear, an unusual subspecies of the black bear, is produced when the parents each have a recessive gene that results in an all-white bear. Minnesota may not have had polar bears when the legends developed, but there were black bears, and who knows, the white bear in the legends just may have been a rare glacier bear.

JOHN CARBUTT AND COMPANY

It was not until May of 1823 that navigation of the upper Mississippi River from St. Louis to Fort Snelling was successfully completed by Captain Richards aboard his steam vessel *Virginia*. He had piloted the *Virginia* through the Rock Island rapids, which were thought to be unnavigable, a feat that took four days.

The first regular navigation of the river began in 1847 when the Galena Packet Company began running river boats from Galena to Mendota and Fort Snelling. During the period from 1849 through 1851, the boats were making two trips per week, and three trips per week by 1852. Time and technology multiplied river traffic on the Mississippi from a scant fifteen steamboats during the period from 1823 through 1826 to 1,068 steamboats in 1858.

Around 1866 the Northwestern Union Packet Company was organized and the Galena Packet Company closed its doors. John Carbutt, one of America's earliest landscape photographers, was hired in the fall of 1865 to publicize the Northwestern Union Packet Company's fleet of steamships that ran daily from Illinois to St. Paul on the upper Mississippi.

This was not the first time that Carbutt had photographed the Minnesota area. In 1864 his work had been prominently displayed in the *Philadelphia Photographer*, the premier photographic magazine of that era, which was created and published by Edward L. Wilson. Wilson and Carbutt would become lifelong friends as a result of their shared passion for photography.

During the fall of 1866 Carbutt took a holiday excursion, taking the same steamships that he had been hired to advertise the previous year. John Carbutt, along with his wife, Mollie, shared the sights with Edward L. Wilson and his wife. It was then that John Carbutt and party visited White Bear Lake.

Upon reaching St. Paul the group hired a wagon to carry them and all their photographic gear on their adventure. They would have traveled primitive dirt roads out to White Bear Lake, where accommodations were probably obtained at one of only three hotels standing at that time: the Leip House, the Murray House, or the South Shore House. The area was just beginning to be developed by the 278 people who resided there. St. John in the Wilderness Church, in its original location in what is now the Episcopal Cemetery, had just been built. It must have been quite the sight as one approached the lake from the south, as it truly was a church in the "wilderness." If the group was lucky enough, they may have seen boat builder Duncan Ross at the helm of the first sailboat to glide over the vast expanse of water. In 1866 there was no bridge to Manitou Island, and the railroad to White Bear would not exist for another two years.

The following four stereoviews are from the Carbutt-Wilson trip in the fall of 1866.

Courtesy of Cynthia Vadnais

The Picnic

Shown are Edward L. Wilson, his wife, and Carbutt's wife, Mollie, on the right. Manitou Island is in the background.

Courtesy of Cynthia Vadnais

The Boat Ride

It is not known where along the lakeshore this stereoview was taken. Pictured are Edward L. Wilson, his wife, and Mollie Carbutt. Possibly the fourth person is the photographer himself, John Carbutt.

Courtesy of Cynthia Vadnais

Views of White Bear Lake, through the Trees

Both Mrs. Carbutt and Mrs. Wilson are in these two very similar stereoviews taken from approximately the same vantage point along the lakeshore. Manitou Island appears off in the distance.

Courtesy of Cynthia Vadnais

Indian Mound Versus Progress

The largest of ten Indian mounds stood in the area near the end of Shady Lane and Lake Avenue. A survey conducted in 1881 showed that this mound was about twelve feet high, with a base diameter of about eighty-four feet. At the time of the survey, it was determined that the other mounds in the group did survive intact, most having been partially removed.

The question of who created these mounds has never definitively been answered but the *Pioneer Press* dated May 30, 1886, reported, "One-legged Jim, a brother of Old Betts, asserted that the large mound was built by his forefathers as a burial place of some celebrated chief." Whether or not there is any truth to that assertion, the Indian association cannot be disputed.

Courtesy of the White Bear Lake Area Historical Society

Old Betts – "The Oldest Squaw in the State"

Many photographs of Old Betts were distributed carrying the appellation, "A Sioux Squaw 120 years old, who will long be remembered with gratitude by many of the Minnesota Captives for her kindness to them while among the Sioux in 1862 [during the Sioux uprising]."

Courtesy of the White Bear Lake Area Historical Society

William Markoe – Circa 1856

Courtesy of the White Bear Lake Area Historical Society

Mound Cottage – Summer Home of William Markoe – Shady Lane

In 1873 William Markoe purchased most of the Indian mound land. Mound Cottage was located on this land near the largest of the Indian mounds.

William Markoe Summerhouse Atop the Indian Mound – Circa 1880

Courtesy of the White Bear Lake Area Historical Society

Courtesy of Cynthia Vadnais

Distant View of the Indian Mound Summerhouse

William F. Markoe, son of William Markoe, built a rustic summerhouse on top of the Indian mound, which was a prominent landmark. He worked much of his vacation doing so as he had to shape 480 pieces of tamarack, around fifteen inches long, to form the walls. The casements of the windows and doors were decorated with U.S. shields, the roof with a simple cross, and the interior was furnished with a round table and circular seats. It was quite a showplace, in addition to being a great vantage point from which to view the lake. During the early years of the village's history, hundreds of people would travel to White Bear by train and rush to the mound to picnic and relax. Sadly, the summerhouse was blown down by a severe storm during 1887 and the mound itself did not survive much longer.

Courtesy of Cynthia Vadnais

The Largest of the Indian Mounds – A Relaxing Place to View the Lake – 1885

Among the visitors to the mound was a scientist from New York who was studying Indian mounds. He talked with Mr. Markoe about transporting the mound, using a raft, to New York's Central Park. He told him that if this could be done, the city council of New York would gladly sign a check for $1,000,000. This wildly ambitious feat never happened as the mound was destined for another fate.

What led to the removal of this ancient mound? One story suggests that the permanent residents of the village were anxious to build White Bear into a great city, and in doing so "make St. Paul its back door." This desire for progress heightened the belief that the mound was a dangerous place for teams and drivers to pass. According to an article in the August 4, 1888 *Lake Breeze*, "Charles Wheeler, a young man aged about 24, from the vicinity of Stillwater, was driving along Lake avenue,… with a team of horses and carriage containing besides himself, his sister and a young lady named Belle Delano, the team became frightened at the shriek of a locomotive and started on a run. Before proceeding far the carriage came into collision with a tree and threw the occupants out. Mr. Wheeler was dragged quite a distance and struck another tree with his head with terrific force, killing him almost instantly, and Miss Delano suffered a fracture of the collar bone, while, Miss Wheeler escaped with a bruised knee... The accident is rendered all the sadder from the fact that the young man and Miss Delano were betrothed and about to be married." The village was sued unsuccessfully for damages. In 1927, William F. Markoe replied to some articles regarding the Indian mound. He stated, "The chief objectors to the ancient land mark were Col. Wm. Leip, proprietor of White Bear's largest hotel, who imported several carloads of beer annually on Decoration day and July 4th, and protested that getting 'around' the mound obscured (momentarily) the view of his popular caravansary and the other objectors were the village council whose policy in those days was to make White Bear, not what Providence had made it, namely, the most popular summer resort and watering place in Minnesota, …but a 'big city,' and St. Paul, to use their own slogan, White Bear's back yard." Whatever the reason, it was eventually decided that the mound be removed to make way for a wider public road to be built along the lake. The decision was hotly debated.

Courtesy of the White Bear Lake Area Historical Society

An Ancient Land Mark – Looking West down Lake Avenue

In a letter written on May 13, 1887, J. Fletcher Williams, representing the Minnesota Historical Society of St. Paul, pled,

> Remove not the ancient land mark… It has for 30 years been an object of interest to both citizens and strangers. We have all looked on it as a feature of the lake, as a notable point of interest and curiosity, we have all taken friends to see it and, they have admitted it is a truly historical relic. It is, an attraction to the lake, a feature that gives charm and interest to it, and looked at simply as a business matter, should not be destroyed but left as one of the notable points on the lake, to point out to visitors as an attraction.
>
> We feel sure that if it is now cut down those who come here after will feel indignant at such a mistake. There are many places in this region which are advertising themselves as summer resorts that would cheerfully give a large sum for such a curiosity, provided it were genuine as the White Bear mound undoubtedly is. It certainly is not good policy for the authorities at White Bear to suffer this interesting relic to be destroyed. It will cause no little regret and perhaps indignation at such action, as there are thousands of persons who have seen the mound, who consider it in some sense public property in which they have an interest…

Despite the strong argument made by Williams, and the fact that Markoe had been able to protect his property for several years by means of an injunction, public support to have the mound destroyed prevailed.

For more than a month, road commissioner Albert Clewett and workmen were engaged in tearing down the mound. It would be totally gone by the end of April, 1889. Teams of horses, ploughs, picks and shovels were used to level the enormous mound. One resident stood guard over his property to protect his trees from destruction. Tensions were high.

William F. Markoe wrote of the mound and how it was "built with rich black loam" adding that it was "not till the workmen reached the natural level of the ground did they begin to realize the gruesome character of the work they were engaged in." In the mound they found nineteen complete skeletons that were "so well preserved – especially their teeth – that they were thought to have been young braves." Three stones in a cloverleaf formation were found near each skeleton, causing someone to comment that maybe they were "Irish Indians!"

A variety of artifacts were also found in the excavation of the mound: flint arrowheads, paint pots, tomahawks, war clubs, a bone scoop, a bone needle or hairpin, a curious right-angled bone, a cake of blue pigment, and some red coloring matter in powder. It is hard to say if all of these items were actually found in the mound, as the accounts vary quite a bit. If there were more relics, that too is unknown, as it was reported that spectators carried off many of them, even though they had all been promised to the Minnesota Historical Society.

It was suggested to the *Lake Breeze* that the Indian bones be placed in a box and then buried in the center of Railroad Park with a suitable monument erected, but when the people realized the damage they had done, no further steps were taken to perpetuate the memory of the mound.

However, according to William F. Markoe, "The nineteen skeletons were hauled to the museum, but the society declined to receive them, and they were hauled back to White Bear and buried in a single grave in the southwestern corner of Union Cemetery. Besides the skeletons, many skulls, thighbones, shinbones, etc., were gathered together by Mr. Markoe and his grandchildren, and buried in a new grave on his property at a spot known only to them."

Helen Johnston Stickley, in her *Story of White Bear Indian Mound* wrote,

> In the Fall following the tearing down of the mound, a tribe, presumably descendents of the original mound builders, passed through here on their way to Rice Lake, where they annually harvested the wild rice. They became greatly excited on finding their sacred burying ground torn down and instead of going on their way, they halted on the spot where the old ice houses stood and held council. For several days their attitude was decidedly warlike, war dances were held around camp fires and it looked as though they contemplated a wholesale massacre of the whites, who had so little respect for their religion. But finally they smoked pipes of peace and went on their way.

The other mounds in the group did not garner the same notoriety as the largest mound. Francis Whitaker wrote, "The other mounds of this group were much lower and less noticeable. However, they were also destroyed in some ruthless manner all except one and that one rises about two feet above the surrounding ground. About fifty or sixty feet west of the home of Mr. Dougherty on Lake Avenue, there is a slight elevation of ground upon which he has placed his flagpole. This is what now remains of the once famous Indian mounds which formerly stood on the shore of White Bear Lake."

As William F. Markoe so aptly stated, "...all regret that act of vandalism and agree that the destruction of White Bear's Indian Mound was the 'crime of the century'!"

Manitou Island

"Spirit" Manitou Island – Circa 1870

Courtesy of Cynthia Vadnais

William Henry Illingworth, a St. Paul photographer, left his initials in the sand when he photographed this stereoview of Manitou Island in the early 1870s.

An Indian legend about the creation of Manitou Island is offered in Molly Bigelow McMillan and Susan S. Wolsfeld's book *The History of Manitou Island*: "…for many nights, Manitou, the Great Spirit of the Indians, restlessly roamed the lake shore unsuccessfully searching for a permanent home. One moonless night, unaware of the Manitou's search, Indians slept soundly in a lake shore camp. They awoke the next morning to a sky brilliant with pink and purple to discover this large perfect piece of land, the island, rising upward out of the lake waters where no land had been the day before. It was believed that the Manitou created this land in the waters to provide his resting place. The early tribes considered it a sacred place and called it Manitou which translates to 'He is God'. Early settlers called it Spirit Island."

Before the island was developed, it passed through the hands of several different owners. William W. Sweeney and Jonathan E. McKusick, a lumber baron from Stillwater, laid claim to the island in 1852. Sweeney and McKusick were probably partners in the purchase, and it is reported that McKusick purchased the island for $1.25 an acre for a total of $66.25. In 1854 they sold the island to William Freeborn, who subsequently sold it to James F. Murray, one of the early settlers of White Bear. For some unknown reason Murray took out a $500 mortgage from Owen Stratton in 1857. Stratton foreclosed on the mortgage in 1860 and sold the island to George Burson on July 23, 1863. At this point the island became known as Burson's Island. In 1871 Mrs. Elsie A. Whitney, wife of Joel Whitney, bought it from Burson. James P. Allen became the next owner of the island in 1876, and he sold it back to Joel Whitney in 1881. On August 24, 1881 Whitney sold the island to William Dean and Reece M. Newport. Newport was the treasurer and auditor of the Northern Pacific Railroad, and Dean, a wholesaler of iron and heavy hardware, was part owner in the St. Paul hardware business of Nichols and Dean. The two purchased the island as representatives of the Manitou Island Land and Improvement Company, which became the Manitou Island Association in 1912.

The original fourteen investors of the Manitou Island Land and Improvement Company were Sylvester M. Cary, a railroad engineer who later founded Robinson and Cary Company, a railroad supply and machinery contracting firm; Reece M. Newport; William B. Dean; Robert N. McLaren, a U. S. Marshall and the Internal Revenue Assessor and Collector; F. B. Clarke, a railroad and land developer; Edward H. Cutler and Charles P. Noyes, partners in Noyes Brothers & Cutler, a wholesaler of a variety of items; Charles H. Bigelow, the president of St. Paul Fire & Marine Insurance; John L. Merriam, an organizer of the First National Bank and later the president of the Merchants National Bank in St. Paul; Joseph A. Wheelock, president of the Pioneer Press Company and editor-in-chief of the *St. Paul Pioneer Press*; Amherst H. Wilder, mercantile businessman and investor in stage, steamboat and railroad transportation; Dwight M. Sabin, a lumberman in Stillwater and machinery manufacturer; Elias F. Drake, vice-president of the Chicago, St. Paul, Minneapolis, Omaha Line; and William R. Merriam, president of Merchants National Bank, one-term governor of Minnesota, and Director of the U. S. Census. These Minnesota magnates all knew each other socially. Several were also, at various times, members of the Minnesota State Senate or the Minnesota House of Representatives. Oddly, only six of these original investors ever built or owned a house on the island.

Courtesy of Cynthia Vadnais

First Bridge to Manitou Island – Early 1880s

In early 1882, the stockholders decided on a number of improvements to the island. These were not to exceed $20,000 and included the "clearing" of the island, construction of a bridge, two barns, and a clubhouse, along with road and harbor improvements.

The bridge to the island was built in the spring of 1882. Before the bridge was constructed, the only way onto the island would have been to swim or take a boat.

In his book *Manitou Island* Carl B. Drake wrote, "There were always enough loose planks in this bridge to produce a sound of distant thunder as the horse drawn vehicles rattled across."

Courtesy of Cynthia Vadnais

1885 – Sketch of Manitou Island Bridge

In 1890 the *St. Paul Pioneer Press* published a tribute to White Bear Lake, saying, "Manitou (or spirit) island is one of the most enchanting and lovely places, consisting as it does of about 60 acres with high and nicely wooded banks, graced thru-out with imposing and picturesque cottages, where dwell, during the summer months, many of St. Paul's most estimable and wealthy people. The island is reached by an arched bridge from the main land, and through out its entire length is a labyrinth of shady, well-kept walks and driveways. An additional interest is lent to this lovely spot by the fact of its previous occupancy, many years ago, by Indian tribes and many are the weird legends told of it."

Courtesy of the Richard Vadnais Family

August 1893 – Bridge to Manitou Island

Winter ice floes damaged the bridge not long after it was built. As a result, in 1888 the bridge was reinforced and an embankment was built up under a portion of the bridge to protect it.

In 1897 a new bridge was authorized, but it is not known whether or not that bridge was ever built, because in 1902 a letter was sent to the Village of White Bear Lake requesting permission to build a new bridge. Permission was given but the cost to replace it was too high. The decision was to repair the existing bridge. Since the minute book of island meetings from 1912 to 1927 is missing, it is not known when a new wooden arch bridge was actually constructed.

Manitou Island Association Clubhouse – 1885

Courtesy of the White Bear Lake Area Historical Society

Early members of the association who built summer cottages on the island included Joseph Wheelock, S. M. Carey, W. B. Dean, Conrad Gotzian, Charles S. Rogers, E. F. Drake, Judge Palmer, Charles P. Noyes, S. J. R. McMillan, and Captain Sanders.

These early cottages, as lovely as they were, did not have kitchens. The clubhouse built in 1884 fulfilled this need (it sat where the tennis courts are currently located). At one end was a large communal dining area and kitchen, with bathrooms located at the other end. Around the outside was a wide, covered porch where members could sit and enjoy the surroundings.

Courtesy of Cynthia Vadnais

For the first two summers meals, were catered for the members, and at other times servants would gather and prepare meals for the residents. With the desire for private, and probably more convenient, kitchen and dining facilities, the residents updated their cottages. Since the clubhouse was no longer needed, it was leased out for three years to a few gentlemen, provided that they remodel it into living quarters and pay the insurance. Cass Gilbert, the architect of several important buildings, including the Minnesota State Capitol, the United States Supreme Court building, and the U. S. Customs House, leased the clubhouse from 1896 through 1899. He had close ties to the island since he purportedly was the architect of nine of the cottages on the island, of which a few still stand today.

One of the more spectacular events to occur on the island happened after the 1899 season when the clubhouse burned to the ground. The island residents were more interested in saving the water tower and ice house because the White Bear Fire Department was directed to pour water on these structures instead of on the burning clubhouse.

Courtesy of Cynthia Vadnais

Donald Taylor's Playhouse – Circa 1895

In 1891 Oscar Taylor built a house at what is now 2548 Manitou Island. For his son Donald he erected a log cabin playhouse on the point, which was a part of his property.

The property was later owned by William McCurdy and then Fredrick E. Weyerhaeuser, who tore down the original house and rebuilt another home, along with a guest house. Donald and Marjorie McNeely purchased the house in 1948. Donald McNeely was still living on the property in 1998.

Entrance to Manitou Island – August 1893

Shown at the end of the road, off to the right, is one of the company barns built during the early 1880s.

Courtesy of the Richard Vadnais Family

The barns were used by all the residents of the island, as they were discouraged from having barns on their own property. With the advent of the automobile, the barns were converted into garages and living quarters for chauffeurs. New garages replaced the barns in 1927.

Courtesy of Cynthia Vadnais

Gateway to Manitou Island

On the island end of the bridge stands a fieldstone entrance with iron gates. For many years the island was only in use during the summer, and one way to dissuade intruders was this gated entrance that could be locked.

Courtesy of the White Bear Lake Area Historical Society

Casper Bloom – the First Caretaker of the Island

From 1888 to 1976 the residents of the island had only four caretakers. The first was Casper Bloom, a Civil War veteran, who took care of the island from 1884 until the spring of 1922. His obituary, printed in the *White Bear Press* in 1922 said,

He and his wife moved to White Bear in 1879. He was engaged at his trade, that of cabinet maker, in White Bear and at Manitou island until July 1, 1884, when he was placed in charge of Manitou island. He was in continuous charge of the island for 38 years, up to the time of his retirement last spring. During the 38 years that he occupied his position he was absent for only five meals and was gone from the island only one Sunday. Year in and year out, summer and winter, he made two trips of inspection over the island, traveling through the deep snows on snowshoes. It was on such a tour of inspection, when a house had been broken into, that he received the injuries that contributed to his death.

After Casper Bloom died, Al Burrows, who had been a steamboat captain and the town marshall of White Bear for ten years, took over the caretaker duties. He was followed by Conrad Johnson, who held the position from 1939 until he retired in 1971, at which time his daughter Bonnie and her husband, Rollie Fasching, took over the position. The Faschings' duties ended about 2000, and since that time the island has not employed a resident caretaker.

The Gatekeeper *Courtesy of the Richard Vadnais Family*

Notice in this view that the gatekeeper, who in all likelihood is Casper Bloom, is holding a gun. Only cottage owners were allowed onto the private island, along with their guests and service people.

The Gatekeeper's Cottage *Courtesy of the Richard Vadnais Family*

The cottage, located on the right side of the road as you come onto the island, was built for Casper Bloom and his family. The structure has changed over the years but was not fully remodeled until 1990. Currently it is rented out.

Courtesy of Cynthia Vadnais

Island Bridge through 2000

The History of Manitou Island states, "It was not until 1947 that bridge replacement was again an agenda item. ... At a special April 1947 meeting, the Board decided to borrow the money to pay for this new bridge. The bridge would be built in the winter, residents were told, necessitating that they drive over the ice during its construction."

Courtesy of Cynthia Vadnais

Current Island Bridge – Summer 2003

After much controversy, a new metal bridge was constructed in 2001.

Summer Resorts and Hotels

Villeroy B. Barnum, one of the first settlers in the area, came to the southwest shore of White Bear Lake in 1852, where he built a primitive cabin covered with elm bark. The next year, he shingled the building and made other improvements. The popularity of the lake was quickly increasing, and in 1854 Barnum opened his house as a hotel for those wanting to fish and hunt in the area. This was the first resort hotel at White Bear Lake.

John Lamb, a St. Paul hotel man and sergeant-at-arms of the territorial legislature, purchased the hotel in 1857 at a cost of $4,000 and proceeded to make improvements to the property. On May 11, 1858, on the very same day that Minnesota became a state, a historic meeting organizing White Bear Township was held at Lamb's Hotel.

The hotel reverted to Barnum in 1860 after a fire partially destroyed the structure. Prices Barnum charged in 1862 were $5 per week for board, 50¢ per day for a rowboat, $1.50 per day for a sailboat and 25¢ per day for a horse. Barnum retained ownership until 1866.

William Leip, the next owner of the hotel, emigrated from Germany in 1846 and by 1855 was running a prosperous wholesale liquor and cigar trade in St. Paul. In 1861 he changed businesses and took up brewing ale and porter. Leip sold his interest in the brewing business in 1865 and in 1866 bought the Leip House from Barnum for $2,500. Leip's ownership of the hotel was the longest and most successful since the railroad to White Bear was built in 1868. The railroad enhanced the area's potential as a resort destination.

Courtesy of Cynthia Vadnais

The Leip House and Surrounding Grounds – 1885

When Leip purchased the hotel, it consisted of ten rooms. By the early 1870s, after having undergone many improvements, the hotel could accommodate up to three-hundred people in the 103 rooms. Over the years Leip added, among other things, a ballroom, bowling alleys, a pavilion, a billiard room, a villa, several cottages, and a sample room (i.e., a bar). The resort was typically open from May 1 to October 1.

For a time Robert Whitaker was the clerk and manager of the Leip Hotel. His son Frederick E. Whitaker Sr. was a bellboy at the hotel from 1881 to 1885. The following excerpts are from Frederick Whitaker's notebook:

> Our Dad... met lots of fine people from around St. Paul but most of them were Southerners who came up on the steamboats in big family parties and stayed all summer... It was a big hotel and Old Man Leip hired colored people to work in the kitchen and dining room. At the peak of the season there were 25 to 30 colored men but all the maids were white. Of course, the hotel had a big and very fine saloon at the end of the big pavilion that was a part of the big rowboat and sailboat dock. There was no good bathing beach right there. A rickety bus and two plugs always met the trains at Lake Shore Station that always had a summer agent, a Miss Maud Johnston, an old maid, and she kept it going until the auto killed the business of the local passengers and the depot was removed. I put in four summers at the magnificent salary of $5 per month and two meals. On the third year I nailed the Old Man for more and he gave me $8. Of course, there were tips quite often and I saved all I could. The Southerners were generous on tips.

These were busy times for the resort. *The American Travelers Journal* reported that on July 14, 1881, "Landlord Leip fed over 800 persons at dinner and supper... He has 258 permanent boarders. The supper began at 5:10 and at 7:50 the dining room closed to be ready for the evening hop, all being done smoothly and without any grumbling of the guests."

Courtesy of Cynthia Vadnais

Leip's Grounds

Captain Vic. Richards, a professional sailor, was in charge of the lake's largest fleet of sailboats and rowboats, located at the Leip House. Fishermen also had access to tackle and bait.

The steamer *Dispatch* provided for large picnic and excursion parties. Often, a barge called the *Clara E. Miller* was pulled behind the steamer and dances were held on her decks.

Also available to those desiring excursions on the lake were the naphtha launches, *Crawford Livingston* and *Don Quixote*, which also docked at the Leip House. The *Crawford Livingston* rented for $3 the first hour and $2 each additional hour. The *Don Quixote* rented for $2 the first hour and $1 for each additional hour.

Having been in the liquor and ale business, Leip probably provided quite well for those visiting his sample room with July 4 being a particularly festive time at the Leip House. In a recollection of the old days in White Bear, William F. Markoe, wrote in 1925, "On July 4th, Col. Leip, the genial proprietor of the Leip house used to bring out two carloads of real beer and the railroad company after borrowing all the passenger coaches it could get from other roads was compelled to haul the overflow of humanity in box cars fitted up with pine planks for seats."

Courtesy of Cynthia Vadnais

The Pleasures of the Sample Room – Circa 1885

Lake Breeze Ad – 1894

Courtesy of the White Bear Lake Area Historical Society

25

In the 1880s the Leip House was considered one of the most popular resorts in the region. Not only did people flock to the lake from the Twin Cities, they also came from all parts of the country to enjoy the fine service and amenities Mr. and Mrs. Leip provided. There was ready access by train with the station conveniently located about 150 yards from the hotel.

In July 1885, *The Northwest* magazine offered an idyllic description of summers at the Leip House: "From almost every room in the house you can see the lake, with a foreground of green leaves; and just across the drive from the hotel front is a long wooden covered platform, where a band plays and where one can sit right on the edge of the water and be happy. You can get into a boat and go fishing or sailing almost at the very doors, and on every side the woodland paths invite one to ramble, while just behind and adjoining the hotel (which has forty acres of property attached) are large baseball, lacrosse and cricket grounds."

Courtesy of Cynthia Vadnais

Leip House Pavilion – 1885

The Leip House pavilion was built in 1880. According to the August 1881 issue of *The American Travellers Journal*, "The pavilion is constructed on an extensive principle, with band and refreshment stands, seats for hundreds of people, and a dancing arena, where dozens of couples can trip the light fantastic toe at one and the same time."

In 1888 a large barn on the property caught fire and burned to the ground, but, not due to a lack of effort on the part of the fire department.

During the 1895 season Leip leased the hotel to J. T. W. Dejong, who ran it under the name Lake Shore Hotel. Leip resumed management of the hotel in 1896.

Lake Breeze Ad – 1896

Hotel Leip and Cottages

WHITE BEAR, MINN.

This Favorite Hotel

FOR LAKE VISITORS WILL BE

OPEN FOR GUESTS ON MAY 1st

For season of 1896. Mr. Wm. Leip having resumed the management it will be fitted up handsomely. Hotel Leip and Cottages are located in a beautiful natural park between White Bear and Wild Goose Lakes, the shores of these lakes forming the boundary of the hotel grounds.

RATES OF BOARD, $2.00 PER DAY.

Liberal Reduction for the Season.

Address WM. LEIP, WHITE BEAR LAKE, MINN

Courtesy of the White Bear Lake Area Historical Society

LEIP HOUSE DINNER BILL OF FARE

SUNDAY, JUNE 27, 1896

SOUP.
Mock Turtle.
FISH.
Baked, Egg Sauce.
JOINTS.
Roast Beef, Brown Gravy.
Spring Chicken on Toast.
Boiled Ham, Mustard Sauce.
ENTREES.
Lobster Salad en Mayonaise.
Queen Fritters.   Chocolate Glace.
VEGETABLES.
New Potatoes with Cream.
Spring Peas.   Mashed Potatoes.
Stewed Tomatoes.
DESSERT.
Apple Pie.   Lemon Pie.
Strawberry Pudding, Whipped Cream.
Vanilla Ice Cream.
Fruit.
Coffee.   Tea.   Milk.

Facsimile of an 1896 *Lake Breeze* Ad

Courtesy of the White Bear Lake Area Historical Society

The hotel was totally destroyed by fire in the fall of 1896 just after having closed for the season. The fire department worked for a number of hours to try to save the building, but by the time the fire was reported, it had already made considerable progress. As a result, very little was recovered before the hotel was lost.

The era of the Leip House had come to an end, but William Leip persevered in the hotel business; by 1898 he had built Lakewood Park Villa and Inn. A 1898 write-up in the *White Bear Life* reported, "The Inn will be a convenient place for travelers to stop for rest and refreshment. Light lunches, choice wines, liquors and cigars, and the celebrated Anhaeuser - Busch Brewing Company's St. Louis beer and malt nutrine will be kept on hand. Meals and board can be obtained at the Leip Villa during the season, and there are six cottages for boarders or housekeeping. The Inn contains some ten or twelve rooms, all nicely papered and decorated." The same year, Leip erected a two-lane bowling alley adjacent to the Inn and provided patrons with a skating rink. Over the next few years he constructed a new boat dock and landing, and he had the bar enlarged.

White Bear Life Ad – 1898

Courtesy of the White Bear Press

In 1905, the new proprietor, J. H. Brown, renovated the Villa. In March 1908, fire struck again. Leip's Inn and Restaurant burned to the ground. When the fire happened, it appears that Leip was leasing the building to a Chris Jenson. However, Leip was the holder of the insurance on the building and he subsequently had it rebuilt a few months later on the same site, with Nick E. Wehr as the manager.

In 1909 Wehr took out a ten-year lease on the buildings and property. He invested several thousand dollars upgrading the hotel and renamed it the Lakeview Inn. The *White Bear Life* wrote, "room and board from $10 a person up" was the rate visitors paid.

William Leip died in White Bear in 1910. He was seventy-eight years old.

In 1912 the St. Paul Automobile Club leased the property from Wehr for one year. The club had also secured a buy option on the property from Mrs. Leip.

Leip's wife, Agnes, continued to live in one of the cottages on the property until 1913, when the property and buildings were sold to the St. Paul Automobile Club for the purpose of constructing a clubhouse. Mrs. Leip died November 23, 1913.

Stereocard Advertisement for the Williams' House

Courtesy of Cynthia Vadnais

John Bryson Murray, son of James F. Murray and brother of James C. Murray, White Bear's first postmaster, moved to White Bear with his family in 1855, and shortly thereafter he built the Murray House, the second resort to open at White Bear. He operated the resort for fourteen years, selling it about 1871 to E. C. Williams, who renamed it the Williams' House.

A Family Portrait outside the Williams House

Courtesy of Cynthia Vadnais

In the 1881 book *Indian Legends of Minnesota Lakes*, T. M. Newson wrote that the Williams House was "an unpretentious building, occupying a beautiful location, and accommodating about 250 customers, and the grounds are valued at about $25,000."

Advertisement for the Williams House

The back of the stereoview shown at the bottom of the previous page.

Courtesy of Cynthia Vadnais

Williams House – Circa 1890

Courtesy of the White Bear Lake Area Historical Society

In July 1885 *The Northwest* magazine described the Williams House property and surroundings this way:

> Half of the hotel building was built fourteen years ago, but it has been enlarged and enlarged to meet increasing demands upon its accommodations, until it is to-day an imposing-looking building, with rooms for a hundred guests. These, however, are not all accommodated in the main building, but close beside it and on the Williams property are three prettily-built cottages, all of which are leased every summer, either to families or in isolated rooms to chance visitors. The whole place – hotel, cottages and lawn – is overshadowed with trees, under which stand garden chairs and benches, which are in great request during the busy times of the hot summer months. Outside the limits of the hotel grounds the property still belongs to Mrs. Williams, and a large stable, a refreshment room and bowling alley are among the buildings thereupon.

Dock at the Williams House – 1880s

Courtesy of the Lawrence R. Whitaker Family

Williams House Pavilion – 1885

Courtesy of the White Bear Lake Area Historical Society

The Williams House,

WHITE BEAR LAKE,

which has been throughly renovated and many improvements made, will be opened May 31. First-class service guaranteed. Special Rates made for the Season.

L. H. HULSE, Proprietor.

White Bear Life Ad – 1900

Courtesy of the White Bear Press

During the late 1890s the house was managed by a few different people, including Mr. and Mrs. W. B. Paton, W. B. Hatton, and Mrs. Bucknam. In April 1898 a group of three gentlemen, named McNair, Zimmerman and Hobe, purchased the Williams House and the surrounding property. That same year the building caught fire and was closed. At that point the owners didn't know if they would do repairs and reopen or simply tear the building down.

An article in the *White Bear Life* in early 1899 announced, "...Messrs. Zimmerman and McNair, who bought the Williams House about a year ago, will erect a fine modern hotel and several cottages, and that the plans are nearly completed, so that work may be begun early in the season." However, this did not happen. Just a few months later, the Williams House was being cleaned up and made ready for visitors. L. H. Hulse had leased the property. The resort faded into obscurity in the early part of the 1900s and was eventually torn down.

Group of Guests Outside the Williams House – 1870s

Courtesy of Cynthia Vadnais

One of the Five Cottages at the South Shore House – Circa 1870

Courtesy of Cynthia Vadnais

Courtesy of Cynthia Vadnais

South Shore House – 1866-1880

In 1866, the year Villeroy Barnum sold his hotel, he also sold part of his property located along the lake (approximately at the narrows between White Bear and Goose Lakes) in Cottage Park to Lucius C. Dunn. That same year, Dunn, a Civil War veteran and the organist for the First Presbyterian Church, opened South Shore House, a hotel that accommodated up to thirty people. This was the first frame building in the area. By 1879 it was called Greenman's Hotel, since a Mr. S. P. Greenman was managing the main building and cottages. In 1880 the hotel burned to the ground leaving five cottages on the property. After the fire, T. M. Newson wrote in his book *Indian Legends of Minnesota Lakes*, "On the south shore of the Lake are five cottages belonging to the Dunn estate, all occupied. This is a charming spot, and will some day be adorned by a large hotel and other accessories of comfort and luxury." His prediction proved true because in 1882 the Cottage Park Association built a clubhouse on the hotel site, and it later was converted into a hotel.

Dunn's Grounds – 1870s

Courtesy of Cynthia Vadnais

Courtesy of Cynthia Vadnais

Group of People Gathered on the Grounds of the South Shore House – 1870s

South Shore House Dock – 1870s

Courtesy of Cynthia Vadnais

Courtesy of Cynthia Vadnais

Views of South Shore House Dock – 1870s

Courtesy of Cynthia Vadnais

Park Place Hotel Ad – 1900 *Courtesy of the White Bear Press*

The Park Place Hotel, open from approximately 1880 until 1910, was located on the northeast corner of Fourth Street and Railroad Avenue. It appears that Mrs. Conroy was the sole proprietor of the establishment. In February 1910, the building was converted into an overall factory.

White Bear House - Circa 1903 *Courtesy of the Robert Vadnais Family*

In 1876 James Waters constructed the White Bear House on the southeast corner of Fourth Street facing Railroad Avenue. Waters, an immigrant from Ireland, first worked as a policeman in St. Paul. He later moved to White Bear while employed with the St. Paul and Duluth railroad as a section boss. The White Bear House could hold thirty-five guests and was often quite busy since it was situated opposite the St. Paul and Duluth Depot. In association with the hotel was a saloon.

WHITE BEAR HOUSE,
WM. SCHUHR, Proprietor.

THIS HOTEL IS REFURNISHED THROUGHOUT.

Good Accommodations to Transients.

Lake Breeze Ad - 1892

Courtesy of the White Bear Lake Area Historical Society

In the mid-1880s Mr. and Mrs. Walter Dunn were running the White Bear House, and by 1892 William and Margaret Schuhr managed the business. In a 1967 *White Bear Press* interview, Rose (Schuhr) LeVasseur recalled, "It was a boarding house with a large stable behind it for the horses and had hitching posts in front. The children, there were seven of them, were never allowed in the saloon or the bar room where men could take their wives or sweethearts... Her father was musically inclined and played the accordion. Because of ill health, he was forced to give up the White Bear House, and the family moved to a home on Division Avenue." Until the turn of the century there were a few different owners: Mrs. W. Dunn in 1895, Emil Schmidt in 1898, Mrs. Fanning in 1899, and in 1900 Levine and Swanson.

White Bear House
BOARDING
By the Day or Week.

MRS. JULIUS LEVINE,
PROPRIETRESS.
Telephone 38.
Cor Railroad Ave and 4th St.

CHAS. REIF
PROPRIETOR
OF . . . .

BAR AND BARN
AT THE
White Bear House.

White Bear Life Ad - 1903

Courtesy of the White Bear Press

Charles Reif, who came to White Bear in 1882, entered the meat business of Reif & Bunghard until 1900. In 1903 he took over the barn and saloon at the White Bear House, while Mrs. Julius Levine ran the boarding house.

In 1921 the Home Trade Store expanded westward into the two front rooms on the Fourth Street side.

Chateaugay Hotel – 1890

Courtesy of the White Bear Lake Area Historical Society

In 1881 T. M. Newson wrote that near the Williams House, off to the right, "is a new and neat building called the Carpenter House built by F. [Frederick] W. Benson, this year — a very desirable locality." Benson soon renamed his resort Hotel Benson. After Benson built another resort on Bald Eagle Lake, naming it Hotel Benson, he renamed the resort on White Bear Lake the Hotel Chateaugay. The Hotel Chateaugay was located on Lake Avenue near Second Street and Stewart Avenue, where the lovely resort drew many people from all walks of life.

Courtesy of the White Bear Lake Area Historical Society

The Hotel Chateaugay

In 1884 William F. Markoe bought the Hotel Chateaugay from Benson for $20,000. He invested another $4,000 in the structure, adding a wing to it.

On May 12, 1884 Markoe reached an agreement with the Erie Telegraph and Telephone Company to have the first phone installed in White Bear at a cost of $60. He was contracted to charge 25¢ for each call made. The telephone proved to be quite an attraction. According to Mr. Markoe, "…on completion of the enterprise the Chateaugay four-horse bus was hitched up and as many as could, scrambled into it and raced for Dellwood to attend a dance by the White Bear Yacht Club, while guests at the hotel gathered at the office and paid 25 cents each to 'listen in' to Stein's orchestra furnishing the dance music at Dellwood."

William F. Markoe – Proprietor of the Chateaugay – 1884 to 1887

Courtesy of Sara Markoe Hanson

Markoe sold the Chateaugay back to Benson in 1887, and in 1890 the hotel came under the ownership of John M. Trealease, a long-time associate of the Sherman House in St. Paul. However, it didn't take long for Benson to become the proprietor once again. He owned the hotel until 1895, when McMichael and Ellis took over the resort, refinishing and refurbishing the place. Benson's on-again, off-again ownership seemed to involve a shortage of funds, a theory that is supported by a *White Bear Life* article reporting, "Mrs. Fred Benson died from self-induced dose of strychnine. The Bensons kept the Chateaugay hotel for a number of years, and lost it, which was felt heavily by Mrs. Benson."

Lake Breeze Ad – 1892

Courtesy of the White Bear Lake Area Historical Society

W. B. Hatton, who had leased the Williams House in 1898, took out a three-year lease on the Chateaugay in 1899. He renamed the hotel Wahbe Maquah, an Indian name for White Bear. The fifty-room hotel was praised as the "finest on the lake."

In 1903 both the Chateaugay Hotel and Abel Leaman's house caught fire from a house that was ablaze next door. The house burned to the ground but the hotel and Leaman's house were saved.

White Bear Life Ad – 1906

Courtesy of the White Bear Press

H. Vierig purchased the hotel in 1906 and renamed it the Oriental Hotel. He invested $5,000 in the resort to fix it up.

The hotel sat empty for a time, and on June 19, 1910 the Oriental Hotel burned to the ground, even though the White Bear Fire Department had answered the call. Firemen Richard G. Brachvogel and Ernest James were trapped in the hotel when the ceiling came crashing in as the chimney fell. The two men were saved from sure death when fellow fireman John Spink rescued them by chopping a hole through the outside wall.

In 1935 Dr. E. R. Sterner purchased the property with the intention of building a home.

Courtesy of the White Bear Lake Area Historical Society

Lakeside Cottage - 1885

Soon after the death of her husband, Mrs. Mary Drake moved to White Bear and proceeded to build the Lakeside Cottage (Hotel). Constructed in 1880, the $2,500 cottage measured thirty-two-by-thirty-four-feet with a twelve-by-sixteen-foot wing. It could accommodate twenty guests. Perched above the water north of Sixth Street on Lake Avenue, it gave guests a perfect vantage point from which to view the lake and surrounding area.

The hotel was open until at least 1917. Just before Mrs. Drake's death on June 15, 1932, at the age of eighty-nine, the Lakeside Cottage was sold to a Mr. Starkey who intended to raze the building.

In 1913 William L. Alden and his family moved to White Bear. That same year he opened the Corner Bar located at 300 Railroad Avenue on the northeast corner of Railroad (Washington) Avenue and Third Street. It appears that he ran the bar until about 1919.

The Alden Apartments located on the northwest corner of Third Street and Stewart Avenue opened in 1920. The property that Alden purchased for this purpose had been the summer home of the Honorable C. D. O'Brien.

The Alden Apartments contained twelve modern furnished apartments each containing two to three bedrooms. Unlike other establishments around the lake, tourists could rent an apartment and do their own housekeeping. There were also three cottages on the grounds, of which only two were for rent, with Mr. and Mrs. Alden living in the third cottage.

Summer Cottage of Hon. C. D. O'Brien

Courtesy of the White Bear Lake Area Historical Society

O'Brien was the mayor of St. Paul in the late 1800s. He also was the attorney for the village of White Bear from 1895 to 1896 and again for a number of years in the early 1900s and the first commodore of the White Bear Yacht Club in 1889. He was known for was his boating club, which was composed of himself and six of his children. Together they would navigate their boat *Hebe* around the lake with the children pulling the oars and O'Brien at the tiller.

In 1925 the Aldens decided to convert the apartment building into a hotel. On January 25, 1925 the *White Bear Press* announced,

> White Bear is to have a hotel. It is to be known as The Alden. February 1 work will begin on remodeling the Alden apartments. The hotel will be opened in the early spring. The hotel is to be modern in every respect. Hot water in each room, also a number of bathes [sic]. The hotel will be open the year round and will have 22 or 24 rooms. An entrance is to be constructed on the Stewart Avenue side as that will be hwy no. 1 when the road is opened north of town. This will be a nice acquisition for White Bear as it now has no hotel within the city limits.

Courtesy of the White Bear Press

White Bear Press Ad – 1925

Courtesy of the Lawrence R. Whitaker Family

Alden Hotel

Dining Room

Courtesy of Cynthia Vadnais

Kitchen

Lobby

Interior Photographs of the Alden Hotel

Courtesy of Cynthia Vadnais

Parlor

Porch

In 1931 the White Bear Lake Church of Christ rented the Alden property. The building was remodeled, becoming the home of the minister, the Bible School, and the congregation. According to an article in the *White Bear Press,* "On September 4, 1931, a tornado that passed through the city badly damaged the building. A portion of the roof was lifted off and dashed to the ground. Temporary repairs were made and later the west wing [the left end of the building] or 'dining room' was torn down entirely. The church acquired the property from the State of Minnesota for $1,334 on February 26, 1938. In the summer of 1943, the church engaged a local contractor to tear down the remainder of the 'Alden Hotel' and a 60 foot by 30 foot basement was constructed, using some of the lumber from the old hotel." The article continued, "In the spring of 1951, the congregation secured a loan and construction was begun on a new superstructure."

Courtesy of Cynthia Vadnais

Great Hope Church of the Nazarene – 2003

The church as it currently looks. The Great Hope Church has occupied the site since 1997.

Business Card for Spring Park Villa

Courtesy of Ruth Mattlin

Natural Spring at Spring Park Villa Resort

Courtesy of Ruth Mattlin

The ten-acre natural park area on Bald Eagle Lake in the area surrounding the intersection of Park Avenue and Bald Eagle Boulevard East offered its guests a place to stay for a week, a month, or the whole season.

Ruth C. Mattlin, along with her husband, Carroll, were the last owners of the Spring Park Villa Resort. The following is a brief history of the Villa written by Ruth, which she titled "Spring Park Villa Resort on Bald Eagle Lake."

The Spring Park Villa Resort was built by Charles Davies in 1905. It was situated on the southeastern corner of Bald Eagle Lake in White Bear Township and consisted of a stately hotel and twenty cottages.

The beautiful hotel was three stories high and featured a large lobby, elegant fireplace, and refined stairway leading to six bedrooms and two baths on the second floor. Also in the lobby was a square-grand piano (an 1882 Matheuchek), made in New Haven Connecticut. Other amenities included an exquisite dining room, an enclosed porch on which to serve meals to guests, and a huge wraparound porch where people could sit and convalesce from their hard workaday lives.

For others who were interested in fun and excitement, the Spring Park Villa offered tennis, swimming, sailing, fishing, horseback riding, croquet, and a rousing game of horseshoes. For those seeking a more romantic experience, there were lovely canoes, so one could paddle away to spoon with one's sweetheart. On the beach were a bandstand and a gazebo for sing-a-longs, programs, and just plain relaxing. Also, there was a natural spring that was made into a well. Many early residents used to come there to get their water, hence the name "Spring Park Villa."

The Mahlon D. Miller family owned and operated the resort. They had six children, Grace, Cora, Beatrice, Faith, Mahlon Jr., and Harold. The Senior Mahlon died on May 26, 1907. His wife and children continued to operate the resort, with daughter Grace taking over after her mother's death. During the Depression years and the drought of the 30s, the cottages were turned into housekeeping units, and the hotel then stopped serving meals.

In the spring of 1956, Carroll and Ruth Mattlin, and Harold and Mary Mattlin purchased the Spring Park Villa property, which by then had dwindled to fifteen cottages, and a grand old hotel. Carroll and Ruth Mattlin continued to operate the resort for the next twenty-two years, until 1978, when all the buildings were finally taken down.

A 1924 Northern Pacific Railroad booklet for the hotel advertised, "The Spring Park Villa Hotel accommodates 70 people. Cottages with screened in sleeping porches and housekeeping cottages may be rented from the hotel management. An 18-hole golf course, tennis, dancing, horseback riding, motor-boating and bathing are attractions of the resort, and fishing is good. Board and room costs $3.50 per day and up, or $15 a week and up. Children's rates are $1.50 a day or $7 a week. Cottages completely furnished for housekeeping are rented for $5 a day and up or $12 a week and up. Boats are also rented. The season lasts from June 1st to September 15th."

Courtesy of Ruth Mattlin
The Hotel at Spring Park Villa – Circa 1970

East View – Spring Park Villa – 1909

Courtesy of Cynthia Vadnais

This postcard was sent to a Miss Bertha Largersen in Oakland, California in July of 1909. Harriet, the sender, wrote, "Having a dandy time at this beautiful place on the lake shore and spend most of my time either on or in the water. A big crowd here and all very jolly so there is something going every minute."

Courtesy of Cynthia Vadnais

Spring Park Villa Lakeshore Pavilion
From the pavilion on the lake, guests could relax and take in the many water activities.

The following three pictures show interior scenes of the Spring Park Villa Hotel. They date from around 1910 and give an indication of the elegant style this summer resort provided.

Courtesy of Ruth Mattlin

Reception Room – Spring Park Villa Hotel
In the left foreground is the Matheuchek piano Ruth Mattlin referred to in her story of the resort.

One of the Dining Rooms in the Spring Park Villa Hotel

Courtesy of Ruth Mattlin

A Sitting Porch in the Spring Park Villa Hotel
Shown on the left is Mrs. Mahlon D. Miller, the proprietress,.

Courtesy of Ruth Mattlin

Hotel Benson Ad – 1890

Courtesy of the White Bear Lake Area Historical Society

Circa 1885 Frederick W. Benson was operating the Bald Eagle Lake resort, Hotel Benson, located on the southwest corner of Bald Eagle Avenue and Bald Eagle Boulevard West. Benson had built the Chateaugay on White Bear Lake just a few years before.

The name was changed to Bald Eagle Hotel when C. E. Smith purchased the resort during the early 1900s. Smith's establishment had electric lights, running water, sanitary closets, bath houses, boats, fishing tackle and bait, among other amenities. For almost four decades the Smiths ran or leased out the hotel.

BALD EAGLE HOTEL

Bald Eagle Lake, Minn.

MRS. M. C. STEWART has taken this popular house for the

1911 SEASON

Hotel open for tourists and other guests Sunday, May 21st. All newly decorated; electric lighted; beautiful grounds; fine bathing, boating and fishing. Meals served to automobile parties any time of the day.

Van der Bie's Ice Cream

White Bear Life Ad – 1911

Courtesy of the White Bear Press

> # BALD EAGLE HOTEL
>
> ### MRS. C. E. SMITH
>
> This celebrated Summer Hotel is now Open for Business after being thoroughly renovated and everything made spick and span. Mrs. Smith will run it herself this season, and will be glad to greet old customers and welcome new ones.
>
> French Cook. Best of Accommodations for Boarders, transient or for season. Orders taken for Automobile Parties. Vander Bie's Ice Cream.
>
> Fleet of 35 Row Boats, Fishing Tackle, Bait, Etc.

Courtesy of the White Bear Press

White Bear Life Ad – 1912

During the late 1910s and early 1920s the Smiths had the Smith's Bald Eagle Air Dome at the hotel. They advertised that there were "moving pictures, dances and refreshments" with "dancing every day (Except Sunday)." Dances cost 5¢, for which customers received two dances (per couple). There were also dances that included movies. These had an admission price of 10¢, which included one dance per person.

Courtesy of the White Bear Press

White Bear Press Ad – 1926

In the 1940s Joe Rogowski took over the hotel, converting it into apartments. He opened Rogowski Tavern and Boats on the premises where tourists, and local people, could have a drink, rent a boat, or purchase snacks. The automobile had done away with the need for overnight housing for almost anyone coming from around the Twin Cities area to fish or enjoy other recreation on Bald Eagle Lake.

The hotel was torn down in the 1970s. It had survived for more than eighty years, having escaped the fiery fate that befell so many other of the resorts in the White Bear Lake area.

Courtesy of the White Bear Lake Area Historical Society

White Bear Hotel (the two-story white building) – Clark Avenue – Circa 1920

The White Bear Hotel was open for about fifty years. C. Perry Long was one of the early hostelers of the establishment. Mary Stevens, the last proprietor of the hotel, owned it for fourteen years, from 1923 through 1937. She died and was buried fourteen years to the day after she took over the business. The hotel was sold to Cleo Smith, who in turn sold it to Eli Auger. It was torn down in 1938 to make way for a garage addition to Smith Chevrolet.

> When you think of
>
> **FOOD**
>
> think of
>
> ## The White Bear Hotel
>
> Home Cooking - Smiling Service
>
> CHICKEN DINNERS OUR SPECIALTY
>
> When on the road drop in at any time that you are hungry-- you will not have to wait for regular meal hours.
>
> Half block from depot   Mary Stevens
>
> Phone 431

Courtesy of the White Bear Press

White Bear Press Ad – 1927

Cottage Park Clubhouse

Courtesy of Cynthia Vadnais

Entrance to Cottage Park and the Cottage Park Clubhouse – 1880s

In 1882, two years after the South Shore House burned, the Cottage Park Association had contractor David Hanna build the Cottage Park Clubhouse at the same location. D. W. Millard was the designer of the building. The association fenced in the exclusive area and sold land to its privileged members for building cottages. The clubhouse not only provided the members with stables and carriage houses, but also gave them a place to gather to visit and have meals, since most cottages at that time did not have cooking facilities. By mid-1887, with members building their own dining and kitchen facilities, the clubhouse no longer had a purpose. An auction was held and all was sold off.

Robert Mannheimer was one of the initial members of the Cottage Park Association. This prominent businessman ran a popular dry goods store, located at Sixth and Robert Streets in St. Paul, called Mannheimer Bros.

J. E. Ramaley purchased the cottage in 1909 with the intention of making it his home.

Although the cottage no longer stands in Cottage Park, part of it does exist as the Wiberg home on the northeast corner of Fourth Street and Campbell Avenue.

Courtesy of the White Bear Lake Area Historical Society

Robert Mannheimer Cottage – 1885

1910 to 1912 White Bear Hospital & Sanatorium *Courtesy of Cynthia Vadnais*

The clubhouse stood vacant for several years. Thomas C. Fulton and J. E. Ramaley purchased it with the intent to remodel it and make it into a hospital and sanitorium. It became the White Bear Hospital and Sanatorium under the direction of Dr. Hopkins, a woman. The sanatorium could care for up to thirty people in its twenty rooms and two wards. In addition, the hospital had an operating room and laboratory.

1910 Ad for the White Bear Hospital and Sanitorium

WHITE BEAR HOSPITAL AND SANITORIUM.

An up to date, thoroughly equipped, ethically conducted Hospital and Sanitorium.

Accommodations for 30 patients.

Private rooms from $10.00 to $20.00 per week, ward beds $1.00 per day, nursing and board included.

For full information address

SUPERINTENDENT OF HOSPITAL,
WHITE BEAR LAKE, MINN.

Courtesy of the White Bear Press

1912 Ad for the Minnesota Eye, Ear, Nose and Throat Hospital

On February 23, 1912 the White Bear Hospital and Sanatorium became the Minnesota Eye, Ear, Nose and Throat Hospital.

Courtesy of the White Bear Press

Courtesy of the White Bear Press

1914 to 1918 Lake Shore Sanitarium

The Minnesota Eye, Ear, Nose and Throat Hospital lasted but a few years before it became the Lake Shore Sanitarium. Dr. Adolph E. Voges, a local physician, was one of the doctors who took care of the many patients between 1914 and 1918. The sanitarium closed in 1918.

1920 to 1935 Lake Shore Inn

Courtesy of the White Bear Press

Around 1920 Charles Bennett took over the unused property, remodeling and renovating the building into an inn with thirty rooms and a large dining area that had seating for two-hundred. He offered "an opportunity to summer visitors who can not or do not wish to occupy cottages." The inn was popular in the late 1920s for people attending parties at the Ramaley Pavilion (Ramaley's Winter Garden).

A 1924 advertisement for the Northern Pacific Railroad noted, "Lake Shore Inn, near the village of White Bear, accommodates 50 guests, at rates of $3-$5 a day, and half rates for children. Rowboats are free. A large, open air dining room overlooks the lake, and 25 of the bedrooms are outside rooms. There is also a large sleeping porch. Charles Bennett is the proprietor."

By 1932 Charles Bennett's son, Carl, and his wife were running the business.

Collett's Lake Shore Inn

Opening Saturday Evening for Dinner, August 24.

Featuring
Fried Chicken and Steak Dinners

Special attention given to reservations for dinners and parties.

———MUSIC———

Excellent Hotel and Tourist Accomodations.

———Phone 536———

White Bear Press Ad – 1935

Mr. and Mrs. W. B. Collett took over the operation of the Lake Shore Inn in 1935 and renamed it Colletts' Lake Shore Inn. The Colletts ran the hotel for a few years, after which it stood empty for a while.

Courtesy of the White Bear Press

Lake Shore Inn

Courtesy of Bob Thein

Prior to opening in September 1941, Mrs. I. O'Leary advertised the inn as a "large hotel with over 20 rooms." However, by 1942, it appears that it had mainly been turned into a boarding house with banquet facilities. This venture lasted a few years at most.

LAKE SHORE INN
NOW OPEN

APARTMENTS AND MEALS

Rooms by Day, Week or Month.

Dinner Parties, Large or Small Splendidly Served.

MRS. I. O'LEARY

Cottage Park, White Bear   Phone: White Bear 605

Courtesy of the White Bear Press

White Bear Press Ad – 1942

Courtesy of the Lawrence R. Whitaker Family

The Original Cottage Park Clubhouse

Courtesy of Cynthia Vadnais

A Portion of the Cottage Park Clubhouse?

Attempts were made to utilize the building as a rest home and still later as an apartment building but, because of zoning laws, both enterprises failed, and the building was demolished in 1946, according to the *White Bear Press*. However, a portion of the residence on the southwest corner of Cottage Park and Circle Drives has a structure that resembles the old Cottage Park Clubhouse. Former owners maintain that part of the clubhouse had been incorporated into their family home.

Dolce Far Niente

Courtesy of Cynthia Vadnais

White Bear Picnic Grounds – Circa 1880

Courtesy of Cynthia Vadnais

Damascus Commandery Dancing Pavilion – Late 1800s

The following eight photographs were taken in August, September and October of 1893 at Dr. Welch's cottage on White Bear Lake. Dr. Welch, a dentist from St. Paul, was commodore of the White Bear Yacht Club in 1894.

Dr. Welch's Cottage

Courtesy of the Richard Vadnais Family

"Dolce Far Niente" (Sweet Doing Nothing)

Courtesy of the Richard Vadnais Family

Enjoying the Afternoon out on the Porch

Courtesy of the Richard Vadnais Family

There's Nothing Like a Good Watermelon

Courtesy of the Richard Vadnais Family

Courtesy of the Richard Vadnais Family
A Relaxing Conversation

Courtesy of the Richard Vadnais Family
Winter is Just Around the Corner

Courtesy of the Richard Vadnais Family
Taking a Dip – September 1893 – 621 Lake Avenue at Seventh Street

Canoeing on White Bear Lake – 1911

The woman who sent this custom-made postcard wrote, "This was taken I assure you when the sun was shining brightly."

Courtesy of Cynthia Vadnais

After a Pleasant Sail – Early 1900s

Courtesy of Cynthia Vadnais

Waiting for the Swimmers – 1916

For a number of years the St. Paul Athletic Club sponsored a swimming contest from Wildwood to the bay by Amundson's Boat Works (shown at the top right). This large group of people seem to be anxiously awaiting the arrival of the swimmers.

Courtesy of Bob Thein

Lake Shore Lunch Room

Shown in front of the former Lake Shore Bowling Alleys are (from left to right) Jack Beamis, Tom Hodskins, Mrs. Chapman, and Minnie Taylor.

Courtesy of the White Bear Lake Area Historical Society

White Bear Life Ad – 1908

Bowling alleys were built in various locations in White Bear as early as the 1880s. A popular activity, William Leip joined in on the fun in 1898 when he built the Lake Shore Bowling Alleys adjoining his Lakewood Park Inn. In 1908 the business was still in operation under A. J. Diamon.

Lake Shore Bowling Alleys

These fine Alleys are now open for the season. Ladies and gentlemen will find bowling on them a delightful and healthy pastime.

Courtesy of the White Bear Press

An Outing to the Peninsula – 1889

Courtesy of the White Bear Lake Area Historical Society

Boating on White Bear Lake – 1909

The description on the back of this postcard states, "This beautiful lake is situated about ten miles N. E. of the center of the city of St. Paul, and affords a fine resort for the city people during the summer months. Its entire shore line of many miles is lined with cottages and villages, the largest of which is White Bear…"

Courtesy of Cynthia Vadnais

Courtesy of the White Bear Press

Winter Activities on White Bear Lake

A December 4, 1896 article in the *White Bear Life* reported, "Ice-boating is the most exciting and exhilarating of all winter amusements, and tobogganing and skating are akin to it. White Bear Lake offers ample opportunities for the enjoyment of all these sports."

Ice Boat on White Bear Lake – Early 1900s

Courtesy of the Robert Vadnais Family

A Group of Ice Boating Enthusiasts – 1918

Courtesy of the White Bear Lake Area Historical Society

Going With the Wind

Courtesy of the White Bear Lake Area Historical Society

Modern Ice Boats near Johnson Boat Works – 1975

Courtesy of the White Bear Press

THE RED CHALET

Fillebrown House – Summer 2000 *Courtesy of Cynthia Vadnais*

The Victorian stick architecture house, reminiscent of a Swiss chalet, was built in 1879 as a summer cottage for Charles P. Noyes, proprietor and cofounder of a wholesale dry goods business in St. Paul, Noyes Brothers & Cutler. Around 1882 Noyes bought land on Manitou Island and built a cottage designed by Cass Gilbert. He subsequently sold the Swiss chalet to District Judge George Young.

Shown is the entrance room in the house where the staircase is located. Notice how the doorway in the foreground is covered with drapery, allowing isolated heating of the general area.

Courtesy of the White Bear Lake Area Historical Society
Judge Young's Cottage – Interior – Circa 1885

Jonas Walter Fillebrown, owner of a fruit company in St. Paul, purchased the cottage from Young around 1905. The Fillebrowns were not new to White Bear, having spent time in Mrs. Fillebrown's father's tent on Clark Avenue in 1883.

Over a number of years the Fillebrowns turned the summer cottage into a year-round residence achieving the final step in 1920 when they moved the small cottage, called Pollywog, at the back of the house, forward and attached it to the rear of the home, creating a kitchen area with a studio above it. In an interview conducted by the *St. Paul Pioneer Press* in 1940, Miss Helen Kendrick Fillebrown reminisced, "We fitted Pollywog onto roller skates and it skated along very neatly to join the Chalet. Naturally we would not have chosen exactly that time for the weather's drop to 15 degrees below zero while repairs kept the house wide open, but probably that spiced the experience."

The cottage became the permanent residence of the Fillebrown family: Jonas, his wife, Harriet Eleanor, son, Arthur, and daughter, Helen.

Jonas Walter Fillebrown and Harriet E. (Coxe) Fillebrown – Wedding Day – 1881

Courtesy of the White Bear Press

Mr. & Mrs. J. W. Fillebrown

Jonas Walter Fillebrown was born August 12, 1850 and died September 25, 1937. His wife, Harriet, was born in 1854 and died in July 1935.

Courtesy of the White Bear Lake Area Historical Society

Arthur Kingsbury Fillebrown

Courtesy of the White Bear Lake Area Historical Society

Helen Kendrick Fillebrown

Helen Fillebrown was born in 1884 and died in 1977. Arthur Fillebrown was born in 1892 and died in 1978. Neither Arthur or Helen ever married.

Courtesy of the White Bear Lake Area Historical Society
Dock at the Fillebrown House
Shown from left to right are Mrs. Fillebrown, Dr. Garvin, and Helen Fillebrown.

    In early 1934 Miss Helen Fillebrown opened a tearoom in her home called "The Chalet." The house was rearranged and decorated to accommodate groups for breakfast, lunch, tea, or dinner. On warmer days the front porch was also utilized. According to the *White Bear Press*, "Miss Fillebrown was assisted at first by Mrs. Charles Buckbee, who waited on tables, and two cooks. The second year a Mrs. Alexander assisted, and Miss Fillebrown hired a different cook, but the third year meals were served on reservation only and hired cooks to come in when they were needed." Because Miss Fillebrown was operating a business in her home, a Mr. T. L. Schweitzer sought an injunction, but at that time there was no ordinance, and hence no case. The tearoom operated until around 1937.

    From 1946 to 1956 the house served as a nursery school called Miss Amy's. It was the first of its kind in the area.

    Helen was an accomplished pianist and spent many years teaching piano. Her home also served as a concert hall, and many recitals were given on the Steinway concert grand piano in the piano room.

Interior of the Fillebrown House Showing the Steinway Concert Grand Piano

Courtesy of the White Bear Lake Area Historical Society

Courtesy of Cynthia Vadnais

The Chalet as Seen from the Back Entrance

Through the generosity of Helen and Arthur, while they were alive, the house was deeded to the White Bear Lake Area Historical Society in 1971 with the stipulation that it remain their home until they no longer required its use. In 1977 it became the property of the historical society and was put on the National Historic Register. Today, events, tours, teas and various other functions are held at the house throughout the year.

Mr. Wilkinson's Cottage

The historic photographs shown here give a feel for upper-class Victorian cottage decor in the late nineteenth century. The pictures were taken in October of 1893.

Rosalie E. and Albert Wilkinson, the first owners, bought the cottage located on the northeast corner of Sixth Street and Johnson Avenue on November 10, 1887. By 1890 the Wilkinsons owned the cottage outright. They sold the cottage May 12, 1900 to John and Tina McCulloch, and on June 9, 1904 McCulloch sold it to Charles F. and Agnes Arrow. The same day, Mary Mattimore bought the house. On September 30, 1905 Mattimore sold it to Henry Warner. He then sold it to Stella E. Benson, a single woman, on June 16, 1936, who in turn sold it to Ellen P. Warner the very same day. Warner sold it to Richard and Clara Wagner March 15, 1941. David and Joanna Vail bought the house November 1961, and the current owners are Garrett Vail, a son of David and Joanna, and his wife, Renee. The house could more aptly be named the "Vail House" as the Vail family has had ownership of the house longer than any of the previous tenants.

The Wilkinsons had a cottage on Manitou Island by 1899. It is not known whether they rented or owned the place.

Courtesy of the Richard Vadnais Family

Mr. Wilkinson's Cottage as Seen from Sixth Street

Reception Hall

Courtesy of the Richard Vadnais Family

A Corner in Mr. Wilkinson's Cottage

Courtesy of the Richard Vadnais Family

Mr. Wilkinson's Dining Room

Courtesy of the Richard Vadnais Family

Trains to Automobiles

Courtesy of Cynthia Vadnais

The First Railroad Depot at White Bear Lake – Circa 1870

The railroad was a major factor in the development of White Bear Lake as both a resort area and as a town. White Bear's railroad history began March 1, 1864 when Minnesota Senator Alexander Ramsey presented an amendment to a bonding bill during the 38th Congress of the United States, resulting in a land grant to the Lake Superior and Mississippi Railroad (LS&MRR) for the purpose of constructing a railroad from St. Paul to Duluth. Construction began in 1867 under the watchful eye of William L. Banning, president (also the namesake of Banning Avenue) of the LS&MRR, the railroad reached White Bear in 1868.

At White Bear the railroad company constructed a red twenty-four-by-sixty-foot clapboard depot to which a twelve-by-twenty-four-foot baggage room was later added.

A special excursion and basket picnic was given on September 10, 1868 to celebrate the grand opening of the first division of the LS&MRR. The celebration was an opportunity for the railroad company to show the public the progress it was making on construction of the railroad, and to showcase the beautiful countryside through which the new railroad would pass. Five-hundred people from St. Paul, along with numerous dignitaries, rode on the train the twelve miles out to White Bear. What used to be a three-hour buggy trip would now take only thirty minutes by train.

On Friday, September 11, 1868, the *St. Paul Daily Pioneer* reported on the special excursion the previous day:

> The train consisted of 10 platform cars and 4 passenger cars which were reserved for the ladies of whom there were about 200… The head engine was named "William L. Banning" and the rear engine, "William R. Marshall."
>
> The train was delayed a few minutes until the arrival of Mr. Lott Moffat, a distinguished townsman. At 9:20 a.m. the train moved off midst the firing of cannon, the screeching of the two engines, the cheering of the

peoples, waving of handkerchiefs, and the music of a band. A more happy excursion party never left the city. Along the bluffs had gathered persons who signified their enjoyment by waving handkerchiefs and cheering. Farther along the road farmers and their families assembled to cheer on the "iron horse". In the country were fertile acres of corn in the shock, scattered over fields were rich golden hued pumpkins, flocks of prairie chicken and duck were seen, and beyond Little Canada two or three deer were spied seeking the covers.

As the train arrived at the lake it was greeted with firing of cannon, cheering by men, and waving of handkerchiefs by ladies who had gathered at the depot. After arriving at the shore of the lake some sought the groves, others the sailboats of which there were many, and others strolled around as they pleased. The largest part of those present gathered around the platform for the speechmakers and dancers. The people were called to order by Gen. McLaren, and a program of speeches and music was put on. Those speaking were: W. L. Banning, president of the Lake Superior & Mississippi Railroad; Dr. J. H. Stewart, Mayor of St. Paul; Hon. Alexander Ramsey, U. S. Senator; Hon. Ignatius Donnelly, representative in congress; Mr. B. P. Bradford, president of the Philadelphia & Trenton Railroad; Hon. James Smith, Jr.; Dr. Foster of Superior; Col. Taylor, superintendent of Indian affairs; and Hon. William P. Murray, state senator.

Courtesy of the Lawrence R. Whitaker Family

Lake Superior and Mississippi Railroad Depot at White Bear Lake – Circa 1870

Soon after the excursion to White Bear the railroad began regular operations. Superintendent Gates A. Johnson, in a *St. Paul Daily Pioneer* ad, announced that "The first division of the Lake Superior & Mississippi Railroad is now completed and ready for freight and passenger business. On and after Tuesday, October 6, (1868) and until further notice, a passenger and freight train will run as follows: Going north: Trains will leave St. Paul daily, Sunday excepted, at 7 a.m. Going south: Trains will leave White Bear daily, Sunday excepted, at 5 p.m. For information in regard to freight and passenger service apply to the company's depot on Third Street, St. Paul."

The first station agent at White Bear for the LS&MRR was James C. Murray, one of the early settlers of White Bear, who had also established the post office in White Bear.

Courtesy of Cynthia Vadnais

Train Wreck at White Bear Lake – Circa 1880

The convenience of the railroad intensified the traffic through, and the growth of, White Bear. The resorts boomed, people from St. Paul took day trips to the lake for pleasure, and more and more people bought land and built summer and year-round homes. In addition, the Pillsbury Company decided that it would be more cost effective to transport their flour to Duluth by train and then ship it east using the Great Lakes. As a result, they paid the LS&MRR to build a line connecting the mills at St. Anthony to White Bear. The grain was transported to Duluth, with coal as the cargo on the return trip.

By 1872 Jay Cooke, the Philadelphia banker who had funded the building of the railroad in 1867, decided to combine the Northern Pacific Railroad lines with the LS&MRR lines. The next year Cooke went bankrupt, as did the LS&MRR. A group, that included James J. Hill, purchased the railroad company at a foreclosure sale and renamed it the St. Paul and Duluth Railroad (St. P & D Ry.).

White Bear became a terminal for the St. Paul and Duluth Railroad resulting in the building of a turntable bed and roundhouse in 1874. The building faced southeasterly and was located about 150 feet south of Second Street and Miller Avenue.

Courtesy of Bob Thein

Six-Stall Engine House – Late 1920s

Courtesy of Cynthia Vadnais

Lake Park Depot – Circa 1890

Lake Park Depot, also known as Lake Shore Depot and as Cottage Park Depot, was built by the St. Paul and Duluth Railroad (St. P & D Ry.) in 1885 and functioned until 1925, when it was torn down. The ornate building, located near what is now the White Bear Shopping Center, was a stopping-off point for those going to the lake to picnic, to boat, or to stay at one of the resorts. A walkway extended from the depot to Ramaley's Pavilion, which was only a few steps away.

By 1887 there were thirteen tracks through White Bear with thirty-six passenger and eight freight trains plying the tracks each day. Six extra passenger trains ran on Sunday. Passenger trains turned around at the roundhouse. Despite all the trains, there were just two mail deliveries each day, one from each direction morning and evening.

Several changes to the railroad infrastructure occurred in 1888. The unsightly warehouse and old engine house that stood at the foot of Third Street on Clark Avenue were removed. C. W. Staehle was making plans to move his lunch house as the freight depot was soon to be placed at the corner of Fourth Street and Railroad (Washington) Avenue. The platform on the depot was extended about one-hundred feet so that when four trains met, there would be ample room on the platform for all of the passengers. A baggage room was added and a ladies' waiting room was made ready. However, the most exciting change was the addition of bee-line steel double tracks from St. Paul to White Bear to accommodate trains that left every hour from St. Paul to depots at Lake Shore, Bald Eagle, White Bear Beach, Dellwood, and Mahtomedi.

The year 1890 saw the start of special "theatre trains" that ran for the benefit of those wanting to attend theatre, lodges, parties, and other events in St. Paul, Minneapolis, or Stillwater. The round trip from White Bear to any of the three cities was 30¢ with a commutation book and 50¢ without one.

Dellwood Depot
This depot was leveled in 1935

Courtesy of Julie Ahlman

Mahtomedi Depot
Altogether there were nine smaller stations that the trains stopped at along a three-mile distance on the line between White Bear Lake and Mahtomedi.

Courtesy of the White Bear Lake Area Historical Society

Bald Eagle Junction – September 1893
Courtesy of the Richard Vadnais Family

Bald Eagle Junction Depot was constructed by the railroad in 1886 to better serve the Bald Eagle Lake area. The depot was conveniently situated at the junction of two rail lines about a half-mile north of the village. The Minneapolis, St. Paul & Sault Sainte Marie line (the "Soo" line) crossed with the St. Paul & Duluth line at this depot.

Courtesy of the Richard Vadnais Family

Tenth Street Station – August 1893

    The Tenth Street Station was erected in 1889 at Tenth Street across Highway 61 from the current McDonalds. The depot caught on fire from a passing freight engine in 1900; before anyone could tell where the fire was, the small depot had burned to the ground.

Courtesy of the Lawrence R. Whitaker Family

The Enormous Shed Roof of the White Bear Depot – Circa 1915

    In 1893 a two-hundred-foot shed roof was added to the south end of the White Bear Depot. It was updated the very next year with electric lights that were installed by the White Bear Electric Company.

Engine #540 Derailed near White Bear Lake – Early 1900s

Courtesy of the Robert Vadnais Family

In 1896 the White Bear Lake Depot was painted a light blue, the official color of St. P & D Ry. depots at that time. By 1921 it had been repainted using the Northern Pacific Railroad (NPRR) colors.

James J. Hill's Northern Pacific Railroad took over the operation of the St. Paul & Duluth in 1900. The line from St. Paul to Duluth became known as the "Short Line" or "Skally Line."

The NPRR Company continued to invest in the line. In 1906 the baggage room in the depot was moved and the building enlarged to twenty-four-by-ninety-three feet. In 1912 the company built a new one-hundred-thousand gallon water tower on the "triangle" at Fourth Street and Washington Avenue. In 1914, they built a pump house, as well as a depot near Bald Eagle Lake. The NPRR also maintained a freight house between Third and Fourth Streets, an icehouse, and an oil house north of Fourth Street.

Courtesy of Bob Thein

Northern Pacific Railroad Depot at White Bear Lake

Courtesy of the Richard Vadnais Family

Northern Pacific Caboose #1436 At White Bear Lake

Courtesy of the Robert Vadnais Family

Northern Pacific Engine #536 and Crew

    Despite all the additions, by 1923 the railroad filed to discontinue ten passenger trains to Taylors Falls and points around the lake. The convenience of streetcars, busses and automobiles gave the railroad too much competition. Application was made in 1926 to remove three more trains between St. Paul and Wyoming, with fifteen trains removed from the schedule in 1927. In 1927 it was reported that in ten days three trains carried only seventeen revenue passengers.

Courtesy of Bob Thein

White Bear Depot and Surrounding Rail Yard – Circa 1910

Permission was solicited in 1926 to close the Bald Eagle Depot. The Mahtomedi Depot was also on the verge of being closed due to lack of passenger and freight business. However, the quaint old White Bear Lake Depot was not going to disappear quietly. The long shed associated with many depots of the time had gone out of style and the NPRR started to demolish the shed in 1929. The White Bear Association (a group of local business people) petitioned the company to stop. The request was promptly complied with and the shed was repaired and returned to good condition.

A request was made in 1930 for the removal of two mail trains. According to the *White Bear Press* in 1930, "A good service taking the place of these trains has been established through the street car." One by one, locomotives were taken away from White Bear Lake with the roundhouse closing in 1931, after fifty-seven years of service. The heyday of the railroad through White Bear Lake was coming to an end.

Courtesy of the Richard Vadnais Family

Roundhouse in Ruins – Circa 1934

Notice the steeple of St. Mary of the Lake Church in the distance through the opening of the second arch from the left.

The reprieve for the depot, which was often filled to capacity, was short-lived. In the early 1930s plans were underway for the construction of a modern highway through White Bear Lake. In 1935 the depot was torn down to make way for the construction of Highway 61. The last wall fell on August 20; shortly thereafter, the old depot site was covered with pavement. Ironically, the White Bear Association that fought to save the old depot also argued to route Highway 61 through White Bear Lake.

The old depot had done well to survive as long as it did, outlasting the Lake Shore Depot, the White Bear Beach Station, the Dellwood Depot, Tenth Street Station, Peninsula Station, and Echo Station. "The place which once knew them will know them no more," lamented the *White Bear Press*.

A "modern, up-to-date" depot was built in 1935 halfway between Third and Fourth Streets about forty feet southwest of the site of the old depot. Contractor Auger, who also had the contract for demolition of the old roundhouse, built the 20-by-83.5-foot depot. Some forty-thousand of the roundhouse bricks were cleaned and used in the construction of the interior walls in the new depot. It was trimmed out with stained fir and the floor was covered with two-tone asphalt tile. The platform on the east side was 303 feet long.

Courtesy of Bob Thein

The New Depot (left) and the Old Depot (right) – 1935

Courtesy of the White Bear Lake Area Historical Society

The White Bear Association – Front of the Old Depot – 1935

In August of 1935, in commemoration of the old and new Northern Pacific depots, the White Bear Association had their picture taken outside the old depot and then in front of the new depot. About half of the association members appear here. Their names are as follows (from left to right): Otto ——, Fred Epperly, C. J. Zwerenz, Clifford Long, Carl Magnuson, Jack Yost, Robert J. Bloom, P. D. Shirley, A. C. Podvin, H. A. Warner, Cleo C. Smith, Sidney E. Henkel, Louis A. Thauwald, W. A. Stickley, Percy Nash, David Cardinal, Robert Freeman, William Holzheid, J. A. Reed, C. E. Davies, Hubert Bring, Nathan W. Blehart and F. D. Melhorn. Otto —— and Fred Epperly were both Northern Pacific employees who were not members of the association.

Courtesy of Bob Thein

Mesabi Big Boy

Circa 1940, at the White Bear Lake Depot, showing Octave Peltier standing in front of the Mesabi Big Boy engine used to haul iron ore.

Courtesy of Cynthia Vadnais

Northern Pacific Depot – 2003

The Northern Pacific Depot built in 1935 not only serves as a landmark of a bygone era, it is also the home of the White Bear Lake Area Historical Society.

Courtesy of Bob Thein

Streetcar Passing by the Fire Station – Circa 1930

By 1904 the Twin City Lines was laying streetcar track from Wildwood into White Bear with a second track laid to St. Paul. At the height of their popularity, the streetcars were jammed to capacity day and night, with people battling to get on and off.

The line into White Bear came around the lake by the shore of what is now White Bear Shopping Center, continuing over to the present day Highway 61. At Second Street it headed east over to Banning Avenue, where it turned north, ending at Banning Avenue and Sixth Street, where a wye was located.

Enough people were using the White Bear line by 1914 that people demanded to have the streetcar show the "White Bear" sign into St. Paul instead of being labeled "Wildwood."

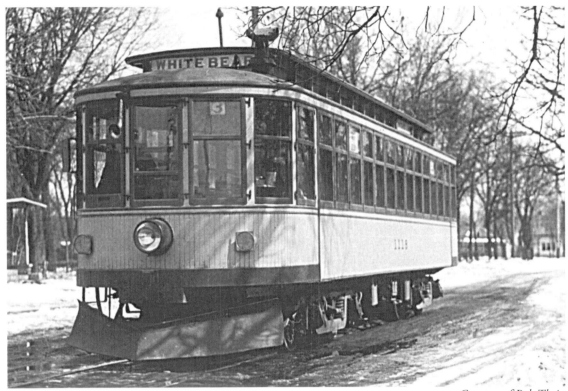

Courtesy of Bob Thein

"White Bear" Streetcar

Despite the streetcars' popularity, within a few decades they would share the same fate as the passenger train. A meeting was held early in 1932 for the purpose of removing the streetcar service from White Bear. The *White Bear Press* gave the following account of the last streetcar run on August 10, 1932: "A number went to Wildwood that evening returning on the last car. At various stations along South Shore, parties of jolly folks - young and older - climbed on and rode to the sixth street wye, and back to their station — having a hilarious time." The paper further commented, saying, "It doesn't seem right not to have the cars charging by. Some got up in the morning when it passed; some set their watches and clocks by it - a few rode it. Anyhow, it was a sign of life, and made one feel that he was 'in town.' However, this is but one indication of the changes going on almost unnoticeable."

Oddly enough, forty years earlier the streetcar company had fought for months to get into town and then in 1932 spent several months fighting to get out of town.

Courtesy of Bob Thein

Streetcar by Priebe's Boat Livery – Late 1920s

Courtesy of the Robert Vadnais Family

Loading the Bus on Fourth Street – Twin City Motor Bus Company

In 1920 Twin City Rapid Transit Company decided it was time to offer motor bus service in White Bear. A deal was made with Jameson and Harrison, the owners of the White Bear Taxi Company, to take over their one-year-old business.

Courtesy of Cynthia Vadnais

Bus Depot Building as it Currently Looks – Summer 2003

By 1926 there was sufficient demand for bus service in White Bear that a bus depot was built on the southwest corner of Banning Avenue and Third Street under the local management of Roy Jameson. The one-story building was constructed of brick and tile extending ninety feet along Third Street and eighty feet along Banning Avenue. The buses would enter from Third Street, loading passengers inside the depot, and would exit on Banning Avenue. Buses continued to Lake Avenue if going to St. Paul or over to Fourth Street if traveling on to Bald Eagle, White Bear Beach or Wildwood. Bus service to Wildwood was discontinued in 1927. The bus depot remained in operation until about 1960.

Truman Ward Ingersoll

About 1887 Truman Ward Ingersoll, a commercial photographer from St. Paul, built a summer home in Dellwood on White Bear Lake, which he named Birch Lodge.

Active in the White Bear Yacht Club, besides being the club photographer, he had at least two sailboats, the *Che-Wa* and the *May B*. In addition to the sailboats, his other lake crafts included a birch bark canoe, a rowboat, a duck boat, and a small steam launch he built himself, which was powered by a one-horsepower, kerosene-fired steam engine.

In 1884 Ingersoll opened his first commercial studio at 160 West Third Street in St. Paul. At that point in time, stereography was the most popular format for images. Ingersoll was a successful stereographer and traveled the world shooting pictures, which canvassers often sold door-to-door; he also sold pictures in his studio. Ingersoll also had the exclusive rights to sell the first Kodak camera when it was patented in 1886. He would eventually be known as the oldest dealer in Kodaks.

As an owner of one of the first automobiles in St. Paul, Ingersoll was also active in the early years of the St. Paul Automobile Club both as an officer and an organizer of excursions.

Ingersoll retired from the photography business in 1909 at the age of forty-seven. He eventually moved to a farm on Buffalo Lake where he and his family operated a wholesale flower business. Ingersoll died on June 9, 1922, at only sixty years of age.

As can be seen from the stereoviews on the next several pages, Mr. Ingersoll delighted in showing the lighter side of life.

Courtesy of Cynthia Vadnais

The Dellwood Short Line Railroad
This stereoview was probably taken during the 1890s. The several children shown appear to be riding on a working train built especially for these "short" people.

Giving Prince a Wash

A late 1890s stereoview of typical life on the lake showing Prince getting a bath.

"I Wonder If I Can Do It That Way."

Copyrighted 1899, this stereoview, like many of Ingersoll's views, shows every day life on White Bear Lake.

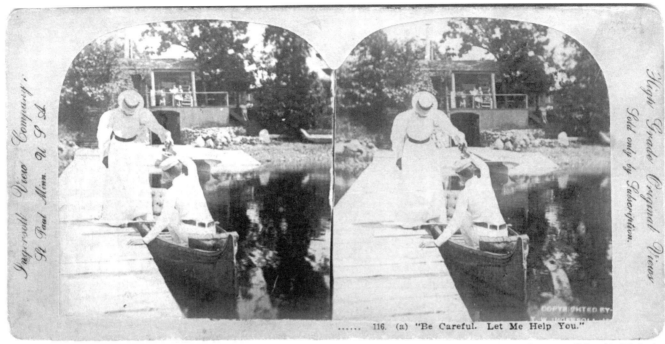

Courtesy of Cynthia Vadnais

"Be Careful. Let Me Help You."
This 1888 short humorous series (this and the stereoview below) using Truman Ingersoll's dock shows Birch Lodge in the background.

Courtesy of Cynthia Vadnais

"Well! I Like the Way You Help Me."
Lucius P. Ordway's cottage can be seen off to the right in this view. Ordway, of the Crane & Ordway Company, a maker of bathroom appliances and furnaces, later became the majority stockholder and president of the Minnesota Mining and Manufacturing Company (3M). Ordway, along with Ingersoll, was one of the first to build a cottage at Dellwood.

Copyrighted 1897, this three-card series, once again, uses Ingersoll's dock and shows Birch Lodge and Ordway's cottage in the background.

Helping – Or the House Maid's Hard Luck

Courtesy of Cynthia Vadnais

Help – Or the House Maid's Hard Luck

Courtesy of Cynthia Vadnais

Courtesy of Cynthia Vadnais

Splash – Or the House Maid's Hard Luck

Courtesy of Cynthia Vadnais

A Genuine Fishing Smack – 1890s

This two-card series showing sailing on White Bear Lake is copyrighted 1899.

Courtesy of Cynthia Vadnais

Pleasures of Sailing – Tending to Business
The woman on the left with her back to the photographer is Emma Hess, Truman Ingersoll's sister-in-law.

Courtesy of Cynthia Vadnais

The Dangers of Sailing – To the Rescue

WHITE BEAR YACHT CLUB

White Bear Yacht Club Dock – 1890s

Courtesy of Cynthia Vadnais

There were two early yacht clubs on White Bear Lake. The first, the original White Bear Yacht Club (WBYC), was organized in the fall of 1889 in Dr. Welch's dentist office in St. Paul. Among those present were John W. Taylor, James P. Elmer, and Dr. Welch. As a result of this first meeting, a constitution and by-laws were established and adopted on December 3, 1890. It was decided that there would be an initiation fee of five dollars with yearly dues of $3. The newly formed organization saw its ranks swell to forty-two new members that first year.

White Bear Yachting Association – Course Map – 1891

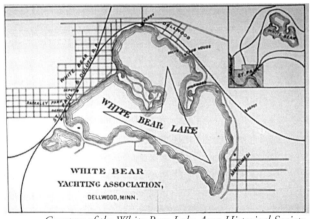

Courtesy of the White Bear Lake Area Historical Society

The Honorable Christopher D. O'Brien, the first commodore of the WBYC, had the distinction of sailing the longest boat, *Victorine*, measuring twenty-five feet in length. Races began at Ramaley Bay from which the boats would sail to Dellwood, then to Wildwood, ending back at Ramaley Bay. The champion for the first two years was Lucius P. Ordway with his twenty-three foot boat, the *Nushka*.

"The inconvenience for the residents of Dellwood of having the start and finish of the races in Ramaley Bay (between the island and Lake Shore) was the excuse given for the withdrawal of a good number of the members from the White Bear Yacht Club and the formation of the White Bear Yachting Association (WBYA) in 1891," according to Dr. Carl B. Drake in his publication *History of the White Bear Yacht Club*.

The one-hundred members of the WBYA elected Lucius P. Ordway as the first commodore. By 1893 the ranks of the WBYA had grown to 125 members with many belonging to both clubs. The primary activity was sailing, but they also promoted many other water sports.

Courtesy of Cynthia Vadnais

The Yachts at the Center Buoy – 1890s

Courtesy of the Richard Vadnais Family

W.B.Y.A. Club House (Kirby Barnum Hotel) – Dellwood –1893

The need for a clubhouse motivated the WBYA to rent the Kirby Barnum summer hotel in Dellwood. The hotel built in 1880 by Byrd Hewitt and Kirby Barnum contained a dining room and a few rooms for guests. It stood on the site of the present sailors' pavilion located at the yacht club. The WBYA held an official opening in their new headquarters on June 20, 1891.

White Bear Yachting Association Dock – 1893

Courtesy of the Richard Vadnais Family

Courtesy of the Richard Vadnais Family

1893 – White Bear Yachting Association Members

Dr. Welch's Cottage – 1893

Courtesy of the Richard Vadnais Family

The *History of the White Bear Yacht Club* recounted, "The White Bear Yachting Association became the more active club from 1891 on and in the spring of 1894 the two clubs were merged under the name of the White Bear Yacht Club [with Dr. Welch being chosen as the commodore]. On March 17, 1894, articles of incorporation, by-laws, sailing rules, and house rules were adopted. One thousand shares of stock at $10 a share were issued. Each stockholder was entitled to one vote, regardless of the number of shares he owned."

In 1897 the club had trouble renewing the lease on the hotel and decided to temporarily move across the lake to Ramaley's Pavilion, where space was provided rent-free by the building's owner, Col. W. W. Price.

Ramaley's Pavilion

Courtesy of Cynthia Vadnais

While the WBYC was headquartered at Ramaley's Pavilion, members decided that recently purchased riparian rights opposite the lot on the corner of Banning and Lake Avenues would provide land where the new clubhouse would be built. It was to be constructed in the summer of 1898 and completed in the summer of 1899 because the club did not want to go into debt. This plan never came to fruition since the residents of White Bear were not happy that the clubhouse would be located in the village. Thus, the group remained at Ramaley's Pavilion during 1898. In early 1899 arrangements were made to buy the original clubhouse in Dellwood. The organization raised $3,000, with $2,500 of that being used to purchase the Kirby Barnum summer hotel.

Courtesy of Cynthia Vadnais

White Bear Yacht Club Clubhouse – Circa 1900

Courtesy of the White Bear Lake Area Historical Society

Once the WBYC owned its own facility, plans were drawn up by club member Allen H. Stem to remodel it to meet the needs of the members. The two-story area at the front of the building was added during the 1899 remodel. The upper-story dance floor was enclosed by large glass windows that could be raised into recesses in the walls, allowing the lake breeze to flow through the room. Above this room was an observation deck and below it were lockers. The remodeled kitchen on the lower level had a dumbwaiter accessing the dining room above it. The second and third floors of the original building were devoted to sleeping rooms. Four small cottages were built behind the clubhouse by Lucius P. Ordway, which were rented to members for $1 per day. The remodeled clubhouse opened July 1, 1899 with the Honorable Christopher D. O'Brien officiating over the festivities. The remodeled summer hotel served as the club's headquarters from 1899 to 1912.

Courtesy of the White Bear Lake Area Historical Society

White Bear Yacht Club Interior Views

Courtesy of the White Bear Lake Area Historical Society

Courtesy of the White Bear Lake Area Historical Society

Yacht Club Dock – Circa 1900
Supposedly the small boat in the right foreground was the first motor boat on White Bear Lake.

Courtesy of the Richard Vadnais Family

Catching the Wind – 1893

Courtesy of the Lawrence R. Whitaker Family

White Bear Yacht Club built in 1912 by Allen H. Stem

In the early 1900s the club expanded to include two clay tennis courts, and by 1912 there was a nine-hole golf course. The need for a larger clubhouse was obvious, and in the fall of 1912 it was decided that the current clubhouse should be torn down to make way for a more modern and suitable structure. The contract for the building was awarded to former club commodore Allen H. Stem, whose firm had designed the Grand Central Station in New York City in 1903. The new clubhouse had hardwood floors throughout, with a ballroom, a large dining room overlooking the lake, and two floors of sleeping rooms. The sleeping rooms had all the modern amenities: electric lights, telephone service, steam heat, and hot and cold running water. Many of the rooms had private baths. The exterior was done in gray stucco with green trim and shutters. The four small cottages that Ordway had built were sold and moved away. The formal opening of the clubhouse was celebrated on Memorial Day, 1913.

The same year, a young F. Scott Fitzgerald, along with the St. Paul Elizabethan Drama Club, appeared at the WBYC in *The Coward*, a play that he had written. In 1914 he again performed at the WBYC, playing a leading role and serving as the stage manager in his play *Assorted Spirits*. It was not until the summer of 1922 that Fitzgerald returned to stay at the WBYC with his wife, Zelda, daughter, Scottie, and Scottie's nurse. In August they were asked to leave because they had worn out their welcome. Fitzgerald, who died of a heart attack in Hollywood in 1940, talked of returning to the yacht club but never did.

By 1914 the membership rolls had three-hundred members. The club encompassed more than two-hundred acres. An eighteen-hole golf course was being laid out and more tennis courts were being built.

White Bear Yacht Club *Courtesy of Cynthia Vadnais*

Courtesy of Ruth Mattlin

White Bear Yacht Club – 1939

In the mid-1930s the club decided to once again build a new structure. The demolition of the old clubhouse never took place, because it burned to the ground October 18, 1937. The fire raged out of control by the time trucks from the White Bear Lake Fire Department arrived. By morning, only the chimneys were left standing.

Club member Stirling (Jack) Horner designed the new clubhouse. C. J. Mattlin was the contractor. Built in a traditional American colonial style, the club's white exterior consisted of brick and shingle accented with blue shutters. At the same time a sixty-five-by-thirty-foot pool, two tennis courts and a sailors' pavilion were built bringing the total cost to more than $120,000. It was in this new clubhouse, which officially opened May 13, 1939, that the members celebrated the club's fiftieth anniversary on September 27, 1940 and the club's seventy-fifth anniversary in 1965.

The clubhouse interior was redecorated in 1988 with the exterior remaining unchanged.

Courtesy of Cynthia Vadnais

Sailors' Pavilion and White Bear Yacht Club — July 2000
The sailors' pavilion shown at left stands on the original location of the first yacht club.

Courtesy of Cynthia Vadnais

White Bear Yacht Club — July 2000
Expanding upon the original 1939 design, the new clubhouse closely mirrors its predecessor.

BOAT BUILDERS

Gustav Amundson, John O. Johnson, Abel E. Leaman, and J. Eugene Ramaley are probably the best-known boat builders whose companies were based in White Bear. Another boat builder whose name does not appear that often is Joseph Dingle, who, during the 1880s, built more yachts than any other builder in the area. He later relocated to St. Paul, where he built motorboats.

Abel Leaman, the first boat builder in White Bear, erected a shop, boathouse and dock near the Williams' House in 1873. He was an experienced builder of several types of boats, including flat-bottomed row boats, which were initially built for the local residents. He owned one of the largest fleets on the lake, which included nearly a hundred rowboats and sailboats.

As a member of the White Bear Yachting Association, Leaman was one of the early participants in yacht racing on the lake. He had at least two yachts, including the *Ben Hur* and the *Nellie,* with the *Nellie* capable of carrying up to forty people.

In 1889 he relocated his boat manufacturing shop to Burson Avenue (one block west of Clark Avenue) where a planing mill was set up. By this time, his son Dean had been working alongside his father for a number of years. Dean would eventually be considered the best rowboat builder in White Bear history. The boat house, fleet, and docks were removed from the Williams' House location in 1899. The boat house was taken to Leaman's boat works site on Burson Avenue, where it was used as a storage shed.

Abel Leaman died in 1908 at the age of seventy-five. Leaman Boat Works continued under the ownership of Abel's son-in-law, Julius A. Haussner.

In 1912 Leaman Boat Works burned to the ground. All was lost, including the shop, warehouse, patterns and material.

Courtesy of the White Bear Lake Area Historical Society

A. E. Leaman Boat Builder – 1890

Courtesy of the White Bear Lake Area Historical Society

Captain Leaman's Launch – 1899

For a small fee, parties would rent a launch to take them on pleasure excursions around White Bear Lake.

White Bear Life Ad – 1909

Courtesy of the White Bear Press

Ramaley Boat Works – Circa 1900 *Courtesy of the White Bear Lake Area Historical Society*

    In 1895 J. E. (Gene) Ramaley opened Ramaley Boat Company on the shores of White Bear Lake near Goose Lake. A larger shop was built in 1899. Ramaley also had another manufacturing plant on Lake Minnetonka in Wayzata. An advertisement for the company boasted, "We build the year around, always having a stock of boats on hand. Write us if you want a canoe, row boat, sail boat, or power boat, for we build all types."

    In 1925 Ramaley moved the entire operation to Lake Minnetonka. He had the large wood-framed building knocked down in the early part of the summer of 1926 to make way for his new venture, Ramaley's Winter Garden. In 1929 the boat works at Lake Minnetonka was sold to a group of investors.

Gustav (Gus) Amundson was born on April 24, 1860 in Oslo, Norway. He was trained in naval architecture while serving in the Norwegian Navy. In 1882 he immigrated to the United States, where he settled in New York. He returned to Norway in 1887 to get married. Upon his return to the United States, that same year, Gus and his wife moved to White Bear.

Amundson opened his first shop behind his homestead at 403 Lincoln Avenue. He was quite successful, and by 1902 90 percent of his yachts were being shipped to New York. Outgrowing his shop at his homestead, he built Amundson Boat Works in 1912, on the lakeshore, where he was joined by his sons Adolph and Edwin.

Courtesy of the White Bear Lake Area Historical Society

Amundson Boat Works

Among many record-winning sail boats that Amundson built was the *Virginia,* owned by T. J. Mendenhall, the commodore of the Oregon Yacht Club. It was written, "The *Virginia* was built by the famous yacht designer, Amundson, in Minnesota, and made for sailing on White Bear lake, near St. Paul. The *Virginia* won the Rose Festival cup and state championship over a five-mile course this year [1914]. She is one of the most graceful of the river fleet." The article also referred to a second boat, saying that, "Another of this class… is the *Grayling,* also built by the noted Amundson for White Bear lake, and shipped, as was the *Virginia,* to Portland. The *Grayling* is owned by Captain H. F. Todd and is a classic among sail boat designs." As was standard, these boats would have been shipped to Oregon by train.

In 1917 Amundson dabbled in building and selling toboggans. White Bear Mercantile carried a sample. Although the enterprising Amundson had spent many years building sail boats, the firm was specializing in outboard motor boats by 1927.

Gus retired in 1935 and died two years later on January 11. His sons carried on the business until August 3, 1957, when the establishment was sold to the Ahren family and renamed White Bear Marine. The Ahrens sold the business to Fletcher Driscoll, who continued in the same location under the name White Bear Lake Boat Yard until 1968. The building was bulldozed in 1971.

Fritjof Amundson, Gustav's son, was quoted in *J. O. Johnson from Norway to White Bear Lake* as saying, "The engine had a six-foot diameter flywheel. At the start of the day my father would stand on the spokes of this flywheel to get the engine to turn over and start. When I walked to school I could hear that engine going 'chug - chug - chug.' All the machines were connected to the overhead drive shaft with leather belts. The leather belts would break and the bandsaw blades would break, but my father was able to repair them."

Courtesy of the White Bear Lake Area Historical Society

Interior of Amundson Boat Works – Late 1890s

White Bear Press Ad – 1914

ROWBOATS

16 ft. Built of White Cedar
finished in spar varnish

PRICE $35.00

Old Boats taken in trade for new ones. Boat Material for repairing.

Oars from $2.00 a Pair up

The Amundson Boat Works

Both Phones

LAKE SHORE, - WHITE BEAR, MINN.

Courtesy of the White Bear Press

Amundson Boat Works Ad – 1927

Courtesy of the White Bear Press

Courtesy of the White Bear Press

Removal of the Old Amundson Boat Works Building – February 1971

Johan Otto Johansen was born January 10, 1875 in Christiania (Oslo) Norway. At the age of fourteen, he met Gus Amundson, in Norway. Amundson told him that if he could get to White Bear there was a job waiting for him. In 1893, at age eighteen, he came to the United States, making his way to White Bear by November of the same year. The Amundsons took him into their home, treating him like a son. Johan worked as a house boy for the Amundsons and soon went to work for Gus in the boat shop behind the house. Johan Americanized his name changing it to John Otto Johnson, probably so that he would better fit in.

Johnson had an innate ability to interpret how boats handled and traveled through the water. After all, he had spent many years of his youth aboard many different types of boats, and during these times he had carefully studied the design of the various boats. He was destined to become a famous boat builder and not remain an employee in someone else's boat works. A few years after going to work for Amundson, Johnson went to work for himself, and in 1900 he came up with a then-revolutionary boat design, a flat bottomed sloop called a scow, which was likened to "a floating pancake or the slice off the end of a loaf of bread." C. Milton Griggs, a prominent St. Paul businessman and investor, as well as a resident of Manitou Island, invested in the new design by having Johnson build him a scow. In its first race, the boat crossed the finish line before the others had barely begun. After this race Griggs named the boat the *Minnezitka,* which was Indian for "water bird." It went on to take the White Bear Yacht Club championship that year.

Johnson Boat Works was started in 1896. At this time, Johnson was using Nicolas Peterson's (his father-in-law's) boat shed. When he built the *Minnezitka*, a larger space was needed, so during the winter of 1899-1900, he utilized his mother-in-law's restaurant building at Lake Shore. In January 1904 he relocated his shop to a shed behind his recently purchased home on the northwest corner of Lincoln and Hinckley Avenues. Johnson Boat Works was moved to its final location at Lake Shore in 1912, where Johnson built a fifty-five-by-one-hundred-foot building partially over the foundation of an old saloon that had previously burned. In 1928 the building was expanded along the front by about fifty feet, with several other additions occurring over the following years.

Just as Amundson's sons went into business with their father, so did Johnson's sons: Milton, Iver and Walter.

Johnson was an extremely creative and forward-thinking man who did much more than build championship boats. In 1910 he designed, built and flew the first motor-powered flying machine in Minnesota to take off from a level surface. However, his most popular invention, on which he held a patent, was a rotary snow plow that he designed, built, and marketed. During the winter of 1922 the *White Bear Press* effused, "The snow plow patented by John Johnson of Lake Shore turned to naught the work of the blizzard when it got in front of a small tractor and started to throw snow. Suddenly the commotion ceased and the famous rotary snow plow that has been perfected by Mr. Johnson came up for air, looked around and again burrowed into the snow. When the little demon gets busy eating snow it is entirely covered with a curtain of snow." His work in clearing the snow amazed both the state and the county officials because there had been so much snow during that winter that its removal had become quite a problem. In 1925 Johnson sold over one-hundred of the "little demons" and almost two-hundred in 1926. He later sold the patent rights making a small fortune off the idea. Versions of his snowplow cleared roads across the northern United States and Canada.

John O. Johnson died February 28, 1968. The last wooden boat was built by the company in 1976, and in 1998, the boat molds were sold to Melges Boat Works in Wisconsin and the city of White Bear Lake purchased the property. When the boat works closed it had been in business more than one-hundred years, longer than any other boat company in the history of White Bear. The company's many contributions to the boating world are undisputed, with the name known around the world.

Courtesy of Bob Thein

Johnson Boat Works – Lake Shore – Circa 1940

Courtesy of the White Bear Lake Area Historical Society

Caulking the Hull of a Sailboat – Circa 1940

White Bear Press Ad – 1927

Courtesy of the White Bear Press

White Bear Boat Works – Summer 2003

Courtesy of Cynthia Vadnais

Ramaley's Lake Shore Pavilion

Courtesy of the White Bear Lake Area Historical Society

Ramaley's Lake Shore Refreshment Pavilion – 1885

In 1879, near the Lake Shore Depot, the St. Paul and Duluth Railroad erected the forty-by-fifty-foot Park Pavilion and, later the same year, a restaurant, both meant for the pleasure of those seeking the sanctuary of the lake. J. D. Ramaley ran the operation that also boasted forty-eight bathrooms. By 1889 the *Manitoba*, a large steamboat owned by Ramaley, kept regular schedules timed with the arrival of the trains, transferring passengers from the depot across the lake to Mahtomedi.

The July 1885 issue of *Northwest Magazine,* a railroad publication, reported,

> Cottage park is the first point at which one strikes the lake, and as the train runs into the station the sheet of clear water lies spread before you, gleaming through the trees which fringe its banks. Here, close by the depot, is naturally the most public part of the lake, as it were, - the place where the majority of casual visitors and pleasure seekers, who are only out for the day, stop to find amusement. And there is amusement and entertainment enough for them. Close in front of the depot, standing upon the very water's edge, is Ramaley's pavilion and lunch room, by far the most popular place of its kind upon the lake. It is in the first place what it calls itself – a pavilion and lunch room, where all manner of fruits and candies and ice creams and cooling harmless drinks tempt the unwary picnicker. The lunch room itself has wide open sides through which the breeze comes to keep it always cool… Outside… runs a wide balcony, and from which one can drop things into the water, which is a delightful place to sit, fronting the lake, upon a cool evening.

Courtesy of the Richard Vadnais Family

Ramaley's Pavilion

In 1890 John D. Ramaley replaced the railroad's pavilion with this majestic refreshment pavilion that was then arguably the finest structure on the lake. This 1893 photograph shows the pavilion in the company of the Lake Shore Depot, part of which is evident in the left foreground.

Courtesy of the White Bear Lake Area Historical Society

Lake Breeze Ad – 1892

White Bear Lake,

SEASON 1890.

We take pleasure in announcing to our friends and lake patrons that our new and elegant

Amusement and Refreshment Pavilion

which we have erected at great expense, to fill a much needed requirement, at this beautiful Lake Resort, will be completed and ready for business about June 1st.

The Auditorium, accommodating over two thousand persons, seated with comfortable Opera Chairs, Proscenium Boxes, and a fully appointed stage 30x40, will compare with any modern opera house.

To at once popularize this place of amusement, we have arranged with the

Celebrated : Seibert : Orchestra,

for a series of twenty semi-weekly **Concerts and Hops**, commencing on **Friday Evening, June 6, 1890**. We shall also endeavor to present numerous other attractions during the season worthy of patronage. It shall be our aim to conduct the "Pavilion" in a first-class manner throughout, and without any objectionable features.

Arrangements have been made with the Saint Paul and Duluth Railroad for special trains on concert nights, at a reduced fare.

J. D. RAMALEY & SON,
MANAGERS
"RAMALEY'S LAKE SHORE PAVILION."

Courtesy of the White Bear Lake Area Historical Society

Courtesy of the White Bear Lake Area Historical Society
Four Horse Tally-Ho in front of Ramaley's Pavilion – Circa 1900

John D. Ramaley built the 150-by-400-foot building, constructed partly on the water, in 1890 at a cost of $40,000. Interior furnishings cost another $35,000. Supposedly the largest pavilion in the west, it was described by some as a "castle in the air." The building contained a large amphitheater that could seat over two-thousand people with a thirty-by-forty-foot stage. It also had a huge dance hall, a lunchroom and rooms to rent that ran all the way around the perimeter of the building.

The proximity to Lake Shore (Cottage Park) Depot made the pavilion a popular gathering place where, among other things, concerts and dances were held weekly.

Courtesy of Cynthia Vadnais
Steamer *White Bear* – Ramaley's Boat Landing and Casino

Many a pleasure tour of the lake originated from Ramaley's Pavilion where 25¢ round-trip tickets could be purchased from Ramaley's White Bear Navigation Company.

Ramaley provided lake excursions, along with transportation to other destinations around the lake, on his steam yachts that included the *Manitoba* (accommodating up to seventy-five people), the *White Bear* and the *Wildwood*.

Ramaley also had a forty-foot launch, an electric launch (the only one on the lake), and a fleet of naphtha launches.

Courtesy of Cynthia Vadnais

Ramaley's Pavilion and the Water Toboggan Slide

One of the summertime water attractions at the pavilion was the water toboggan slide (shown at the far right in the picture). A forty-room bathhouse was added to accommodate guests who wanted to partake in the fun.

In 1888, the *Lake Breeze* enthused, "White Bear turned out in full force to attend the entertainment at Ramaley's pavilion last evening, and the gathering very much resembled some of the summer assemblies in the handsome little theater. All the reserved seats were taken some days previous and the hall and balcony were well filled. The Lady Minstrels laid themselves out to give their friends a good show and were successful in their anticipations and the audience was delighted with the performance of the troupe..."

Courtesy of the White Bear Lake Area Historical Society

Pickle Club Dance – Ramaley's Pavilion

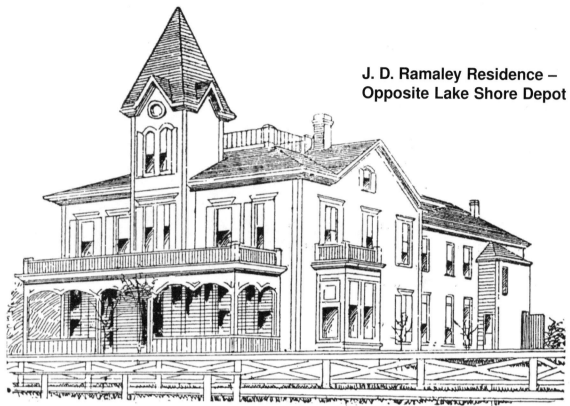

Courtesy of the White Bear Lake Area Historical Society

J. D. Ramaley Residence – Opposite Lake Shore Depot

Ramaley's home, perched high above the lake off to the west, provided him with a perfect vantage point for viewing the activity at his place of business. One part of the home was relocated, between 1900 and 1910, to the southwest corner of Fourth Street and Banning Avenue, with the remainder eventually becoming the present-day Havenor Funeral Home.

Courtesy of Bob Thein

Apartments on Ramaley Pavilion Site – Highway 61 in the Foreground

Ramaley's Pavilion was demolished in 1908 in order to build apartments. The *White Bear Life* reported, "Considerable progress is being made on the demolition of Ramaley Pavilion. Soon, this fine but unprofitable edifice will be a thing of the past." The apartments have since been pulled down and Veterans Memorial Park now occupies the location that Ramaley's Pavilion once dominated.

LAKE STEAMERS AND NAPHTHA LAUNCHES

The simple pleasures that the lake and surrounding area have provided since the late 1800s are the same as those enjoyed today by the people living in White Bear and by those who visit. What has changed is the mode of transportation used on the lake. Gone are the large, steam-powered excursion boats and the smaller naphtha launches. They were replaced by smaller, and often faster, modes of transportation, such as pontoon boats, speedboats, and jet skis. The only local steamboats we see today are on the St. Croix River, Lake Minnetonka, and the Mississippi River where, if one wants, one can recreate the feeling of traveling on a steamboat or naphtha launch on White Bear Lake more than one-hundred years ago.

Courtesy of the Richard Vadnais Family

Steamer *White Bear*

The eighty-foot steamer *White Bear* was built at Ramaley's Boat Works from late 1899 into the spring of 1900. J. E. Ramaley, the boat's captain and owner, launched the double decker steamer in July 1900. This modern boat had electricity throughout, in addition to an electric searchlight, upper-deck dance floor, and a triple expansion engine. At a time when many travelers would come by train to Ramaley's Pavilion to cross the lake to Wildwood Park, the *White Bear* provided swift and comfortable service, taking only fifteen minutes to make the trip. Other captains were Louis Heckel and Thomas Peterson. It was reported that the *White Bear* met its demise in a disastrous fire that sent it to the bottom of White Bear Lake.

Courtesy of Cynthia Vadnais

Steamer *White Bear* Being Built

Although this image is not very sharp, in all likelihood it shows the steamer *White Bear* in slip as it was being built in the bay just south of the VFW.

White Bear Life Ad – 1900

Courtesy of the White Bear Press

NEW STEAMER
WHITE BEAR,
J. E. RAMALEY, Captain.

Time Table.

DAILY—Leaves LAKE SHORE at 10:30 a. m., 2:45 p. m. and 4:30 p. m.

SPECIAL EVENING EXCURSIONS—
Leaves STEAMBOAT LANDING at 7:30 p. m., CLARK STREET at 8 p. m., for Wildwood.

SUNDAY—Leaves every hour at 9:45 a. m.

Steamer Wildwood *Courtesy of the White Bear Lake Area Historical Society*

Both large and small steamers plied the lake from the 1880s into the 1910s. The largest of the steam yachts was the *Dispatch* which was able to carry up to three-hundred passengers. It was often used for parties, evening excursions, and dances. Its accompanying barge, the *Clara E. Miller*, was frequently in tow, providing room for even more passengers. The *Dispatch* had initially been an excursion boat on the local rivers until Al Burrows bought it and moved it to White Bear Lake. Once it had outlived its usefulness, it was dismantled and sunk in the lake. Other sizable steamers of the period included the *White Bear*, the *St. Paul*, the *Manitoba*, and the *Wildwood*.

The *Manitoba*, captained by William Webber, arrived at White Bear Lake in 1888. It was quite a bit smaller than the *Dispatch* and held only fifty to seventy-five passengers.

The *Wildwood*, like the *White Bear*, had been built at White Bear Lake by Harry Darling, a retired riverboat pilot and master on the upper Mississippi River. He is also credited with building the side wheeler *L. P. Ordway* at White Bear Lake. Darling, along with partner A. J. Diamon, owned a garage at Lake Shore where the talented machinist repaired "gas and steam engines, launches, autos, motorcycles, bicycles and all kinds of machinery." There was a period of time when he built small steam engines for the Great Western Railway. Before coming to White Bear, he had built and launched the river boat *Twin Cities* at the lower levee in St. Paul.

As with the other steamers, the *Wildwood* eventually outlived its usefulness. It was put up for sale in 1914.

H. M. Darling's Garage at Lakeshore

Darling's garage was located just west of the present VFW. In 1928 Darling retired from the general machine business. The building had been leased out to the Carver brothers in 1926. Ed Priebe eventually bought the building, which was razed in 1940. Priebe's house is shown to the right of the garage in this photograph.

Courtesy of Bob Thein

Shown (from left to right): Harry Darling, Timmy Darling, John Smith, and Claro Darling. Both Timmy and Claro were Harry's sons. Claro later worked at Parenteau's Grocery. Harry Darling died at age ninety-two in June 1944. His son Claro had died that same year, just a few months before his father.

Courtesy of the Richard Vadnais Family

Harry Darling in His Workshop

Come Take a Ride

Courtesy of Cynthia Vadnais

A Variety of Pleasure Boats on White Bear Lake

Courtesy of Cynthia Vadnais

Steamer *Maud* – Circa 1900

Courtesy of the White Bear Lake Area Historical Society

Steamer *Maud*

Shown is the *Maud* in the foreground and probably the steamer *Floyd* behind her.

Courtesy of the Lawrence R. Whitaker Family

On July 21, 1901 the fire alarm sounded. The *Maud*, whose owner was Captain Young, was on fire. The fire department worked for thirty-five minutes but all was lost.

In 1899, Young had been the captain of the *May*, at that point in time the largest boat on the lake, carrying up to 125 passengers. Some claim that it later burned.

Besides the *Maud*, and the *May*, lesser known steamers operating on the lake were the *Floyd*, the *Ruby*, the *Abe*, and the *Bristol*. The *Floyd* was operated by Captain Boulter and could hold sixty-five passengers. The *Ruby* was a private pleasure steamer that held only twenty passengers, whereas the *Bristol* was a bit bigger holding thirty passengers. The *Bristol*, owned by A. M. Lawton, had been launched in 1888 and was docked at White Bear Beach.

LAKE STEAMERS
MAY and ABE.

Time Table.

Leaves LAKE SHORE daily at 10:15 a. m., WHITE BEAR, foot of Clark avenue, at 10:30 a. m.

Leaves LAKE SHORE daily at 1:45 p. m., WHITE BEAR at 2 p. m.

Leaves LAKE SHORE daily at 3:45 p. m., WHITE BEAR at 4:00 p. m.

Leaves WILDWOOD daily at 11:15 a. m., 3:15 and 5:15 p. m.

Courtesy of the White Bear Press

White Bear Life Ad – 1900

1890 – Ad for Naphtha Launches

Naphtha launches were also very popular during the same period enjoyed by the steamers on White Bear Lake.

According to John W. Johnson in his book *John O. Johnson from Norway to White Bear Lake*, "Naphtha is a petroleum fuel with a boiling point between gasoline and kerosene. Naphtha is used not only as the fuel for these engines, but also as a vapor to drive the pistons. The steamboat uses steam while this boat uses vaporized naphtha in the engine cylinders."

Courtesy of the White Bear Lake Area Historical Society

Lake Breeze Ad – 1892
Courtesy of the White Bear Lake Area Historical Society

Courtesy of the White Bear Press

One of Leaman's Naphtha Launches

WILDWOOD PARK

In the late 1800s Wildwood was under private management. In addition to the amusement park, the resort offered boating, fishing, bathing, dancing, and lovely wooded grounds where people could picnic or just take a stroll. In 1899 the park became the property of the Twin City Rapid Transit Company.

Lake Breeze Ad – 1893

Courtesy of the White Bear Lake Area Historical Society

Courtesy of the White Bear Lake Area Historical Society

Twin City Rapid Transit Company Streetcar Platform at Wildwood Park

In 1899, when Twin City Rapid Transit Company took over Wildwood, the name was changed to Wildwood Park. It was a very successful endeavor, with up to a thousand people visiting the park each day on the weekend, and four-to-five-hundred people visiting daily during the weekdays. The park was open Memorial Day to Labor Day, from eleven in the morning to eleven at night. The last streetcar would leave for St. Paul at 11:30 p.m.

Traveling to Wildwood Park on the streetcars, each of which held forty-eight passengers, was probably as thrilling as some of the rides at the park; reportedly some of the streetcars would hurtle down the tracks and reach speeds of sixty miles per hour on a few sections.

In the 1920s, passengers were paying 10-15¢ each way to travel from St. Paul out to the park. Employees of the park were given free passes each day. The park itself did not have an admission charge.

Littered Picnic Grounds at Wildwood Park

Courtesy of Julie Ahlman

Streetcar Loading Platform

Courtesy of the Thomas Whitrock Family

According to Henry Castle's *St. Paul and Vicinity*, "The electric trip from St. Paul to Wildwood is through rural scenes whose beauty is the delight of thousands who travel this highway. The line sweeps into Wildwood where one may find comfort, coolness, and kindred delights."

To gain entrance to the park, passengers disembarked onto a raised platform, descended one of two large stairways, and entered a tunnel between the stairways, which passed under the elevated rails. This structure was built in 1900.

White Bear Life reported, "Since Wildwood, that beautiful resort at White Bear Lake has passed under the management and control of the Twin City Rapid Transit Company, it is acquiring great popularity. The Transit company has been generous in its improvements, which have included new bath houses, additions to the pavilion, new walks and above all a new and complete stage for the large auditorium."

Courtesy of the White Bear Lake Area Historical Society
Watching a Baseball Game from the Pavilion Veranda – Early 1900s

Courtesy of the White Bear Lake Area Historical Society
Lakeshore along Wildwood Park – Early 1900s

Courtesy of Cynthia Vadnais

Laughing Gallery and Katzenjammer Castle – 1905

Fire struck the park for the first time in 1908. It started in the kitchen of the pavilion and spread, eventually destroying the entire pavilion, the scenic railroad, the laughing gallery, Katzenjammer Castle, the figure-eight roller coaster and one-hundred rowboats that had been stored in the pavilion.

Courtesy of Cynthia Vadnais

Water Toboggan Slide and Bathhouse

Courtesy of the Thomas Whitrock Family

Wildwood Park had one of the finest beaches in the area with an enticing array of water activities, including swimming, water polo, water baseball, a diving platform with several spring boards and a water toboggan slide. Those using the water toboggan slide sat on a wooden toboggan with wheels that would travel along tracks as it moved down the steep incline, jettisoning the riders out into the lake.

Courtesy of Cynthia Vadnais

Wildwood Park Bathhouse

      Those wishing to use the lake had access to a sizable bathhouse. Ladies had two-hundred rooms in which they could change into their swimwear. Suits were rented for 25¢, stockings for 10¢ and caps for 15¢. Men had access to five-hundred lockers along with six showers and could rent suits for 25¢, while small boys' suits rented for 10¢. Those bringing their own suits were charged 25¢ for a towel and use of the changing rooms.

Courtesy of Cynthia Vadnais

Gay Sport on the Water Toboggan Slide – 1905

The use of the water toboggan slide was free; however, the management of the park posted a sign warning, "The owner would not be responsible for nor guarantee its safety nor the condition of the bed of the lake."

Cooling Off on a Hot Summer Day – Circa 1905

Courtesy of Cynthia Vadnais

Renting a Rowboat

Courtesy of the Thomas Whitrock Family

Wildwood Park Boat House provided rowboats for both pleasure and the more serious business of fishing. Tackle was provided free of charge with a small fee charged for the bait. Boat rental was 25¢ per hour, with special rates arranged for those wanting a boat for the entire day.

Wildwood Park

Courtesy of Cynthia Vadnais

Courtesy of the Lawrence R. Whitaker Family

The Main Pavilion – Rebuilt after the 1908 Fire

The newly built red-brick pavilion, with its hardwood floor dance hall, was probably the most popular attraction in the park. For 10¢, a person gained admission for the entire afternoon or evening dance session, each of which showcased fifteen dances. This price included use of the checkroom. Dances were held on Wednesday, Friday, Saturday and Sunday each week. On Sundays free concerts were given on the veranda. Guy Lombardo, Cliff Perine, Fats Waller, Johnny Erickson's Land O'Lakes Orchestra, A. L. Snyder's Minnesota State Orchestra, Wally Erickson, Norvy Mulligan, and the Coronado Orchestra are among the many groups that played at the park.

At the entrance to the dance hall was the main refreshment stand that sold soda fountain drinks, candy, ice cream, popcorn, and cigars. Patrons could order from the counter or sit at tables on the expansive veranda overlooking the lake and be served by waiters.

The large building also housed the eleven well-equipped bowling alleys that cost 10¢ per person per game.

The park closed in 1932 but the pavilion remained open until 1937.

Courtesy of the White Bear Lake Area Historical Society

Tilt-a-Whirl

Wildwood Park boasted the first tilt-a-whirl invented and built by the Sellner Manufacturing Company in Faribault, Minnesota.

Courtesy of Cynthia Vadnais

Fun Factory and Postal Photo Gallery

The brick building on the right was built after the fire in 1908. This location next to the entrance to the roller coaster had previously been occupied by Katzenjammer Castle and the Laughing Gallery.

The house of mirrors was called the Fun Factory (located on the left side of the brick building). Here people looked into distorted mirrors to view misshapen images of themselves. Admission was 5¢ for children and 10¢ for adults.

For those wanting to create a picture memory of their trip to the park, the Postal Photo Gallery Factory (located on the right side of the brick building) would take a visitor's picture and use it to create three postcards for 25¢ – all while the customer waited. A specialty of the Postal Photo Gallery was to take pictures of picnic parties, in small or panoramic groups, since no outside commercial photographers were allowed on the grounds.

Figure-Eight Roller Coaster – Early 1900s
The figure-eight was the first roller coaster in the park. It was lost in the 1908 fire.

Encased by the Figure-Eight Roller Coaster

The Pippin

Courtesy of the White Bear Press

Courtesy of Julie Ahlman

The Pippin, a five-hundred-foot-long roller coaster that dominated the landscape, replaced the original smaller coaster after it had burned down. Although it was not the only feature at the park, it was by far the most popular with a ride costing a mere 5¢ per person. When the park was dismantled in 1938, the coaster was taken apart and moved to Excelsior Amusement Park, where it was used for many years before being dismantled. (It was not moved to Valley Fair.)

White Bear Press Ad – 1937

One Night Only---
Wednesday, July 28

"FATS" WALLER
AND HIS 15 ARTISTS

A FOUR STAR ATTRACTION!
RADIO - STAGE - SCREEN - RECORDING
World's Greatest Entertainer

Only Appearance in this Territory.

Dancing 9 to 1 a.m.

WILDWOOD
AMUSEMENT PARK
WHITE BEAR LAKE

Courtesy of the White Bear Press

Wildwood Park Bathhouse Rebuilt After the 1908 Fire

Courtesy of Ruth Mattlin

The bathhouse burned to the ground in February of 1936. The Mahtomedi and White Bear firemen worked together, laying 1,600 feet of hose to the nearest hydrant, only to discover that it was dead. The snow was deep enough that any attempt to get to the lake for water would have also failed. Besides, it was determined that even if they could make it to the lake, the ice was so thick they would have had to cut through several feet of it to get to the water. The only choice for the firemen was to return to quarters.

Courtesy of Julie Ahlman

Taking in the Warmth of the Day – Early 1920s

The two bathers on the left are Frank and Ann Wallerick. This picture was taken some time in the early 1920s on the steps of the bathhouse.

Courtesy of Beverly (Wallerick) Vadnais

Courtesy of Cynthia Vadnais

Wildwood Park Picnic Pavilion

Located in the picnic grove, the Picnic Pavilion carried a variety of refreshments, sandwiches, and ice cream that could be bought by the cone for 5¢, or in large quantities for picnic parties. Not everyone was inclined to purchase meals at the park. As a courtesy to patrons, a free picnic kitchen, located in the pavilion, was provided for preparing lunches and coffee. The vast picnic grove was furnished with benches and tables where families could relax, eat, and enjoy the surroundings while the children played on the playgrounds and swings interspersed throughout the area.

Courtesy of the Thomas Whitrock Family

The *Wildwood*

In the early years, most residents, and those traveling out to White Bear by train, would take the trip over to Wildwood Park using one of the steamboats. The Minnetonka and White Bear Navigation Company was incorporated in March 1910 as a subsidiary of the Twin City Rapid Transit Company. As an agent for the company, J. D. Ramaley provided round-trip transportation across the lake to Wildwood Park on board the *Wildwood* and the *White Bear*. In the early 1900s the steamboats ran hourly from Lake Shore (Cottage Park) Depot over to Wildwood Park, with a round trip ticket costing 25¢. By 1914 the steamboat era on the lake was coming to an end. The *White Bear* had burned and sunk to the bottom of the lake and Ramaley Boat Company had put the *Wildwood* up for sale.

Courtesy of Cynthia Vadnais

1907 – The Steamer *Wildwood* at Dock – Wildwood Park

Wildwood Park encompassed twenty acres with two-thousand feet of shoreline.

Steamers Docked at Wildwood waiting for Pleasure Seekers

Courtesy of the White Bear Lake Area Historical Society

Courtesy of Cynthia Vadnais

Over the years many boats transported passengers to and from Wildwood. Among those that made regular trips were the *Wildwood, White Bear, Abe, May, Dispatch, Manitoba, Maud,* and *Floyd.*

Ann and Frank Wallerick spent many a day at Wildwood Park while dating and after marriage. Friends and relatives often accompanied them to the park. The next several photographs of their trips to the park were taken in the early 1900s.

Getting Ready to Go to Wildwood Park on the Twin City Lines Streetcars

Frank and Ann Wallerick (shown on the right) used the streetcar line, as did most, to get to Wildwood Park from the east side of St. Paul, where they resided.

Courtesy of Beverly (Wallerick) Vadnais

Early Beach Wear – 1910s

Notice the streetcar and the wagon and horses in the background.

Courtesy of Beverly (Wallerick) Vadnais

Later, More Revealing Beach Wear – 1920s

Bathing Suit Fashion of the Day – 1920s

Courtesy of Beverly (Wallerick) Vadnais

Wildwood Rowboat #5 with Bathing Beauties

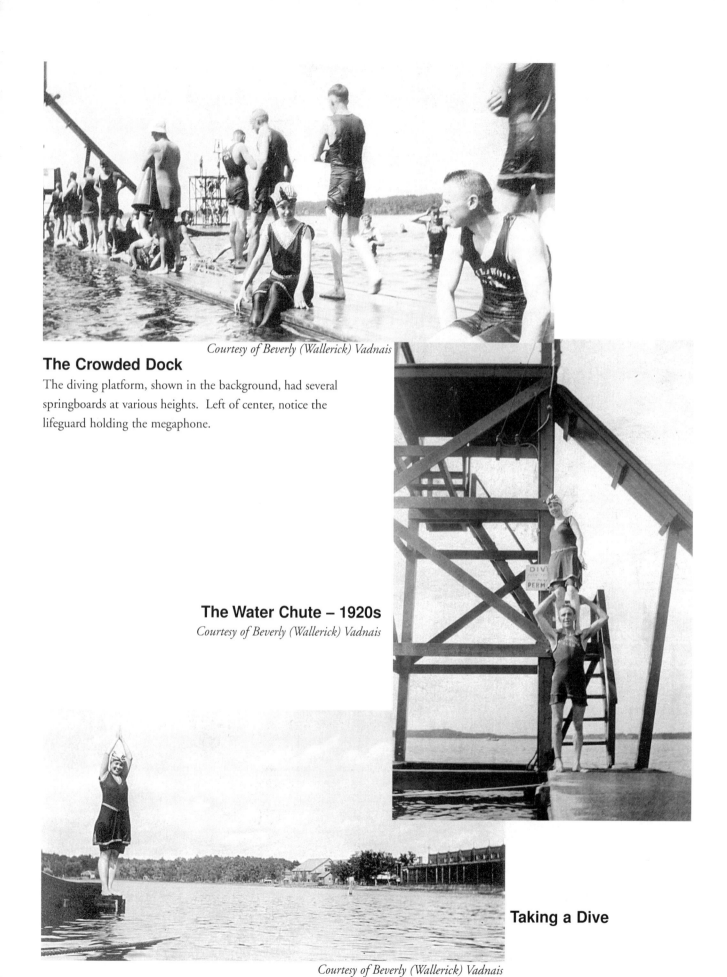

The Crowded Dock

The diving platform, shown in the background, had several springboards at various heights. Left of center, notice the lifeguard holding the megaphone.

Courtesy of Beverly (Wallerick) Vadnais

The Water Chute – 1920s

Courtesy of Beverly (Wallerick) Vadnais

Taking a Dive

Courtesy of Beverly (Wallerick) Vadnais

Enjoying a Soda in the Picnic Grove

Courtesy of Beverly (Wallerick) Vadnais

The Carrousel

The Philadelphia Toboggan Company owned the carrousel at Wildwood Park. It had brightly colored horses, lions, and giraffes to ride while riders grabbed for the brass rings. Seats were provided for those who did not wish to ride on one of the animals.

Courtesy of Beverly (Wallerick) Vadnais

Ready to Head Home

Courtesy of Beverly (Wallerick) Vadnais

Rental Boats, Dance Pavilion and Bathhouse – Circa 1912
Courtesy of Cynthia Vadnais

The water's edge as it looked for many of the years that Wildwood Park was in operation.

Wildwood Beach Area where once stood Wildwood Park
Courtesy of Cynthia Vadnais

In 1938 Wildwood Park was dismantled and many of the amusements were moved to Excelsior Amusement Park on Lake Minnetonka. The two-thousand feet of shoreline became backyards in a housing development.

St. Paul Automobile Club

Courtesy of the White Bear Lake Area Historical Society

First St. Paul Automobile Clubhouse at White Bear Lake – 1912

The St. Paul Automobile Club was organized around 1903 to "promote good roads and protect the motorist against the hostility of pedestrians." In 1912 the St. Paul Automobile Club leased the old Leip property on White Bear Lake for its summer headquarters. During the rest of the year the club had its headquarters at the Ryan Hotel in St. Paul.

At the end of the 1913 season the club purchased the property and contracted with C. E. Davies to erect a new clubhouse. The old clubhouse, along with the cottages located on the property, were to be disposed of upon completion of the new building. The total cost to purchase the land, build, and make improvements came to around $50,000.

White Bear Lake from St. Paul Automobile Club Entrance

Courtesy of the Richard Vadnais Family

Courtesy of the Richard Vadnais Family

St. Paul Automobile Club – Circa 1915

    C. E. Davies finished the construction of the clubhouse designed by H. A. Sullwold in May 1914, at which time there were 957 members on the rolls. The exterior of the building was finished in stucco and tile. The interior contained a cafe, ballroom, private dining rooms, and card rooms on the main level, with a rathskeller and gymnasium located in the basement. The second floor had ten or more sleeping rooms. The building was situated so that there were views of both White Bear Lake and Goose Lake. Arrangements were made to auction off the other buildings on the property. The grounds were to contain a baseball diamond and tennis courts. In 1921 a golf course was added, and by 1927 automobile sheds and trap shooting could be found on the club grounds.

Courtesy of Cynthia Vadnais

Summer Headquarters of the St. Paul Automobile Club

St. Paul Automobile Club Dining Room

The circular dining room was located around the perimeter of the ballroom. Over the years, a number of the White Bear High School junior and senior banquets were held at the automobile club.

Courtesy of the White Bear Press

White Bear Press Ad – 1928

Courtesy of the White Bear Press

Aerial View of the St. Paul Automobile Club – 1921

Courtesy of the White Bear Press

Courtesy of the White Bear Press
First Section of Latticework for the Artificial Beach
Construction of the Latticework

Courtesy of the White Bear Press

Courtesy of the White Bear Press
Distributing the Concrete Onto the Latticework

Courtesy of the White Bear Press
Finishing the Third Section

Placing of the Concrete Slabs

Courtesy of the White Bear Press

    In 1924 the county installed an artificial bathing beach in White Bear Lake, locating it in front of the automobile club. The bottom of the lake in the area was all mud, so the idea was to create a wooden lattice structure that would hold a two-foot-square-by-two-inch-thick slab of sidewalk concrete in each opening. The latticework was built in three parts, floated onto the lake and linked together like a big raft extending 150 feet out. Once laid in place, the concrete tiles sank the wooden structure, effectively covering thirty-two-thousand square feet of the muddy lake bottom. The project started on July 10, 1924 and was completed three weeks later.

Courtesy of Cynthia Vadnais

Resthaven Sanitorium

The clubhouse sat vacant for a few years. Around 1932 Jacques Brouwers used the old automobile sheds as horse stables for White Bear Stables. In 1931 Mrs. Joe Boppre, whose husband owned Boppre Chevrolet, purchased the automobile club. She renovated the clubhouse and grounds, creating Resthaven, a center for the treatment of tuberculosis and other pulmonary diseases.

Resthaven came upon hard times during the Depression. In 1936 the property was scheduled to be cut up into lots. The building fell into disrepair and was further damaged by the tornado that struck White Bear in 1941.

AUCTION SALE
at "RESTHAVEN"
Former Auto Club

ENTIRE FURNISHINGS CONSISTING OF:

Kitchen Equipment	Dining Room Furniture
Wicker Furniture	Hospital Equipment
Office Furniture	Bed Room Furniture
Living Room Furniture	Miscellaneous Equip.

Saturday, Sept. 14
Beginning at 9 a. m.

Julius A. Haussner Consignee for Owner

Chas. A. Haussner, Clerk   Julius A. Haussner, Auctioneer

White Bear Press Ad – 1935

Courtesy of the White Bear Press

Colony Country Club
Old St. Paul Auto Club Bldg.

is running a special of
STEAK or CHICKEN
50c
Orchestra - Beautiful Dance Floor - Always Cool

Also hotel, housekeeping rooms and apartments. Reasonable rates.

White Bear Press Ad – 1937

Courtesy of the White Bear Press

In 1937, for a brief period, the old St. Paul Automobile Clubhouse was used as the Colony Country Club.

Courtesy of the White Bear Lake Area Historical Society

The Beginning of the End – Circa 1959

The automobile club was converted into apartments, which later fell into ruins and was sold off. In 1959 the developer cleared the land to make way for the construction of the White Bear Shopping Center, which has occupied the property ever since.

The Plantation

In 1925 J. E. (Gene) Ramaley, son of J. D. Ramaley, the owner of Ramaley's Pavilion at the turn of the century, moved Ramaley's Boat Works to Lake Minnetonka, converting the old boat house at White Bear into a dance hall. Later the same year, after having demolished the boat works, he erected Ramaley's Winter Garden. It was located about where Lions Park is today. When completed, the facility had parking for up to three-hundred cars and had cost $50,000 to build.

The 1926 *White Bear Press* gave a beautiful description of Ramaley's Winter Garden, saying the building was

> ... a fairylike stucco structure in Spanish style, adorned with flags and a blaze of light outside, and inside containing a spacious dancing pavilion, the fruition of a beautiful dream in which nothing even to the smallest detail has been forgotten or overlooked. The terra cotta color scheme is heightened by myriads of var-colored [sic] lights, baskets of flowers along the wall, and graceful hanging chandeliers, while the slightly arched ceiling suggests the 'grand salon' of a gigantic Atlantic liner. The popular Land of Lakes orchestra from Wildwood discourses sweet music from an aerial platform accompanied by beautiful electric lighting effects. The spacious dancing floor is now as smooth as the first coat of glare ice that forms annually on the lake about Thanksgiving day.

St. Paul Night at Ramaley's Winter Garden
Sat., January 22

Mayor and Mrs. Hodgson and the St. Paul City Council accompanied by their wives will be in attendance and will be received by Mayor and Mrs. Jackson and City Council members and their wives.

The Public is Invited.

Tickets . . . . . 50c the person

Special attraction: Moose Serenaders
Land-o'-the Lakes Orchestra

Special Bus will leave hall at 12:15 for St. Paul

Courtesy of the White Bear Press

During 1927 the business was leased to two separate parties. The first was T. E. Barbeau, who had a radio station, WMBE, hooked up so that the dance music could be broadcast. At this time only Saturday night dances were held. Then a Mr. Mendelshon from Minneapolis took over and renamed the establishment The New Pershing Inn. But neither business lasted, since Ramaley was once again the manager before the end of the year.

White Bear Press Ad – 1927

Courtesy of the White Bear Press

DANCING AT
Ramaley Winter Garden
White Bear Lake

WHITE BEAR NIGHT
SATURDAY, JANUARY 8, 1927
8:15 to 12 o'clock

Ramaley's Winter Garden

J. E. RAMALEY, Prop.

Most Beautiful Dance Pavilion in the Northwest
Located on West Shore of White Bear Lake

Roof Garden, Boats and Launches
in Summer Time

Engagements for Private or Public Parties

Open Every Saturday Night Until Summer Season
Begins When It Will Be Open Every Night

--For Engagements Address or Phone--

J. E. RAMALEY

Wayzata Telephone 5   WAYZATA, MINN.

Courtesy of the White Bear Press

White Bear Press Ad – 1927

DANCE AT White Bear Castle
White Bear Lake

To the Music of
Walt and his Hoodlums, 10 Pieces
Dancing from 9:00 to 1:00 o'clock

Every Wednesday Saturday and Sunday

On Highwey No. 1 — Formerly Ramaley's Winter

Courtesy of the White Bear Press

White Bear Press Ad – 1928

During the 1928-1929 season the dance pavilion was called the White Bear Castle. In 1928, with Larry Johnson managing, dancing costs were 25¢ for ladies and 50¢ for gents.

In 1928 the radio station installed in 1927 was removed and donated to White Bear High School.

DANCE EVERY SATURDAY NITE at White Bear Castle

Now Under New Management with

Mel and his Harmony Bears
of The White Bear Motor Sales

Refreshments - 9 to 1 - Checking

Courtesy of the White Bear Press

White Bear Press Ad – 1928
Mechanics by day, musicians by night!

White Bear Press Ad – 1929
In 1929 the White Bear Castle was under the management of W. L. Dragert and C. O. Breen.

Courtesy of the White Bear Press

147

Courtesy of the White Bear Lake Area Historical Society

The Plantation

On July 2, 1930 the newly remodeled and renamed dance hall, The Plantation, opened with an invitation-only premier party with music provided by an orchestra from New York. The improvements had cost at least $10,000. The interior had been decorated like a scene from a plantation. According to the *White Bear Press*, "Beautiful trees spread their branches, forming a canopy, and creating a bower of foliage. The check room is a splendid replica of an old shed, in one corner of the plantation." The chef, Chris Gade, had been with the White Bear Yacht Club for eight years and had also, raved the *White Bear Press*, "delighted the exacting connoisseurs of Hollywood, Los Angeles, and other coast cities." KSTP radio was connected and the music broadcast for half an hour each evening, five days a week.

From 1930 to 1933 the Plantation was under the management of Ben Harris, who was supposedly connected to the Barker-Karpis gang. The Plantation soon became a hangout for many types of gangsters. According to Paul Maccabee, in his book *John Dillinger Slept Here*, "Hoover [J. Edgar] was infuriated that the gangsters felt so safe they didn't bother to hide from his agents but lived openly in White Bear Lake, partying uproariously at local nightclubs." He goes on to say, "Among the Plantation's patrons during the summers of 1931 and 1932 were local thugs like fixer Jack Peifer and bootlegger Morris Roisner, nationally known bank robbers Jimmy Keating and Tommy Holden, and Capone gunman Fred Goetz." Frank Nash, a gangster out of Oklahoma, frequented the club during the summer of 1931. It was reported that he won $6,000 in just one night of gambling. Although liquor was not served, patrons brought in bootlegged gin and whiskey with the club providing the setups. Armed guards stood outside the entrance to the gambling casino. Robert "Frisco Dutch" Steinhardt, who had been arrested more than eighteen times for various reasons, served as a bouncer and gambling consultant. By 1932 White Bear mayor Buckbee denounced the Plantation, calling it "a rendezvous place for gangsters."

Harris closed the Plantation at the end of the 1933 season. He said, "In 1930 and '31 I did well, but the Depression hit everybody so hard they couldn't keep up their patronage. 1932 was bad but 1933 was worse." In 1934 Ben Harris pled guilty to running a roulette wheel.

White Bear Press Ad – 1933

Courtesy of the White Bear Press

Courtesy of the White Bear Press

White Bear Press Ad – 1935

In 1935 Ramaley decided to reopen the Plantation. The bill of fare was a wholesome, all-family-members-allowed barn dance at a bargain admission price of 35¢. The club was to be open six nights a week with four different orchestras performing each week. WTCN was the radio station that broadcast the dance music.

During the late 1930s and into the early 1940s, the Plantation was open sporadically. It remained closed during World War II.

In 1946, three ex-GI's purchased the building and turned it into the Plantation Playhouse. The community theater seated four-hundred, with plays performed by University of Minnesota students. Although the theater was run on a shoestring budget it did manage to last for at least three seasons, after which the building stood vacant until 1950.

Courtesy of the White Bear Press

White Bear Press Ad –1937

Plantation Boat Livery & Drive-In

"EVERY BITE A DELIGHT"

CHICKEN IN A BASKET

Hamburgers   French Fries

Steak Sandwiches

Dairy Dip   Cold Drinks

For extra fast service to take out, phone in advance Open 12 Noon to 11:00 P. M. Every Day, Except Friday and Saturday. Open Friday and Saturday 12 Noon to 12:00 P. M.

4400 WHITE BEAR AVE.   W.B. 160M

White Bear Press Ad – 1954   *Courtesy of the White Bear Press*

In 1950, Arthur Allen purchased the building and razed most of the main structure. The building was remodeled into a drive-in shaped like a boat. The Plantation Boat Livery & Drive-In opened for business on May 12, 1951. Allen had purchased boats for hire from Amundson Boat Works, and with his family they successfully operated the business until about 1959.

The Plantation – 1974   *Courtesy of the White Bear Press*

The building that was once one of the liveliest places in White Bear Lake was purchased by the city of White Bear Lake on May 31, 1974. The long-forgotten and much-deteriorated structure was demolished the same year. Lions Park now occupies the site.

Sir Aubrey John Paul and Lady Laura Paul

Early citizens of White Bear did not know that the English couple, Mr. and Mrs. John Aubrey, were really English nobility. The couple's generosity masked the shame they must have felt because of the hard times that had besieged Mr. Aubrey's family back in England.

In 1851, Sir Aubrey John Paul, son of Sir John Dean Paul of Gloucester, married Laura Kaye, the second daughter of Sir Lester Kaye of Yorkshire. Misfortune fell upon the family when Sir John Dean Paul's bank failed, resulting in his exile to Australia for fourteen years. Disgraced, Sir Aubrey and Lady Paul decided to leave and go to Canada, where they secured their anonymity by using the names John and Laura Aubrey. They moved to White Bear in 1857 after their home in Superior, Wisconsin burned.

Around 1858 they purchased a tract of land from Villeroy B. Barnum, the proprietor of Barnum's Hotel, where they had lived since their arrival. The land extended between White Bear and Goose Lakes extending down along the shore of Goose Lake. It was here where a Mr. Ashton of St. Paul constructed a home for the Aubreys. The two-story wooden shake home was the first house in White Bear not built of logs.

Aubrey became one of the best hunters and trappers in the area. It was a common sight to see him roaming the countryside accompanied by his two hunting dogs "Powder" and "Shot." When not hunting, he built some of the first sailboats to ply White Bear Lake, with the help of Duncan Ross.

Courtesy of the White Bear Lake Area Historical Society
Lady Laura Paul

Courtesy of the White Bear Lake Area Historical Society
Sir Aubrey John Paul

Mrs. Aubrey's benevolent nature led to educational and religious progress in White Bear. She taught school, without pay, in her home and at the log schoolhouse after it was built. Later, she donated land and raised money for a church, St. John in the Wilderness, to be built. Her friends in the U.S. and in England contributed to the cause, with one English gentleman sending $500. Upon the dedication of the church in 1862, the one-hundred or so in attendance were invited to dinner at Mrs. Aubrey's home.

It was late in 1868 that Aubrey received a telegram about his father's death on September 7, 1868 in Australia. Sir Aubrey and Lady Paul decided to return to the family manor home, near Dean Forest in England, to take their rightful place in society. The townspeople had been quite fortunate, if only for a short time, that the Aubreys had given so much to the advancement of the young community of White Bear. Sir Aubrey John Paul died in June 1890 and his wife, Lady Laura Paul, died in May of 1924 at the age of ninety-five.

Courtesy of Cynthia Vadnais

Aubrey Home – Cottage Park Road – December 2003

Duncan Ross, who spent time with Mr. Aubrey, was brought back into the minds of the people of White Bear long after he was gone. It seems that Mr. Ross and others had been buried at a location outside the cemetery. When the Union Cemetery was established, all but two of the bodies were relocated, but those two could not be found.

In 1937, while the city was doing sewer work, a skeleton was uncovered. Mr. W. W. Webber had known Ross and described him as being "a man below medium stature, about 60 or 65 years of age." When a full-length picture of Ross was produced, it matched the characteristics given by Mr. Webber. The newspaper article about the identity of the mystery skeleton went on to say, "The bones unearthed indicated a man of the described size of Ross, and the teeth tallied with his age." From this information, it was decided that the unknown remains were those of Duncan Ross and he was given a proper burial in Union Cemetery.

Duncan Ross had been a Mississippi river sailor before coming to White Bear. Also a religious man, in 1860 Duncan Ross became the first Sunday School superintendent of the Union Sunday School, a nondenominational Sunday School that included instruction from Presbyterian, Episcopal, Baptist and Methodist clergymen. The first meeting of the Sunday School was opened with the prayer "that they would have the intelligence not to annoy each other with the minor differences in the religions but would rather think to instruct the children in the Bible here in order to make them useful and good as they grow up in life." The prayer was given by James F. Murray, also known as Father Murray.

Courtesy of the White Bear Press

Duncan Ross – Builder and Sailor of First Boat on White Bear Lake

Early Community Churches

> "Show me your churches and schools and I will tell you what sort of a community you have."
> *Anonymous*

Mr. and Mrs. Aubrey were the principal organizers of the Episcopal Church at White Bear. Around 1858 services were being held at the log schoolhouse located on Murray Avenue near Second Street, with the Reverend Van Ingen from Christ Church, St. Paul officiating. A desire for a permanent location led to the building, in 1861, of the fifteen-by-twenty-five-foot Episcopal Church, St. John in the Wilderness.

St. John in the Wilderness was located on land donated by the Aubreys inside what is now the Episcopal Cemetery. The eighteenth century Hanoverian style church was constructed with money raised by the Aubreys and materials provided by the James C. Murray family at Bald Eagle. Trees were cut on the Murray property and gathered together out on the ice of Bald Eagle Lake. The following day the intention was to load the timbers onto sleds for the trip to the site of the new church, but this became quite a chore when, during the night, the weight of the logs had sunk the ice, flooding the surface and soaking the logs. The water-laden logs were hauled to the construction site with great effort.

John Aubrey hired Cyrus Greaves (Grieves?) to build the church. Greaves started work on the church in the spring of 1861, each day carrying a scale model of the church to the site and home again in the evening. The church was built through the effort of the community. It was finished with a coat of dark-red paint.

Courtesy of St. John in the Wilderness Episcopal Church

St. John in the Wilderness Church in its Original Location

When the church first opened, tamarack boughs were used to cover the windows, as there were no window sashes. Sashes were donated later when Christ Church in St. Paul was torn down. The simply furnished interior contained plain benches with no backs.

Courtesy of the Lawrence R. Whitaker Family

William & Emily Stiles House – Cottage Park

This photograph of the Stiles house was taken by William H. Whitaker.

(Samuel) William Stiles was married to V. B. Barnum's daughter Emily. In 1861 Barnum sold Stiles a strip of land just north of the Aubrey's home, where they built this house. The building stood until about 1910. On October 5, 1868 a funeral service was held for Samuel William Stiles. This was the first funeral service held at St. John in the Wilderness Church.

Depiction of the Moving of St. John in the Wilderness Church

The drawing shows a steeple already in place. The steeple was not constructed until after the church was relocated.

Over time many of the parishioners were settling on the other side of the lake. To better serve the needs of the growing population, the church, with the aid of Mrs. Benson, Mr. Harry Getty, Mrs. Leip, and Mrs. Williams, among other supporters, raised money to purchase a lot for $300 on the northeast corner of Clark Avenue and First Street and to have the church relocated. In the winter of 1874 the church was transported, at a cost of $300, across the lake by Mr. Craig to the foot of Clark Avenue, where it was jacked up to street level and moved to its new location. There, a steeple was added, and in 1877 a bell donated by Cooper Fulton's father, Thomas C. Fulton, was installed.

Courtesy of St. John in the Wilderness Episcopal Church

St. John in the Wilderness Church – Clark Avenue

With the rector having to travel a long distance, services were held but once a month. None were held during the winter months, since the small stove located in the center of the building did not supply sufficient heat. Regular services began after April 26, 1897 when Rev. H. S. Streetar became the first clergyman of the parish to reside in White Bear.

Eventually the simple wooden benches were replaced with pews donated by Mrs. William R. Merriam, the then-governor's wife. Other contributions included an altar donated in 1880, a lectern donated in 1883 by Mrs. Hoyt and Mrs. E. C. Williams in honor of their brother Captain Eugene B. Gibbs, and a marble font donated in 1887 by Mrs. E. C. Williams in honor of her husband. All of these are still in use today.

Courtesy of St. John in the Wilderness Episcopal Church

The Choir – 1910

Members (from left to right): Lucy Francis, Ruth Torinus, Rev. C. Herbert Shutt, Beth Warner, Nellie Freeman, Mrs. H. A. Warner Sr., Marie Hansen, Sophie Holzheid, and Margaret Benson.

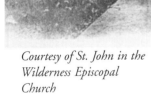

Courtesy of St. John in the Wilderness Episcopal Church

Interior of the First St. John in the Wilderness Church

Courtesy of St. John in the Wilderness Episcopal Church

St. John in the Wilderness Episcopal Church Choir – 1925

Members of the choir are, from left to right: (first row) Dorothy Wentworth, Burr Brosious, Harriet Bloom, Marie Hamilton, Rev. William Temple, Rt. Rev. Frank A. McElwain, Arthur Parcells, Mr. Bonham, Mr. Webb, Sterling Price, William Bonham; (second row) Marian Price, Naomi Bowen, Nellie Fulton, Virginia Dungan, Mrs. Webb, Louis Nash Jr., Harold Mattlin, Ruddy Brosious, —— Bloom, Robert Bloom; (last row) Jane Fulton, Eleanor Jones, Louise Dungan, Charles Price, Ione Green, Charlotte Harding, and Jim Fulton.

Over the years St. John in the Wilderness was remodeled three times. It was not until 1901 that electric lighting was installed. Contractor John Mackenhausen did the last remodel in 1914 when a vestry room was added. On May 12, 1925 the little red church was deconsecrated, and the last service was held in the building on July 26, 1925. Most of the building was torn down, with a small portion being carted off and incorporated as a part of a summer cottage.

C. E. Van Kirk was the architect and C. E. Davies the contractor of the new Gothic-style church and parish house. Construction on the limestone building started in 1925 and Bishop McElwain dedicated the church on June 20, 1926. The interior was furnished with the altar and woodwork from the original church. In 1960 a parish hall and classroom wing was added; otherwise, the church remains as it was built in 1925.

White Bear Press Ad – 1915

Besides being a house builder, Davies built many notable structures in White Bear, including the Y.M.C.A./Auditorium (1907), the St. Paul Automobile Club (1913-1914), and the Carnegie Library (1914-1915).

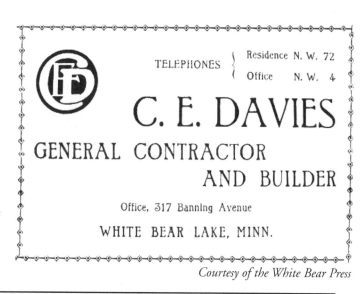

Courtesy of the White Bear Press

Courtesy of Cynthia Vadnais

St. John in the Wilderness Church – 2000

First Presbyterian Church – 1890

Courtesy of the White Bear Lake Area Historical Society

Reverend J. C. Caldwell and Reverend J. G. Reihldaffer organized the First Presbyterian Church on May 28, 1864. There were eight charter members: James Murray, Amelia Murray, Jacob Long, Mary Long, Daniel Getty, Mark K. Getty, Edward Long, and Ernestine Long.

Before the church was organized, services were held at various homes. In 1864 the log schoolhouse was used for services. From 1870 to 1873 services were held at West Side School.

Around 1870 the church received a gift of $100, which was used to purchase a lot near the railroad, but it was deemed unsuitable for the building of a church. In 1871, Dr. J. H. Stewart of St. Paul donated a more suitable site at what was then 701 Second Street just east of Clark Avenue.

Funds were raised and building started in 1871 on the second church to be built in White Bear. The cornerstone was laid on November 8 of that same year. The church was partly enclosed by the spring of 1872. At this point the interior was furnished with crude benches so services could be held during the summer. The thirty-three-by-fifty-foot structure was completed on November 11, 1873 at a cost of $2,500, and on August 23, 1877, with Reverend Reihldaffer presiding, the church was dedicated.

In 1881 two lots and a house were purchased for $400. The house, which was located at Third Street and Banning Avenue, was remodeled into a parsonage for the first resident pastor, Reverend J. C. Robinson. In August 1914 the church bought another house and property, at Fifth Street and Stewart Avenue, at which time they traded in the original property. This new parsonage was still in use in 1937.

Over the years many improvements were made to the church. These included the installation of a bell and carpeting in 1877, building of a lecture room, papering and carpeting of the church, and the siding and painting of the building in 1886; in 1896, the church was reroofed and repapered. In 1919 the church was enlarged to accommodate up to two-hundred people, and a pipe organ was installed. In 1937 a basement for Sunday school classes was added.

The Presbyterian Church Choir – 1929

Shown from left to right: (first row) Mrs. C. H. Christenson, Evelyn Bacon, Mrs. E. R. Cunningham, Mrs. F. D. Parker, organist; Helen Lafond, Dorathea Peltier, Helen Fisher; (second row) Mrs. Wesley Parcells, Mrs. C. G. Smith, Mrs. T. W. Bacon, Edwin G. Amundson, director; Mrs. H. Anderson, Mrs. Ga. A. Silloway, Mrs. I. E. Long; (third row) Wesley Parcells, Kenneth Rippel, Cleo G. Smith, C. H. Christenson, Harry Anderson, Harry Hauglie.

Courtesy of the White Bear Lake Area Historical Society

Lucius C. Dunn, a Civil War veteran and owner of the South Shore House, was one of the early organists for the First Presbyterian Church. From 1918 to 1930, Mrs. Emma Guipe Parker was the organist for the church.

Mrs. Parker – Organist at the First Presbyterian Church

Courtesy of the White Bear Press

First Presbyterian Church – Circa 1920

The last services were held in the old First Presbyterian Church building in 1959. Groundbreaking for a new church, located on the northwest corner of Fifth Street and Bloom Avenue, was held in 1958, and on September 27, 1959 the first service was held in the new building. Services have been held in the same location ever since.

Courtesy of the White Bear Lake Area Historical Society

Courtesy of Cynthia Vadnais

First Presbyterian Church – Northwest Corner of Bloom Avenue and Fifth Street

The Gutted Shell of What Was Once the First Presbyterian Church Building – 1969

Courtesy of the White Bear Press

The First Presbyterian Church property and building on Second Street were sold to the Lakeshore Players in 1957. In November 1969 the building caught fire, damaging it to the point where it had to be razed. It was almost one-hundred years old. This was the second, but fatal, brush with fire for this building. In 1928, when a fire destroyed a barn that stood near the back of the church, the building had survived with minimal damage. The area where the church once stood is now a part of the easternmost end of the US Bank parking lot.

Mound Cottage – Shady Lane

Courtesy of Bob Thein

Although White Bear did not have a Catholic church, the spiritual needs of those in White Bear were attended to by Father Goiffon of Little Canada. As early as 1865, Father Goiffon celebrated Low Mass in private homes and on occasion at the log schoolhouse.

In 1873, Father Koop, a frequent visitor to the Markoe cottage, celebrated mass at the log schoolhouse, which had been converted into a chapel for the occasion. The celebration of mass by Father Koop was the first High Mass to be celebrated in White Bear Lake. A choir from St. Mary's Church in St. Paul participated in the event.

In 1874 the Markoe cottage, also known as the "Mound" cottage because of its proximity to the largest of the Indian mounds, was blessed and became central to the growth of the church. Over the next six years daily mass was celebrated, confessions heard, and Holy Communion received in the small and often crowded cottage.

St. Mary of the Lake Church – 1880 to 1926

Various efforts were made to establish a Catholic church at White Bear Lake, none of which succeeded until near the end of the 1870s, when Bishop Grace instructed Father Goiffon to build a church. The church was erected during the spring of 1880 on Bald Eagle Avenue at Birch Lake Avenue. Father Goiffon and the parishioners hauled stones from the lake, laying the foundation in only four days. Those who could not provide money for the cause were asked to donate time. Father Goiffon, acting as the architect, supervisor, and one of the laborers, had the church up and ready for plaster in just two months – surely a remarkable feat for a man with one partial leg and but half a foot on the other. The thirty-by-sixty-foot wood structure had been built for just $1,000. Although not completely finished, the church was blessed on August 15, 1880 using a makeshift altar constructed of packing boxes.

St. Mary of the Lake Church was the third church to be constructed in the village of White Bear.

Courtesy of Cynthia Vadnais

Courtesy of Bob Thein

Father Joseph Goiffon – Circa 1908

Joseph Goiffon was born in France on March 13, 1824. Ordained in 1852, he came to Minnesota in 1857, where he became a missionary at Pembina on the Red River. It was during a return trip from St. Paul that he was stranded in an early winter snowstorm. His horse froze, and he most certainly would have frozen too if he had not been rescued. His injuries from frostbite resulted in the loss of a good portion of his right leg and part of his other foot. Father Goiffon whittled a peg leg and foot (over his life he made more than one of these devices) that he attached using a leather harness around his hips. He died on May 6, 1910 at age eighty-six at his nephew's house in Hugo and is buried in Calvary Cemetery.

Father Goiffon formally served as the pastor of St. Mary's Parish from July 24, 1881 to August 20, 1882. At that time there were forty or fifty Catholic families in the area. It was not until 1883 that St. Mary of the Lake Church went from French to English sermons.

In the late 1880s the pastor was Father Robert, who arranged for a large bell to be shipped from France and installed in the steeple of the church. The only problem was that the structure was not strong enough to hold the weight of the bell. Instead, a stand was erected directly behind the church on which the bell was suspended. To pay for the bell, parishioners were allowed to ring the bell a certain number of times based on the amount they had donated. W. H. Jackson erected a bell tower on the church in 1902.

In 1897, under the direction of Father P. R. Cunningham, the main part of the church was cut in half, pulled apart, and expanded in length from sixty feet to eighty feet. The interior was frescoed, a new furnace was put in, and the woodwork was painted. The building could now seat 360, making it the largest church building in White Bear at that time. A stained glass window in the church memorialized the name of the contractor, U. S. Myers, who had performed the job.

Interior of St. Mary of the Lake Church – Easter Sunday 1926

This photograph was taken on the last Easter Sunday celebrated in the original church. Father John Fahey is shown.

Courtesy of Bob Thein

First Parish House for St. Mary of the Lake Church

The parish house was erected about 1885 on the lot just south of the church (notice the church steeple in the left side of the picture). Around 1925 the house was moved to Fourth Street just off Bald Eagle Avenue to make way for the new convent being erected next to the school. The house still stands just to the west of Roger Vadnais Plumbing on Fourth Street.

Having outgrown the little church built in 1880, St. Mary's Parish embarked on constructing a new one on the west side of Bald Eagle Avenue between Third and Fourth Streets located on the site of the then parish house (which was moved to the south end of the site). The church was built in 1925. The building, along with the interior furnishings, were a gift from James J. Hill's three daughters, whose wish was to have a replica of St. Mary's Church in downtown St. Paul, which they had attended as children. The church was dedicated on November 27, 1926 by the Bishop of St. Paul, Reverend James J. Byrne. The original church was to be put up for auction that same year.

Father John Fahey
St. Mary of the Lake pastor from 1915 to 1939. He died in 1942 when he was seventy-one.

Courtesy of the Richard Vadnais Family

Courtesy of the Richard Vadnais Family

Second Parish House for St. Mary of the Lake Church
Purchased about 1920 from Fred F. Campbell at a cost of $10,000, the house was relocated to the northwest corner of Bald Eagle Avenue and Third Street when the new church was built in 1925. Father John Fahey, the priest at that time, moved into the house, providing the sisters teaching at St. Mary's School a home in the original parish house.

Courtesy of Cynthia Vadnais

St. Mary of the Lake Church – 2000
The church was remodeled in 1988 with the exterior retaining most of its original architecture.

Reverend Orville K. Bosse
Reverend Bosse was the first resident pastor at Zion Evangelical Lutheran Church. He served from 1925 to 1929.

Courtesy of the White Bear Press

Courtesy of the White Bear Press

Zion Evangelical Lutheran Church

The German Lutheran congregation of thirteen members was organized in 1888 by Reverend A. F. Winter. West Side School was used for services during 1888 and Webster School was used for services from 1889 to 1891.

When the congregation desired a permanent home they purchased a lot at the corner of Seventh Street and Stewart Avenue for $400. On September 7, 1891, builder W. H. Jackson was awarded the contract to build the $1,300 church for the congregation. It was dedicated on November 15, 1891.

A full basement and furnace were added in 1922, while a bell, a new organ and a hardwood floor in the basement were added in 1926. George Jungblut built and donated an altar.

By 1917 services were given in English. Services were discontinued in May of 1929 and the church subsequently merged with the First Lutheran Church.

The church was moved but the property was retained, and in 1937 a six-room bungalow costing $4,000 was built on the land as a parsonage for the First Lutheran pastor.

When the Swedish Evangelical Lutheran Church was organized in 1888, Reverend Gus Wahlund delivered a sermon to the faithful who had gathered at the Hotel Chateaugay. Building began on the southeast corner of Sixth Street and Stewart Avenue that same year. The $1,600, thirty-by-fifty-foot structure, including tower and chancel, was finished in June 1889. The lot had cost $760.

The church was renamed Faith Lutheran in 1923, changing once again on November 5, 1925 to First English Evangelical Lutheran Augustana Synod of North America.

Up until about 1923 sermons were given in Swedish, and then until around 1925 part Swedish, part English. Sermons were given entirely in English by 1925.

The bell in the tower had come from a church in Ainsworth, Iowa founded by Captain W. Stickley's grandfather.

A merger occurred with the German Lutheran Church on March 14, 1929.

The church that began with just eighteen members had grown to around 435 members by 1936.

Courtesy of the White Bear Lake Area Historical Society
Swedish Evangelical Lutheran Church

Courtesy of the Lawrence R. Whitaker Family

First English Lutheran Church

In August of 1939 a chancel, sacristy, and choir room were added to the church increasing the floor space in the building by more than 2,200 square feet. It was once again remodeled in 1950.

Courtesy of the White Bear Press

First Evangelical Lutheran Church – ELCA

On May 25, 1959 the church building on Sixth Street and Stewart Avenue was sold to the First Baptist Church. A new building was built at Highway 61 and County Road F. Services began four months before the dedication date of April 26, 1964.

Courtesy of the White Bear Press

First Baptist Church

The First Baptist Church began meeting in various members' homes in 1948. Upon formal organization in 1950, Reverend Bill Murray held services in the armory. In 1951 a church was built on East Highway 96. The First Lutheran Church property became the new home of the First Baptist Church on May 25, 1959. Services were held at this location through 1969, at which time the property was sold to the Lakeshore Players, a community theater group. The First Baptist Church, now called Eagle Brook Church, moved to the northeast corner of Highway 61 and Buffalo Street where they built a new ediface.

The Methodist Episcopal Church was organized in 1892. A church was built on the west side of Clark Avenue between Second and Third Streets in 1894. Reverend Samuel White was the pastor in 1895. This early religious organization in White Bear did not survive, and for a number of years the church stood empty.

Courtesy of Cynthia Vadnais

First Church of Christ Scientist of White Bear Lake

Pupils of the Christian Science religion began to meet in White Bear in 1916. The home of Mrs. Griffith at Bald Eagle was used in 1916, and Mrs. Morrissey's home at Cook Avenue and Second Street was used in 1917. As the membership grew, the I.O.O.F. Hall at Banning Avenue and Fourth Street (above Gerken's Hardware) was rented.

On January 27, 1918 the group became an authorized Christian Science Society and elected J. A. Bazille president. There were sixteen charter members. By February 1918 a Christian Science Sunday School had been organized.

The society purchased the unused Methodist Episcopal Church building on Clark Avenue for $1,200, August 26, 1918. The first service was held September 1 the same year, with William D. Kilpatrick delivering the first Christian Science lecture the summer of 1919. That same summer a reading room was added.

The society formally became the First Church of Christ Scientist of White Bear Lake in January 1925, with Mrs. Amy Binswanger becoming the first registered Christian Science practitioner to serve the community.

The church building changed over the years: it was turned sideways and remodeled in 1938, and in 1941 it was remodeled again at a cost of more than $9,000. A reading room was added on the northeast corner of the white colonial structure in 1966.

The First Church of Christ Scientist of White Bear Lake has been in the same location for over eighty-five years.

Church of Christ – 1972

Courtesy of the White Bear Press

Services for the Church of Christ were first held in 1928 in the Masonic Temple. When the church was formally organized in 1931, the Alden Hotel on the northwest corner of Third Street and Stewart Avenue was rented for services. The state seized the hotel for back taxes in February of 1937, and in February of the next year the church purchased the building from the state for $1,334.

By this time the building was run down. A furnace was added in 1939 but not much more would be done to the old hotel. On September 4, 1941 a tornado struck White Bear, tearing a portion of the roof from the building and causing other damage. Two years later, in the summer of 1943, the remainder of the hotel was torn down and a new church was built. The first services were held November 14, 1943.

A new superstructure was erected in the spring of 1951, with the first services held in the new sixty-five-by-thirty-foot sanctuary on December 2, 1951. Brother Dean Hardy became the church's first full-time minister in 1958. In 1997 the church became the Great Hope Church of the Nazarene.

Courtesy of Ruth Mattlin

Bald Eagle Union Church Play Program Ad – 1907

From 1903 to 1905 the twenty members of the Bald Eagle Union Church held services during the summer at E. A. Warren's Bald Eagle Lake summer home, *Arcadia,* and during the winter, services were held at H. H. Griffith's home, also on Bald Eagle Lake. In 1905, the church constructed a thirty-by-sixty-foot building at the head of Elk Street on Park Avenue. The land was part of the Mahlon D. Miller Spring Park Villa property and the building materials had been contributed by the Bald Eagle Improvement Association. The church was dedicated on September 10, 1905. In 1910 a $300 bell tower was built to house the forty-four-inch diameter, 1,790 pound bell. By 1925 the church had eighty-five regular members.

The nondenominational church not only provided for the religious needs of the Bald Eagle residents, it also was a gathering area for social events and organizations. Sadly, church services stopped in 1928 because automobiles made it easier for residents to attend the church of their denomination. However, the church was used from 1928 through 1935 for Sunday School and by the Community Club of Bald Eagle. The church reverted to the Miller estate in 1935 and the building was subsequently torn down.

Schools

Courtesy of the White Bear Lake Area Historical Society

First School House in White Bear – Built in 1857

The log school, a primitive structure of tamarack only twenty feet square with two windows on each side, was built in 1857 for about $100. It was located near the southeast corner of Murray Avenue and Third Street on land donated by James F. Murray, one of the original settlers of White Bear. During cold weather, animal skins were hung over the windows to fend off the cold. Later on, a lean-to was added to the back and window sashes with glass were installed.

At that time there were many Indians living across the region. A school must have been a very curious sight and it was reported that Indians would ofttimes peer through the windows.

The first teacher was Mrs. John Aubrey who taught until 1868. Upon the formation of the White Bear Lake School district, the first paid teacher was Joann Burson in September, 1862. Other log school house teachers include: Addie Dean, Emma L. Kelly, Dora Gibson, Hester Chrysler, Ruth Miller, and Kate C. Taylor.

The school was in use until 1870, when it became the Lonergan cabin. Frank Lonergan was born there on May 14, 1882.

West Side Schoolhouse – Open from 1868 to 1895

Courtesy of the White Bear Lake Area Historical Society

Increasing enrollments caused the little log schoolhouse to become obsolete. The problem was temporarily solved with the erection of West Side School in 1868. The structure, built along Murray Avenue at Second Street, was a twenty-by-forty-foot, one-story wood structure that cost $1,400. White Bear continued to grow, as did the desire for children to be educated, so a second story was added in 1878 at a cost of $1,000. There were, on average, about sixty students a day in 1881. By 1887 West Side school was bursting at the seams. The school remained in use through the 1895 school year.

In January 1896 the school became known as Forester Hall and it was used as the meeting place for the Catholic Order of Foresters, St. Mary's Court, #570. The purpose of the organization was "social, welfare of families, fraternal, and insurance for families." It was also the home of the Lake Theater, which was controlled by the License Motion Picture Patent Company. The theater was open from 1911 through 1912. Movies were shown in the Hardy Hall in 1911 and in the Forester Hall in 1912. The Foresters sold the old school house in 1920, donating the land to St. Mary's Catholic School. The building was razed in 1924.

White Bear Life Ad – 1912

Courtesy of the White Bear Press

Courtesy of the Richard Vadnais Family

First, Second, and Third Grades – West Side School – 1895

The year 1895 was the last year that West Side School was used for classes. At the end of the year, classes transferred to Washington School.

Frederick E. Whitaker attended the West Side School and later reminisced,

> The building was divided into two rooms which were light and airy, especially in the winter, as far as I know, never had a storm window on any window and although they were well-fitted there were some of the wintry blasts fought to come in and get warm.
>
> The entrance was over a three-foot flight of steps into a nice hallway from which a flight of steps went up into the coat rooms for both sexes. The upstairs classroom was a duplicate of the downstairs room except that it was made for larger pupils. There never was a lamp of any kind in the school because it was too far over on the "West Side" to walk for School Board meetings.
>
> When I first went there the seats were mostly homemade of pine lumber. They would have been a very uncomfortable proposition even for an outdoor park bench only they had a projecting overhang on the back of the bench where you were supposed to keep your books and supplies—also your lunch or any contraband. The room was partially equipped with some of the new models of the iron framed desks like the modern ones so it was quite a Duke's mixture.
>
> I got two educations, one from my seat mate, Albert (Hammer) Taylor and one from the "school marm." Hammer was French and he taught me French... We had a snap downstairs with Miss Lottie (Charlotte) Murray, later Mrs. Harry Getty and I guess she was also allowed to do the janitor duties. All the boys liked her and they brought in the wood for her.
>
> Some of the children came from one to one and a half miles every day–snow, rain or sun–and were a pretty tough bunch. They had to be or go under...

It wasn't "grades" in those days, it was First Reader, Second Reader, Third and Fourth Reading book. Then you went upstairs into the Fifth Reader classes, and had Geography, Spelling, Arithmetic, Grammar, Writing and maybe something else.

I was a good student and held my own with the other students, some of them were twice as big as I was. I liked spelling and we sometimes had "spell-downs"... they were pretty hot contests and the children showed plenty of enthusiasm over the contest and we learned how to spell.

They had a big "Charter Oak" stove which was about five or six feet long with one of the old fashioned hollow drums that had the stove pipes on the same end as the door... The heat came from the back of the stove, circled through the drum and then went through the 30 foot smoke pipe at the top of the room, into the chimney and outside. The stove had a big frame like a box under and around the stove to insulate the floor so we would not catch fire and some pupil was the fireman. "Jack Tracy, will please fix the fire." Jack was a good fireman and tried to roast us out but on this day everybody got as close to the stove as possible.

School Vaccination Certificate for William Vadnais

Courtesy of the Robert Vadnais Family

F. E. Whitaker also wrote about the smallpox vaccination needed for school in 1880:

This was an almost new process in the rural sections and was supposed to be performed by an M.D. or some medical authority. Doctor Jim Murray was a horse doctor and a general all around good fellow and if you didn't have the 25 cents to pay, he forgot to collect. He took both boys and girls, raised their sleeves as high as the muscle of the upper left arm, scratched back and forth to make the skin thin and jabbed the vaccine points into the arm and when it had stopped bleeding you were allowed to lower your sleeve. The vaccination was a safeguard because every so often there was a flurry of smallpox and most of the time it seemed to originate in the vicinity of Centerville or Hugo.

Courtesy of Cynthia Vadnais

Hester Chrysler and Former Log School Students – 1923

In October 1923 Mrs. William Freeman, the former Hester Chrysler, had a reunion with her former "old log school" students from fifty-five years earlier at her home in White Bear. She is the center woman in white holding the book.

Courtesy of the Lawrence R. Whitaker Family

Webster School from Fifth Street – 1889

In response to burgeoning enrollments, a new school was built in 1888. Webster School was erected along Fifth Street between Cook and Stewart Avenues on land donated by J. D. Ramaley. D. W. Millard designed the building, and contractor David Hanna of White Bear built the modern two-hundred student schoolhouse at a total cost of about $14,000. The two-story veneered brick building had four classrooms with up-to-date improvements, including heating, ventilation, water and sanitary facilities. The doors, wainscoting, and interior woodwork were of Georgia and white pine, all finished with oil, the floors all of hardwood. The lot was enclosed on the east and south sides by a three-rail gas pipe fence. The proud community of White Bear had a lovely new school and had the distinction of being the first schoolhouse in Minnesota to fly the American flag from its peak.

Courtesy of Cynthia Vadnais

Webster School – Circa 1910

Courtesy of the Robert Vadnais Family

Webster School Students and Teachers – Early 1900s

When Webster School first opened, only two of the four rooms were used, with John F. Mackay, the principal of both Webster and West Side, having charge of the higher room and Miss Carrie M. Gundlach the lower. As more rooms opened in the new school, more teachers were added. Mary C. Dunn, Martha R. Elliott, and Ida E. Couvillion are among those who taught classes in those early years.

At first students on the west side of town attended West Side School, while those on the east side attended Webster School. By 1927 Webster School housed only the primary grades.

Courtesy of the White Bear Press

Webster Elementary School – Artist's Rendition 1951

In 1952 Webster Elementary School was opened on the northeast corner of Cook Avenue and Fifth Street. The old school was demolished on August 8, 1961, with authorities stating that it was too old to remodel in addition to being a wood frame structure. The new school was open until 1982.

Courtesy of the White Bear Lake Area Historical Society

Washington School – Circa 1900

It was not until the 1890s that students could receive an education beyond the eighth grade without traveling to St. Paul to go to school. About 1892 the first high school classes were held in the Hardy Hall, the upstairs meeting room of the then Hardy Building located on the southeast corner of Banning Avenue and Third Street.

By 1895, with the student population growing, along with a desire for students to be able to attend all grades through high school, it was deemed necessary to have a new building. David Hanna built Washington School in 1895 on property situated along Fourth Street, between Murray and Miller Avenues. It cost $22,000. On July 10, 1895 the cornerstone was laid in an elaborate ceremony.

The red brick structure started with six rooms seating 300 students and as enrollment increased the school was expanded, via additions, to twelve rooms and still later to sixteen rooms. W. H. Jackson built the second addition in 1906.

According to the *White Bear Life*, "The schools are graded as follows: Primary department, first and second grades; Intermediate department, third, fourth and fifth grades; Grammar department, sixth, seventh and eighth grades." In addition, Washington School was the high school and, in one of the rooms on the third floor, there was a normal school (teacher's training) program.

In 1896 all students were transferred from West Side School, as it no longer was being used. That same year Miss Francis Whitaker was the first graduate of White Bear High School. *White Bear Life* stated, "No pupils are allowed to graduate unless they have done the full amount of work required for entrance to the State University." The rigorous high school program saw two graduates in 1897 and by 1909 had eleven graduates, the largest class to that date.

From 1892 to 1899 the number of teachers increased from six to nine, while the average daily attendance during the same time period went from 250 to 350. By 1901 women teachers were being paid $48.89 per month, while men were paid $111.11 per month. In 1903 the high school course alone had 460 pupils. Washington School was full to overflowing.

Professor F. F. Farrar – First Superintendent of Schools in White Bear

Miss Abigail Stough – First Principal of White Bear High School

Courtesy of Cynthia Vadnais

Both of these educators came to White Bear in the later part of the 1800s. Farrar became the principal of Washington School while Miss Stough was the vice-principal. In 1893 Farrar was elected as the first superintendent of schools in White Bear. During his term he was instrumental in the movement to erect a new high school. He held the post until 1921 and retired in 1922. Miss Stough went on to become the first principal of White Bear High School.

Class of Students with Teacher – Washington School – Early 1900s

Professor Farrar is standing on the left side near the back.

Courtesy of the Robert Vadnais Family

Teacher and Students – West Steps of Washington School – Early 1900s

Courtesy of the Richard Vadnais Family

Courtesy of the Robert Vadnais Family

Washington School after Two Additions

Washington School served many roles during its lifetime. When it opened, its main function was to serve as a high school. Not long after it was built, a postgraduate course for training teachers was integrated into the program. After the construction of a new high school in 1918, Washington School switched its focus to elementary through the eighth grade. From 1967 to 1969 it served as the temporary home of Lakewood State Junior College. In the early 1970s it was used as an administrative office annex for the school district, in addition to being used by the fire department for fire drills.

Razing Washington School

Courtesy of Lorraine Billingsley

Ted Glasrud purchased the property for $80,000 and the building was demolished during the summer of 1978. Glasrud erected Washington Square, a housing unit for seniors, on the property.

Courtesy of Ruth Mattlin

White Bear High School – Circa 1920

In 1913 the school board was authorized to buy land for a school site not less than four-hundred-feet square facing on Bald Eagle Avenue. Work began on the new White Bear High School in 1918, with wings added on the north and south ends in the summer of 1924. No cornerstone was laid until the two wings were added. The high school opened a library that could accommodate thirty students at a time in 1924.

By 1927 the total enrollment in the White Bear schools was 790. The enrollment in the high school alone was 290, with the number of boys in high school being equal to the number of girls in high school over the two previous years.

Courtesy of Cynthia Vadnais

White Bear High School – 1928

Courtesy of Ruth Mattlin

White Bear High School – 1938

The high school was expanded on the south end in 1935 to include a 132-foot-by-111-foot auditorium-gymnasium that could seat 1,200 people, a cafeteria, and eight more classrooms. The eighty-foot-wide-by-fifty-foot deep auditorium stage hosted many basketball games, dances, plays, community events, etc. The auditorium has continued to serve the community well over the many decades since it was built.

Courtesy of Cynthia Vadnais

Running Track – Circa 1931

School athletics were relatively new in the early part of the 1900s. Basketball began in 1912 and was played on hard-packed ground outside of Washington School. Practice was held wherever it was convenient, including the attic of Washington School and Billy Baer's blacksmith shop. It wasn't until 1913 that White Bear High School had an official football team. The team won their first game against South St. Paul, 36-6. Other early sports included tennis and hockey. Of course, hockey was a winter staple. Early on there were few school teams since they did not have ice rinks. White Bear was among the few with a rink, which was located at Webster School and later at the Hippodrome.

White Bear High School Mascot – 1934

Courtesy of Cynthia Vadnais

White Bear High School Football Team – Early 1940s

Courtesy of Jack Vadnais

All Decorated for Homecoming – 1934

Courtesy of Cynthia Vadnais

White Bear School Band – 1934

Courtesy of Cynthia Vadnais

The members of the 1934 band shown are: (front row) R. Helgeson, J. Mattlin, R. Hansen, D. Rippel, Mr. Williams Behrns, F. Harper, H. Merches, J. Marier, M. Helke; (second row) O. Wood, H. Becker, F. Crever, De Wayne Sickler, T. Peltier, H. VanVoorhis, D. Chapin, S. Ross, C. Bibeau; (third row) J. Anderson, A. Crawford, F. Nickolaus, D. Becker, R. Cochran, W. Parcells, S. Pautenberg, H. Foote; (top row) E. Kulkey, R. Long, R. Rautenberg, W. O'Gorman, J. Morissey, R. MacDougal, B. Barth, B. Robertson.

About 1914 Herbert J. Keeler organized the White Bear School Band consisting of about twelve members. It was the pride of the community. John G. Gerken took over after two or three years, followed two years later by Mr. H. G. Hauglie. In 1919 there were just three members but by 1922 the band had fifty-four members ranging in age from nine to twenty years old. Besides playing at football and basketball games, the band would give concerts in the park during the summer months.

Courtesy of Cynthia Vadnais

White Bear High School and Athletic Field – Circa 1954

The addition on the north end of the school was built in 1954 at a cost of $1,000,000. O. U. Johansen, the principal of the school, commented at that time, "This building will outlive us all. We hope that posterity will say that we built wisely and well."

The athletic field (Price Field) floodlights were installed in 1948 at a cost of $25,000. The stands seated one-thousand people.

White Bear High School – 1964

The new White Bear High School was the first completely circular high school in the Twin Cities. Located to the north of the old high school, the circular school was completed in 1964 at a cost of $3,000,000 and could accommodate 1,800 students.

Courtesy of the White Bear Press

Courtesy of the Robert Vadnais Family

St. Mary's School and Church – Circa 1916

There are several things to notice in this image. West Side School is partially showing to the left. By this time it was known as Forester Hall. Also, directly in front of the doors to St. Mary's School at the edge of the street is a short flight of concrete stairs. These were used to help access a wagon or a buggy.

General contractor and local builder William H. Jackson built St. Mary's School in 1914 from plans St. Paul architect E. J. Donohue developed. The one-story red-brick school, located right next door to St. Mary's Church, on Bald Eagle Avenue between First and Second Streets, cost a total of $22,624.87. Archbishop Ireland had the honor of laying the cornerstone. In 1916 a second story was added to the school.

When the school opened the students had blackboards, chalk, erasers, and tablets to work with, but no books. With no public transportation, the children walked to school, with relief from the cold occurring when a farmer would collect and deliver them using his horse and hay rig. During the first year almost two-hundred children attended the school.

The Sisters of St. Joseph provided education at the parochial school, where they taught the eight lower grades. Upon the opening of the school there were four sisters teaching under the direction of Sister Mary Thomas. By 1927 there were about three-hundred students and seven teachers beside the Mother Superior.

**Sixth Grade Class
St. Mary's School
– Circa 1925**

Courtesy of the Robert Vadnais Family

Those identified in the back row, third, fourth and fifth from the left are Robert Vadnais, Frank Reibel and George Vadnais, second from the right in the back row is — Mingo. In the front row (from left to right): Marion VanVoorhis, ——, Catherine Collette, ——, Elizabeth Thein, Ann Dougherty, Helen LeVasseur, Fran Miller Basch, Margaret Vadnais, ——.

Courtesy of the Lawrence R. Whitaker Family

St. Mary's School – Circa 1952

In 1951 the Walter Butler Company extended the school, adding classrooms, a library, a nurse's room, and a combination dining room/auditorium-gymnasium. The addition cost approximately $175,000 and was dedicated on October 21, 1951. The school was remodeled in the late 1960s and began a major renovation in 2003.

The pupils started to wear uniforms in the fall of 1952. Girls wore white blouses and navy-blue jumpers bearing the monogram of St. Mary's School. Boys wore slacks and white shirts.

St. Mary's Convent

Courtesy of Bob Thein

Without a permanent place to live, the sisters initially stayed at the A. J. Diamon home on Lincoln Avenue and later rented the Baldwin cottage on the lakeshore. It was 1925 before the red brick convent was built, giving the Sisters of St. Joseph a permanent home. Both the original church and first parish house were torn down or moved to allow for the expansion and addition. The convent contained more than twenty rooms with accommodations for twelve or more sisters. From 1972 to 1992 the convent went by the name Northeast Residence and was a home for disabled people. It was last used as a shelter for women and children called the Hill Home. The building was torn down in October 2002 to make way for the new addition to the school, which is now called St. Mary of the Lake Parish Center and School.

Courtesy of Bob Thein

White Bear Beach School – Circa 1953

School District #26 was organized May 1, 1883, with the first school building located on what was then the Brachvogel farm. In 1898 the school discontinued at that site and relocated on Portland Avenue, about half a mile from the lake, where a new one-room school was built.

It was about 1924 when W. H. Jackson built White Bear Beach School, which had an exterior with brick on the lower portion and tile on the upper portion. It was situated on a hill midway between White Bear Lake and Bald Eagle Lake, where it provided an education for those students in the White Bear Beach area as well as those in the Bald Eagle area.

In addition to a library, the two teacher school had two classrooms on the upper floor, which held seventy students. The lower floor contained a 125-seat auditorium and a kitchen. Two more classrooms were added in 1948.

Looking Down Railroad (Washington) Avenue

Courtesy of Cynthia Vadnais

Panoramic View of Railroad Avenue and Park – Circa 1905

Courtesy of Cynthia Vadnais

Railroad Avenue Looking Toward Third Street – Circa 1905
On the left is the White Bear House and next to it is the First State Bank Building. The G. H. Lemon Hardware business was housed in the third building from the left. The brick building with the circular sign housed the Reif and Clewett Meat Market.

Courtesy of the White Bear Lake Area Historical Society

White Bear House, First State Bank and George H. Lemon's Hardware Store – Circa 1910

In 1903, a Mr. P. H. Simms started a small private bank at the First State Bank location. Having purchased the property for $500, the McGrath Saloon and Boarding House that sat on the property was moved over and a brick building was built. H. A. Warner of Little Falls, Minnesota bought the bank in 1904, reorganizing it under the name First State Bank.

During its first thirty years in service, the bank was robbed three times: in 1909, 1917, and again in 1931. As detailed by the *White Bear Press* in 1931, "This is the third time the First State Bank has been held up. Many will remember the battle with the bandit at Sixth Street and Banning Avenue in 1909. When he killed two and wounded two of our citizens and he was killed by Richard Brachvogel. Alfred Auger was alone in the bank then. The second one was about 12 years ago [1917] when the robber got away. He took Mr. Warner's watch, which was recovered a long time after in Chicago. This same bandit was hanged in Kansas City two or three years ago for murder." The 1931 robbery resulted in cashier Mr. Allyn Warner's being shot through the lung. The total amount taken in the three bank robberies was approximately $6,251: $598 in the first robbery, $5,000 in the second robbery, and $653 in the third robbery. Despite the notoriety of the bank, it was advertised as a "homey place, where your wants are cared for in a careful but cheerful way and you go out satisfied."

The bank building was remodeled about 1909 and was used by the bank until 1936, when they relocated to the First National Bank Building near the south end of Railroad Avenue.

George H. Lemon started his business in the Getty Block on Third Street about 1892. For a brief time, around 1900, he was located in the Mackenhausen Building, which is currently the last building standing on the south end of Washington Avenue. By 1902 his store was on Fourth Street, and shortly thereafter he located to the property just south of the First State Bank. In 1915 he was once again on Fourth Street in the Bacon Building. Lemon went out of business in 1919 and died May 10, 1921.

The White Bear Bowling Alleys occupied the Lemon Building on Railroad Avenue around 1904. The bowling alleys advertised that one would get "The best exercise in cool weather for ladies or gentlemen in the 'old but good' game of BOWLING," and furthermore, "Just now it is all the rage and getting more popular every day."

In 1920 H. M. Clark opened his billiard parlor/barber shop in the Lemon Building. It was open until 1934, when Martin Berghammer remodeled it and renamed it Marty Berghammer's Saloon. Larry Johnson, who had managed the White Bear Castle and the Beach Tavern, opened a saloon and liquor store at the location in 1936 and was in business until about 1939, when the building was removed to make way for P. J. LeVasseur's new grocery store.

H. M. CLARK BILLIARD PARLOR

FIRST CLASS
BARBER SHOP IN CONNECTION
SOFT DRINKS, CIGARS,
CIGARETTES,
TOBACCO'S and SMOKERS' SUPPLIES

Courtesy of the White Bear Press

White Bear Press Ad – 1927

Meet me at LARRY JOHNSON'S LIQUOR STORE
(Formerly Marty Berghammer's)

And we will have a quiet chat and friendly glass.

White Bear Press Ad – 1936

Courtesy of Cynthia Vadnais

Railroad Avenue – Circa 1915

Proprietors Nathan W. Blehert and C. A. Brache opened the Home Trade Store on April 17, 1915 in a remodeled portion of the White Bear House on the southeastern corner of Railroad Avenue and Fourth Street. Mainly a clothing and shoe shop, the store was remodeled in 1921, adding a ladies' department that was run by Lillian Henkel. That same year Brache sold his interest in the business to Blehert. The small shop was expanded again in 1927, giving it four times the area it had when the store opened. It was expanded once more in 1928.

From the mid-1920s on, a number of different businesses were housed in the rear of the store. These included Harry R. Pierce's radio shop in 1925, Arthur Parenteau's bicycle shop in 1926, Stephen Stancui's shoe rebuilding shop in 1927, H. Horne's tailor shop in 1932, and finally, George Goulette's barber shop in 1933.

On December 14, 1939 Nathan Blehert went into Goulette's barber shop with the newspaper to sit a moment, read and visit. He sat down, coughed heavily, and fell over dead.

From 1940 to 1949 Mr. and Mrs. Sam Kaufman owned the business. In 1946 the property was sold to Archie LeMire, at which time a section of the store, on the side facing Washington Avenue, was remodeled and became Jim Swanson's Liquor Store. The Kaufmans sold the business to Mitch Parenteau in 1949. This marked the beginning of Parenteau's Clothing.

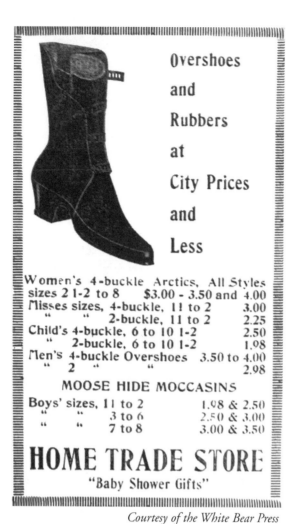

Courtesy of the White Bear Press

White Bear Press Ad – 1928

White Bear Press Ad – 1941

William Alden's Cafe opened in the recently vacated First State Bank Building in 1937. Alden died in 1938, at which time it was bought by Mr. Vogel. It was renamed Vogel's Coffee Shop sometime around 1940 and remained open through 1942. Soon thereafter a Mr. Coffin opened a dry-cleaning business in the building.

Courtesy of the White Bear Press

Benny Schmalzbaurer opened his barber shop in the Kohler Building in April of 1936. In 1945 he bought the First State Bank Building and relocated his shop, initially sharing the space with Mr. Coffin's dry-cleaning business. He remained in this location into the late 1980s, when he sold the business and retired.

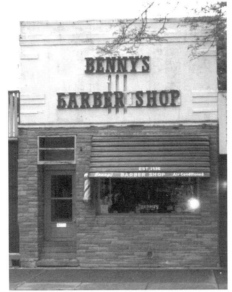

Benny's Barber Shop Building – May 2004

Courtesy of Cynthia Vadnais

BENNY'S BARBER SHOP
Now Open in The New Kohler Bldg.

Strictly Modern in Every Respect.

Special Attention to Ladies and Children.

Shoe Shining Stand.

Laundry Agency.

Benny Schmalzbaurer

White Bear Press Ad – 1936

Courtesy of the White Bear Press

Grand Opening......
'THE MALT SHOPPE'
330 Washington Avenue
MONDAY, JUNE 2

Free CAKE WITH EACH DISH OF ICE CREAM

SANDWICHES • COFFEE • FOUNTAIN SERVICE

Bill Jantzen, Proprietor

White Bear Press Ad – 1928

Courtesy of the White Bear Press

Archie LeMire bought the White Bear House property in 1946, building the Malt Shoppe shortly thereafter on the southern portion of the property facing Washington Avenue. This location is currently the home of the Cobblestone Cafe.

Courtesy of Bob Thein

The Malt Shoppe Interior

Shown are waitresses Shirley Blackbird and Alice McConnel.

Union Meat Market Ad – 1890

Courtesy of the White Bear Lake Area Historical Society

Courtesy of the Lawrence R. Whitaker Family

Reif & Clewett Meat Market – Circa 1906
The Louis Van Avery Bar is shown to the left of the meat market.

Starting in 1882 Charles Reif was in partnership with John Bunghard in the meat market business. The Railroad Avenue meat market building was built in 1886 to house the growing enterprise. The partnership of Reif and Bunghard was dissolved in 1889 and the market was renamed the Union Meat Market. By the late 1890s the business was Reif Brothers Meat Market (Charles and Frank J.). In 1900 Frank J. Reif and Reuben N. Clewett were in partnership, with the name changing to Reif & Clewett Meat Market. Frank J. Reif went to work for the White Bear State Bank as a cashier in 1913. It appears that he retained possession of the meat market property but not the business for two reasons. By 1913 the name had changed to Hubman & Clewett Meat Market, but it was Reif who built a large barn at the rear of the building, which burned in 1914. Sometime before 1920, King & Company took over the building, selling out to C. J. Zwerenz in 1920.

Reif & Clewett Meat Market Interior

Shown (from left to right): Emory Clewett, Miss Ella Lindgren, Louis M. Reif, and ——.

Courtesy of the White Bear Lake Area Historical Society

White Bear Life Ad – 1911

Courtesy of the White Bear Press

Reif & Clewett Meat Market Interior

Shown (from left to right): Alton Taylor, Miss Ella Lindgren, Emory Clewett and the Hubman brothers (one of which is Julius).

Courtesy of the White Bear Lake Area Historical Society

Norman Taylor Home Ice Delivery Wagon – 1904

Courtesy of the Richard Vadnais Family

The picture above was taken on Railroad Avenue just south of Greengard's Restaurant, which is shown to the left. Taylor sold his ice business to Reuben N. Clewett in 1912. Shown (from left to right): Alton Taylor, Norman Taylor, and Felix Auger.

Courtesy of the White Bear Lake Area Historical Society

The Hub – Circa 1915

The two-story brick building adjacent to Reif & Clewett's Meat Market on the north side was owned by the Hamm's Brewing Company. One of the earliest known tenants was J. S. Peterson, who had a sample room (the early name for a bar) and built a beer garden on the adjoining lot to the north. Others followed, and in 1905 Louis Van Avery took over the saloon and beer gardens from a man named Borsch. Hugh Hamilton had Hamilton Hardware here in the early 1910s. The Hub, run by Joseph L. Fournelle, started sometime around 1913 and was open under Fournelle's management through 1917; then Joseph Miller ran it under the same name for about a year. Hamilton was again located here until 1920. William Hartzell purchased the building from the brewing company in 1920, whereupon he moved his grocery store, the People's Meat Market, to this location. He sold the business to L. A. Markeson, and his son, Donald, in 1936. They continued with the name Markeson & Sons People's Market until 1945, when George Mayer took over the business, calling it the People's Market.

Courtesy of the Robert Vadnais Family

Railroad Avenue Looking North from Third Street – Circa 1920

An electric clock was installed on the outside of the First State Bank Building on the north end of the block in 1916. The clock, which struck every hour and chimed every fifteen minutes, became a landmark for the bank. The shorter white building, behind the telephone pole near the center of the picture above and also shown below, is the White Bear State Bank.

The White Bear State Bank was organized by James C. Fulton, Frederick H. Murray and Frank J. Reif and opened December 22, 1913. In 1921 the building was moved to the north side of Third Street between Railroad and Banning Avenues to make way for the construction of a new bank building. The bank remained in the building during the move.

The White Bear State Bank was not immune to the rash of bank robberies occurring during the early part of the 1900s. On May 9, 1919 Mr. Kidder, the assistant cashier, was robbed. The *White Bear Press* gave the following report of the robbery:

> All had left the bank and Mr. Kidder was just putting away the cash and preparing to close when a stranger approached him and placing a nickel-plated gun – not a very large one – to Kidder's side ordering him to "dig up the cash". Mr. Kidder becoming indignant at the audacity of the fellow was about to wallop his assailant, when the robber introduced another gun. Kidder states that the appearance of the big blue gun was too much for him and he had no further argument. Scooping up the currency and placing the silver in a bag, the robber

Courtesy of Bob Thein

James Cooper Fulton Outside the White Bear State Bank – Circa 1915

went out. It didn't take Kidder long to spread the sad news. The bandit was seen cutting across the park in the direction of the fire station. Art Long who claims to be quite a hunter of jack-snipers seized his rifle and started out for game. Arriving at the fire station, Second and Clark, Art halted the gentleman, who was then at Second and Milner and still hanging onto the $400 of silver in a bag, but had strewn the currency from Getty block all along the way. He didn't propose to stop, whereupon Art "drew a bead" on his man and "pulled." The bullet burned the bandit's scalp just above the right ear and [he] thought he was shot. He gave up and Art marched him back to the bank. All the cash was recovered and Mr. Kidder balanced his books that evening without any trouble.

James Cooper Fulton

Mr. Fulton, born in Pittsburgh, first came to White Bear with his family, who maintained a summer home at White Bear. Around 1894, when Fulton was about twenty years old, his family made White Bear their permanent home. Fulton was one of the founders of the White Bear Association, the precursor to the Chamber of Commerce. He was probably better known in his role as one of the organizers of the White Bear State Bank, of which he was president. Fulton died August 23, 1929.

Courtesy of the White Bear Press

Frederick H. Murray

Frederick Murray, the son of James C. Murray, the first postmaster in White Bear, was born on February 13, 1870 at the H. K. Getty homestead on Lake Avenue. On June 10, 1912 he married June M. Fulton, the sister of James Cooper Fulton. Murray was mayor of White Bear from 1910 to 1915. He was also the first manager of the White Bear Elevator Company, the first vice-president of the St. Paul Automobile Club, a director of the Ramsey County Agricultural Society, and the first vice-president of the White Bear State Bank, which he also helped to organize.

Courtesy of the White Bear Press

The small wood frame building housing the First National Bank of White Bear (formerly White Bear State Bank) was replaced in 1921 with a distinguished-looking stone building designed by architect C. E. Van Kirk. The front featured Dunville stones with the pediment heavily carved Dunville and Bedford stone that illustrated a horn of plenty with fruits and products of the state set off by a large white bear, the symbol of the bank. The small portion of the roof that could be viewed from the street was covered in red Spanish tile. The interior of the bank was finished throughout with marble and mahogany. Today, the exterior appears almost unchanged.

The New First National Bank – Circa 1922

Courtesy of Bob Thein

From 1901 to around 1905 the building to the south of the bank was occupied by Fournelle's White Front Saloon, run by Peter Fournelle. He and his bride, Janette Auger, took up residence above the bar in 1902. In 1920 Arthur Johnson opened the Park Sweet Shop at this location. Carl Reif and Arthur Johnson remodeled the building in 1922, with Reif bowing out of the partnership in 1924. Johnson moved the sweet shop to the northeast corner of Railroad Avenue and Third Street in December of 1926, then sold to Melvon Kirkby in 1927. The shop offered many items, including ice cream, cigars, cigarettes, lunches, and confectionery. When the sweet shop building on Railroad Avenue was scheduled for destruction, Kirkby relocated to the east compartment of the new Avalon Theater Building, where he was in business, under the name Mel Kirkby's Sweet Shop, until about 1934, when the 617 Liquor Store opened in that location.

Park Sweet Shop Interior
Shown is Gladys St. Sauver Mackenhausen. She worked in the Park Sweet Shop in the late 1920s, when it was located on the corner of Railroad Avenue and Third Street.

Courtesy of Bob Thein

One of the earliest occupants of the northeast corner of Railroad Avenue and Third Street was John Macey, with his sample room, the French Resort. Although the Maceys continued to own the building until 1912, other people managed bars in the building. In 1892 John Hartmann ran the Stillwater Headquarters, and in the later 1890s Louis Kuhn had his saloon in the building. Nick M. Henkel opened his saloon in 1898, remaining in the building until sometime around 1906 when William L. Alden, the eventual owner of the Alden Hotel, opened the Corner Bar. Alden bought the building from Joseph Macey in 1912 for $6,000. The Corner Bar was open until about 1918 when it became Anderson's Restaurant and then in 1920 the Corner Restaurant, run by Miss Clara Burrows and Mrs. William Lundy. Clara Burrows became the sole proprietor in 1925, and in 1926 Arthur Johnson moved the Park Sweet Shop to the location. The sweet shop was the last business to occupy the building before it was torn down in 1930 to make way for a gasoline station.

Courtesy of the White Bear Lake Area Historical Society

Lake Breeze Ad – 1887

Henkel Saloon Interior

Courtesy of the White Bear Lake Area Historical Society

N. M. Henkel Saloon – Circa 1900

Courtesy of the White Bear Lake Area Historical Society

South End Railroad Avenue – Circa 1925

Of the five buildings shown in this photograph, only the three on the left remain. The businesses occupying these buildings in the mid-1920s (from left to right) are the First National Bank, Park Sweet Shop, Greengard's Restaurant, Long's Grocery, and the White Bear Cafe.

Courtesy of the Robert Vadnais Family

Courtesy of the White Bear Lake Area Historical Society

M. J. Mackenhausen & Son Hardware Store – 1890s

Mackenhausen Hardware Store was located in the First National Bank Building on Railroad Avenue in 1887. In 1889 the brickwork commenced on Mackenhausen's new building. This building is now the last building standing on the south end of Washington Avenue. When it was built, such a large workforce was employed that it was thought that the brickwork would be completed in just eight days barring any inclement weather.

About 1890 J. N. Bies, a baker, was located in Mackenhausen's building while he waited for the Cobb Block, located on Railroad Avenue north of Fourth Street, to be built.

Just south of Mackenhausen's Hardware was the house Joseph Macey owned. N. M. Henkel lived there around 1900 and William L. Alden also lived there around 1910. The house disappeared sometime after that.

Greengard's Restaurant and Bakery – Early 1900s

Courtesy of the White Bear Lake Area Historical Society

Interior of Greengard's – 1912

Courtesy of the White Bear Lake Area Historical Society

  In 1904 Phil Greengard, a pioneer businessman, purchased the Mackenhausen Building on Railroad Avenue. Greengard had a bakery, soda fountain and lunchroom, and sold cigars, tobaccos, and confectionery. By 1907 Fournelle and Bloom, Hardy's, West Side Grocery, and the Mahtomedi Store were carrying Greengard's baked goods. Daily deliveries began in 1913. In 1920 the *White Bear Press* described the rebuilt soda fountain area, saying, "There are 8 new syrup faucets, a root beer dispenser, a brick ice cream refrigerating receptacle and other conveniences. It looks quite gay and is a decided improvement." Mrs. Kenneth Burgdorf recalled in an interview in 1960, "Mr. Greengard and his brother, Jim, did all the baking themselves and their baking business became very extensive – their clientele extending as far as Duluth." She went on to say that she "remembers standing with other children by the windows watching the baking activity until the mouth watering morsels were taken from the ovens. Then their waiting was rewarded by Mr. Greengard distributing any of the donuts or cakes which were broken when taken from the ovens."

The *White Bear Press* wrote about the "Greengard Rush" in 1923. The Press teased, Phil Greengard says he is going to furnish free scholarships admitting certain parties to night school long enough for them to learn to read. He says pushing is all right but a pull is better – especially on the screen door to his restaurant. Hardly a day passes that someone does not insist on pushing the said door in, notwithstanding the fact that there is a "pull" sign on the door and the pushing is hard and the pulling is easy. Phil admits that they are all in a hurry to get to his tables, but he did not know his "eats" were so attractive that they would break down the doors to get in.

Courtesy of the White Bear Press

White Bear Press Ad – 1922

Mrs. Greengard passed away in 1945 and Phil Greengard died in 1952. Their son, Phil, and his wife ran the business until about 1953, after which the building stood empty for a few years. In 1956 the building was used as the local headquarters for the Adlai Stevenson Democratic presidential campaign, and in 1960 Mr. Harvey Chapman remodeled the building for occupancy by the Appleton Real Estate Company and the Hillman Insurance Agency.

Railroad Avenue about 1928

Courtesy of Bob Thein

The Henkel home stood on the site of the second building from the right in the late 1800s and early 1900s. Sometime after that the building shown above was erected. Arthur R. Long had his grocery store here from 1923 to 1927. George Goulette, who is probably the man standing outside the barber shop, moved his business here from Third Street in 1927, opening a branch of the Elk Laundry that same year. Above the barber shop was the LaRose Payette Beauty Parlor. Goulette, like his neighbor Art Johnson at the Park Sweet Shop, was forced to move in 1930 so that the two buildings on the far right could be razed. Goulette moved first to the Flatiron Building on Clark Avenue and Third Street, then in 1933 to the rear of the Home Trade Store on the corner of Washington Avenue and Fourth Street, facing Fourth Street.

Texaco Station – Northeast Corner of Washington Avenue and Third Street

Courtesy of Bob Thein

In 1932 the Daughters of the American Revolution (DAR) petitioned the town to change the names of Railroad Avenue and Railroad Park to Washington Avenue and Washington Park, respectively, in honor of the bicentennial birth year of George Washington.

After Goulette's Barber Shop and the Park Sweet Shop were torn down, a Texaco station was built. By 1936 it was under the management of Bernard Letourneau. White Bear Oil Company owned the station from the early 1940s until shortly after George, the oldest of the Vadnais brothers who ran the station, retired in 1974.

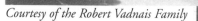

Washington Avenue Looking North

In 1936, in the midst of the Depression, the First State Bank bought First National Bank and relocated to the First National Bank Building. The stone bear was removed to make way for the landmark First State Bank clock. The bank continued business at this location until 1961, when new quarters were built on the northeast corner of Clark Avenue and Second Street. Drive-through banking started in 1965 and the bank was once again expanded in 1969. Currently the bank is owned by US Bank.

The White Bear Drug store was located just north of the bank. Clarence J. Zwerenz bought the business from King & Company on July 13, 1920, changing the name to White Bear Drug. For just over thirty years Zwerenz, a pharmacist, ran a thriving business that included a popular soda fountain installed in 1925. He retired in the spring of 1951 and died at the age of eighty-two on July 24, 1974.

Courtesy of the Robert Vadnais Family

First State Bank Clark Avenue Artist's Rendition – 1960

Courtesy of the White Bear Press

Courtesy of Bob Thein

White Bear Drug Store – Circa 1926
George Vadnais, a soda jerk, and store owner Clarence Zwerenz are shown in the entrance to the store.

```
Postcard
Scenes
in
White Bear
18 beautifully colored
scenes in White Bear.
Printed in France.

2 for 5c

Send some to your friends
and show them what a
beautiful city we have.

THE
WHITE
BEAR
DRUG
STORE
Always a registered
Pharmacist in Charge
```

Courtesy of the White Bear Press
White Bear Press Ad – 1928

We make our own
Ice Cream fresh
daily.

══ 30 FLAVORS ══
To Choose From.
A box of Cookies free with each quart.

Kohler's Romance
Phone 5

White Bear Press Ad – 1937
Courtesy of the White Bear Press

    Two doors north of the White Bear Drug was Kohler Dairy, later known as Kohler's Romance Parlors. Aloys and Henry Kohler bought the Schnorr Dairy business in 1924. At that time the building contained a creamery department and a retail area. From the late 1800s into the second decade of the twentieth century, the site was the location of a beer garden last associated with the Hub Saloon. When the cellar of the Kohler Building was excavated in 1931, there were two large oak stumps that were removed. These once mighty oaks had provided shade to the patrons of the drinking establishment.

    The Kohler brothers went into the ice cream mix business in 1929, manufacturing their own ice cream mix for the first counter freezer installed in the state of Minnesota. By 1930 the building was enlarged to 140 feet in length to accommodate the growing demand for their products. A new English-style front was put on the building, and the retail area was converted into a refreshment parlor with a soda fountain and seating for twenty. In 1935 the *White Bear Press* reported, "The firm now is serving lunches and has quite a run in that line. The booths are often crowded to that extent that more room has been found necessary. This week they removed a partition and are remodeling a former storeroom, which will be an extension of the booth department."

In 1936 the Kohler brothers once again expanded the building and incorporated the production business. Henry took charge of the manufacturing end, naming it Kohler Ice Cream Mix Incorporated, and Aloys ran Kohler's Romance Parlors. Aloys extended and remodeled the building again in 1940, adding sixty feet and booths, while Henry moved the mix company to the old Masonic Temple Building on Banning Avenue north of Fourth Street. Henry sold the manufacturing business in 1953 and retired in 1954. He died August 11, 1974. His sons, Clifford, Donald, and Walter, bought the business back in 1960, building a manufacturing plant on the west side of Highway 61 just past County Road F. The *White Bear Press* wrote, "Perhaps Kohler Mix Specialties' biggest success was in 1986, when it adapted its recipes to be used in a non refrigerated mix product with a long shelf life, something that was practically unheard of in the field of ice cream."

In 1955 Aloys sold the parlors to Mr. and Mrs. John VanGilder, who sold the shop in 1959 to Vera and Dean Schreiner. They renamed the business Dean's Ice Cream Parlor. Dean's closed in the early 1970s.

Many people have fond memories of the murals on the walls, which depicted special sundaes for each month of the year. Al Kohler and Ross Moore painted them, and many still exist today in the hands of private collectors.

Courtesy of Lorraine Billingsley
Lorraine Hogan outside Kohler's Romance Parlors

Courtesy of the White Bear Lake Area Historical Society
Interior of Kohler's Romance Parlors – 1936
Shown are Delia Thein and Aloys Kohler.

Delivery Trucks for Kohler's Ice Cream Mix Incorporated

Shown, from left to right, are Jack Quinn, Arman Abresch, and Reinhard Kohler. They are on a once-vacant lot on Fourth Street across from the Avalon Theater.

Courtesy of the White Bear Press

Courtesy of the White Bear Lake Area Historical Society

Cyrus Cobb's Lumber, Real Estate, and Insurance Office
Courtesy of the White Bear Lake Area Historical Society

Cyrus B. Cobb, who was an agent for the St. Paul and Duluth Railroad for seven years after coming to White Bear in 1879, was also in the lumber business, dealing not only in lumber but also lath, building materials, coal, and lime. In addition to his lumber business, he sold real estate and insurance. In 1888 his office was relocated to the southeast corner of Railroad Avenue and Fifth Street to be closer to his coal and lumber business – Cobb Lumberyard. He died in early July of 1888.

Cobb's legacy was the Cobb Block, which began posthumously in 1889. According to the *Lake Breeze*, the new block "will be a structure similar to the plan of the Forepaugh building in St. Paul. The building will be located just north of the Park Place Hotel with a frontage of fifty feet on Railroad Avenue, and running sixty feet back. The block will consist of two stories and a double basement, and the floor of the first story being raised about four feet above the line of the street will substantially make it equivalent to a three-story building. The north half of the basement will be occupied by a cigar manufacturer from Wyoming, while J. N. Bies will occupy the south half with his bakery." The location described is that area just north of the gas station at the intersection of Fourth Street and Railroad Avenue. The plans were greatly simplified.

GEO. E. TORINUS,
—DEALER IN—
LUMBER,
Lath, Shingles, Sash, Doors,
BLINDS,
Coal, Wood,
Brick, Lime and Cement.

All Orders Promptly Filled.

Courtesy of the White Bear Lake Area Historical Society

Lake Breeze Ad – 1892

In 1891 George E. Torinus became the successor to Cobb's Lumberyard. Torinus came by the business naturally because his father had been a prominent lumberman in Stillwater. By 1894 Torinus had moved the lumber office to Fourth Street and Banning Avenue.

1890 Ad for Otto J. Troseth Grocery Store

Upon completion of the Cobb Block, tenants included the post office, the *Lake Breeze*, and Otto J. Troseth Groceries.

Troseth sold foreign and domestic groceries from his storefront and from a covered wagon. He also erected a building at the rear of the grocery store for his flour and feed business.

The Cobb Block burned down on July 11, 1894.

OTTO J. TROSETH,
—DEALER IN—
Foreign AND Domestic Groceries,
PROVISIONS,
Fruits, Vegetables, Fresh Eggs,
Choice Dairy and Crescent Creamery Butter,
FLOUR AND FEED.

ORDERS CALLED FOR AND DELIVERED FREE OF CHARGE.

Cobb's Block, Next Door to P. O.,   WHITE BEAR, MINN.

Courtesy of the White Bear Lake Area Historical Society

Courtesy of the White Bear Lake Area Historical Society

Cyrus B. Cobb Home – Circa 1888

In 1885 the Cobb home was built on the northwest corner of First Street and Banning Avenue. The Victorian-style home was one of the first built in White Bear as a year-round residence.

The religious Cyrus Cobb was active in the church, becoming the superintendent of Sabbath School at St. John in the Wilderness. His home served as the first rectory for St. John in the Wilderness Church in the early 1900s.

The 1941 tornado that struck White Bear blew the second-story porch off the home. It had been located on the upper left side of the building as it appears in the photograph.

The Edward Holtz family purchased the home in 1954 and have lived there since.

The house stands today as one of the most complete Victorian homes left in White Bear Lake. Very little has changed since it was built.

Courtesy of Cynthia Vadnais

Holtz Home – 2000

Inter-State Lumber Company – Circa 1914

Courtesy of the White Bear Lake Area Historical Society

Inter-State Lumber Company – 1950s

Courtesy of the White Bear Press

Inter-State Lumber Company was incorporated in 1899 and started operating in White Bear in 1907 at the corner of Railroad Avenue and Fifth Street. When the new highway was put through White Bear in 1935 a few of the buildings and the coal sheds of the company had to be moved or taken down. A new five-thousand-square-foot building was erected in 1951, with the company remaining in business in White Bear into the late 1980s. Frattallone's Ace Hardware remodeled the building and has since occupied the location.

Frank E. Lindgren – 1915

Courtesy of the White Bear Press

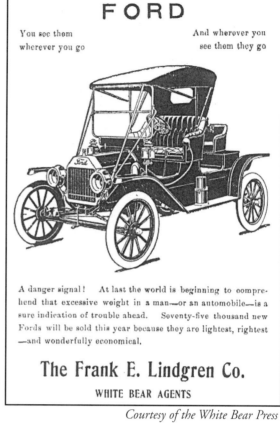

White Bear Life Ad – 1912

Courtesy of the White Bear Press

    Frank E. Lindgren started out in the hardware business with G. H. Lemon, one of the pioneer merchants of White Bear. Lindgren first organized his own business as the Frank E. Lindgren Company; the name was changed in 1914 to the White Bear Implement Company, with Lindgren as manager. The company was located in the stone building on the southern end of Railroad Avenue between Fourth and Fifth Streets. Lindgren dissolved his partnership with Herman Benson in 1916; that same year M. J. Mackenhausen Sr., the owner of the building, put it up for sale. In 1918 E. J. Lindquist bought the Implement Company from Lindgren, while William Baer purchased the building. The White Bear Implement Company was reformed in 1937 under the ownership of B. J. Schafer and William A. Larson, opening for business in the Harris Perron Building on the south side of Inter-State Lumber Company.

Courtesy of the White Bear Press

Delivery of Fourteen Manure Spreaders to White Bear Implement Company – 1914

This photograph looks north on Railroad Avenue from Fourth Street. The White Bear Implement Company was located in the brick building with the flag on it. The small wood frame building adjoining it on the north is the Harris Perron Building. In the early 1890s, this location was part of the Cobb Block that housed the post office and *Lake Breeze* newspaper. After the Cobb Block burned down, the Harris Perron Building was erected on that site.

Parading the Fourteen Manure Spreaders down Railroad Avenue – 1914

According to the newspaper, those who purchased one of the manure spreaders were Dolphus Cardinal, Louie LeRoux, Henry Charpentier, Archie Laventiers, F. L. Glassco, H. D. Glassco, George LeMay, Leonard Webber, E. J. Houle, William Rehbine, and J. C. Laken.

William (Billy) N. Baer bought the Mackenhausen Building in 1918 and opened a blacksmith shop. His assistant was S. R. Bortie. Baer adapted to the changing times, learning acetylene welding techniques to repair automobile springs and framework as well as other types of machinery. In 1932 a fire completely destroyed the Harris Perron Building next to Baer's shop. Inter-State Lumber Company to the north was threatened by the fire, but Baer's was protected since the walls were cement and the roof was metal. Baer died September 24, 1956.

BLACKSMITH

I do all kinds of Blacksmithing.   Repairing Promptly done.

HORSE SHOEING A SPECIALTY
All My Work is Guaranteed

Your Patronage Solicited

W. N. BAER

4th Street across the tracks from Depot

Courtesy of the White Bear Press

White Bear Press Ad – 1915

Courtesy of Bob Thein

Baer Blacksmith Shop – Billy and Elmer Baer Standing

Courtesy of Cynthia Vadnais

The Beulke Building – Summer 2003

The exterior of the old Baer Blacksmith Shop has changed very little since the 1950s. Currently, Gordy Beulke has his insurance offices on the north side of the building, while The Mane Tease, a hair salon, is located in the south side of the building.

Jacob A. Reed and his son Harold bought Peter Fournelle's station on the northeast corner of Railroad Avenue and Fourth Street in 1919, naming the establishment J. A. Reed Oil Company. The *White Bear Press* reported, "They don't sell cars but they run a real garage with mechanics on hand 24 hours every day in the year – just a garage, that's all." Over the years the company was affiliated with Skelly, the Pyramid Oil Company, and Chevrolet.

The business prospered and by 1940 the first major remodeling occurred when the front of the station was set back twenty-five feet. J. A. died in 1943 and Jack joined his father Harold in running the business in 1946. In 1962 the building was torn down and a modern, three-bay service station was constructed on the site. J. A. Reed Oil Company ceased doing business in February of 1981. Although not owned by the Reed family, the corner still has a gas station on it.

Courtesy of the White Bear Press

White Bear Press Ad – 1924

Original J. A. Reed Oil Company

Courtesy of Bob Thein

J. A. Reed Oil Company after 1940 Remodel

Courtesy of Bob Thein

Courtesy of the White Bear Press

J. A. Reed Oil Company – New Station Built in 1962

Courtesy of the White Bear Lake Area Historical Society

The Eight Brunswick Bowling Alleys at the Sunset Bowling Center

In 1940, O. M. Cherrier, the owner of the White Bear Ice Company, decided to build a recreation center and bar on Washington Avenue between Inter-State Lumber Company and J. A. Reed Oil Company. Perron's Tin Shop stood on the site and was relocated. Carl Mattlin constructed the building at a cost of approximately $32,000. The Sunset Bowling Center opened on October 19, 1940 and became a mecca for bowlers from all over the area for decades to come.

Sunset Bowling Center

Courtesy of Bob Thein

Courtesy of the Lawrence R. Whitaker Family

Washington Avenue, Looking North – Early 1950s

The businesses along Washington Park at this time included (from right to left): Greengard's Restaurant, White Bear Appliance Shop, Cassel's Apparel, First State Bank, White Bear Drug, People's Market, Kohler's Romance Parlors, Benny's Barber Shop, National Food Shop, the Malt Shoppe, and Hazen's Park Liquor Store.

Courtesy of Cynthia Vadnais

Washington Avenue, Looking South from Fourth Street – Circa 1960

The businesses along Washington Park at this time are (from left to right): Hazen's Park Liquor Store, the Malt Shoppe, Benny's Barber Shop, Chamberlain's Clothing Store, Dean's Ice Cream Parlor, Bond Electric, White Bear Drug, First State Bank, ——, Appleton Realty, and Vadnais Mobil Station on the corner.

Courtesy of Cynthia Vadnais

Margaux Limitee Restaurant and the Old First State Bank Building – Summer 2003
 Both the Margaux Limitee Restaurant building and the old First State Bank Building were for sale in 2003. The restaurant building had once housed Reif & Clewett Meat Market and later the White Bear Drug Store.

Courtesy of Cynthia Vadnais

The Nest and Washington Square Bar and Grill – Summer 2003
 The Nest, a needlework shop, was once the location of the Park Sweet Shop and later Cassel's Apparel. The Washington Square Bar and Grill occupies the building that once housed Greengard's Restaurant and Bakery.

Looking Down Third Street

Courtesy of the White Bear Lake Area Historical Society

Third Street, Looking West – 1917
The first building shown on the left is N. M. Henkel & Company Meat Market.

Nick Henkel, along with junior partner, John Flandrick, opened N. M. Henkel & Company Meat Market in the spring of 1888. Henkel was not new to the business. He had worked in St. Paul, then in Charles Reif's Meat Market in White Bear before becoming the junior member of Milner and Henkel Meat Market, located on Clark Avenue just behind the Getty Building. Henkel and Flandrick dissolved their partnership in 1898.

Courtesy of the White Bear Lake Area Historical Society

N. M. Henkel & Co. Meat Market Ad – 1890

Courtesy of the White Bear Lake Area Historical Society

N. M. Henkel & Co. Meat Market – August 25, 1889

Courtesy of Bob Thein

Wayside Cafe – Early 1960s

The Rose Cafe, run by Rose Reibel from 1934 to 1945, was located in the Henkel Meat Market building. In 1945 Louis Leninger took over the business, renaming it Lew's Cafe. Henry Navis was the next proprietor in the building, starting the Wayside Cafe in March of 1946. He was still in business in the early 1960s.

Courtesy of the White Bear Lake Area Historical Society

South Side of Third Street Looking West – 1917
Shown from left to right: N. M. Henkel & Co. Meat Market, Schaefer's Ice Cream Parlor, Hamilton Hardware, Brachvogel Barbershop, and J. A. Flandrick's Meat Market.

Schaefer's Ice Cream Parlor was owned by F. W. Schaefer. It opened in 1916 and was probably in business for just about two years. They advertised the "best cup of coffee in town for five cents."

Joseph Burkard's Blacksmith Shop was located just west of Schaefer's in a two-story brick building. It currently houses Evans Music. Burkard, the first blacksmith in Centerville, opened his shop in White Bear in 1875. He was a horseshoer and general blacksmith. A number of other blacksmiths, including Joe E. Peltier, Joe Lambert, S. J. Hoag, Henry E. Schultz, and William Cody, leased from Burkard or were located in this building in the late 1800s and early 1900s. This building was later occupied by Hamilton Hardware, owned by Hugh Hamilton, and the White Bear Hardware store was owned by John C. Lundgren.

Just east of Burkard's shop was the location of the Brachvogel Barbershop. Richard G. Brachvogel was not only a barber for fifty-six years but also a White Bear fireman for forty-two years and the fire chief for twenty-eight of those years. Brachvogel was in business with William Laub in the late 1890s. Joe Shea, who had worked for him for twenty-one years, bought the business from Brachvogel upon Brachvogel's retirement in 1932. The location would become known as Harry & Joe's Barbershop after Harry LaBelle joined Joe Shea.

John A. Flandrick had come to White Bear in 1882, later going into the meat market business with N. M. Henkel. In 1903 he opened Flandrick's Meat Market on Third Street. He turned the business over to his son George in 1927. In 1929 Arthur R. Long moved his grocery business in with the meat market, but by 1931 Long had moved on and Flandrick added his own line of groceries. The store was later renamed Flandrick's Fine Foods. John A. retired in 1936 and died on January 13, 1947. That same year the business became Bazille's Grocery.

LUNCH ❋ ROOM.

Warm Meals at all Hours.

Sandwiches, Cakes, Pies,
Tea, Coffee and Milk,
And everything generally found in a
first-class Lunch Room. Give
me a call.

Mrs. J. Burkard,
East Third St.,   WHITE BEAR, MINN.

Joseph Burkard,
HORSE SHOER
—AND—
General Blacksmith.

Repairing Done to Order.

East Third Street.
White Bear Lake,   -   Minnesota.

1890 Ad

Courtesy of the White Bear Lake Area Historical Society

Flandrick's Meat Market – Third Street

By 1937 Flandrick's Meat Market was the oldest business in White Bear. Shown in the photograph, from left to right: George Flandrick, John Flandrick, Mr. Conway, Carl Flandrick, and Richard Conway.

Courtesy of the White Bear Lake Area Historical Society

White Bear Life Ad – 1912

J. A. FLANDRICK,
Dealer In All Kinds of
FRESH AND SALT MEATS
POULTRY, FISH, Etc.
Third St., opposite Railroad Park.
WHITE BEAR, MINN.
Telephone N. W. 58-2.   T. C. 15-1.

Courtesy of the White Bear Press

William Goesch's Dry Goods, Millinery,... – 1890s

William Goesch came to White Bear in 1882. Shortly thereafter, along with his dressmaker wife, he opened his store on Third Street. This is the same building that would eventually house Flandrick's Meat Market. According to an 1888 ad, Goesch carried "dry goods, millinery, notions, ready made clothing, hosiery, hats, caps, and furnishing goods of all kinds."

Courtesy of Bob Thein

James M. King was born in 1861 and in 1887, after passing his drug business exams, opened a store in White Bear on Third Street at the head of Railroad Avenue. The business soon included Hiram T. and W. D. King.

The upper story of the store was rented out. In 1887 it was the initial location for Albert H. S. Perkins, the owner of the first newspaper in White Bear, the *Lake Breeze*. Dr. C. L. Clark rented the second story in 1896 and Dr. Voges did the same in 1912.

King and Company moved to 115 S. Railroad Avenue, the building just north of the White Bear State Bank (First National Bank), and in 1920 King sold the business to Clarence J. Zwerenz, who renamed it White Bear Drug.

KING & CO..
Prescription Druggists,
—AND DEALERS IN—
Paints, Oils and Glass,
Imported and Domestic **Cigars,**
Books and Stationery,
Also a full line of Chocolate Creams and Candles.

All Night Calls Answered Promptly.

GETTY BLOCK, E. THIRD ST.,   White Bear Lake, Minn.

Courtesy of the White Bear Lake Area Historical Society

Lake Breeze Ad – 1892

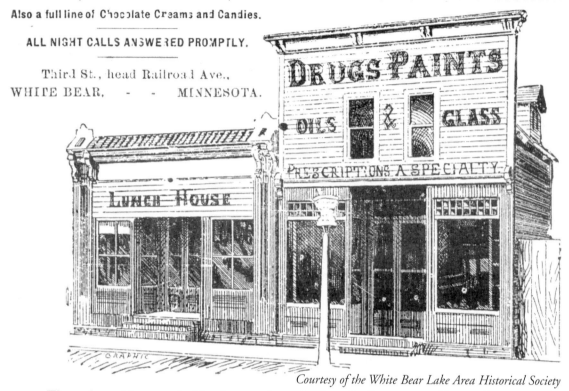

Courtesy of the White Bear Lake Area Historical Society
Theodore Hansen's Restaurant and King & Company Drug Store – 1890

Theodore Hansen started his restaurant in 1884 and was still in business in 1914. He advertised "Warm meals at all hours. A fine line of confectionery, cigars, tobacco, pipes,..."

Courtesy of the White Bear Lake Area Historical Society
***Lake Breeze* Ad – 1892**

Courtesy of the White Bear Press

Third Street at the head of Railroad (Washington) Avenue

This 1917 photograph shows Arthur R. Long's Grocery Store and Bull's Photo Shop in what was then called the Hansen Building.

The remodeled Hansen Building had previously housed Theodore Hansen's Restaurant and King & Company Drug Store. William Bull moved into the building in the early 1900s and relocated to St. Paul in 1917. In 1914 George Cook, from Madison, South Dakota, made his headquarters at the photo shop, where he sold clocks, watches, jewelry and glassware in addition to performing repairs.

The building was remodeled in 1917 to accommodate both Long's Grocery Store, which opened on March 12, 1917, and Cook's Jewelry. Long moved his business to the south end of Railroad Avenue in 1923 and moved two doors north in 1927 to the building on the south side of the old First National Bank (the Odd Fellows Building). Here he took on Cleo Smith as a partner, renaming the business Long & Smith Grocery. Long joined in business with Flandrick's Meat Market in 1929, returning the business to Third Street, one building east of where it had begun. Arthur Long quit business in White Bear in 1931, taking the position as manager of the Lincolntown Mercantile Company on the other side of the lake.

Long's Grocery Delivery Truck

Courtesy of Bob Thein

GEO. COOK
JEWELER

A Guaranteed Stock at
Reasonable Prices.

Expert Watch, Clock and Jewelry Repairing

DIAMONDS RESET PROMPTLY

Kodak Films For Sale and Developed

Patronize Your Home Jeweler
and Save Money.

Courtesy of the White Bear Press

White Bear Press Ad – 1927

In 1921 George Cook retired and L. J. Cook, his son, took over the business. At that point the shop was located at 420 Fourth Street.

Bennett's Cafe
STRICTLY FIRST CLASS

We engage Ex-Dining Car Chef and give Dining Car Service.

ALWAYS OPEN UNTIL MIDNIGHT

*A Better Service
       At Reasonable Price.*

Courtesy of the White Bear Press

White Bear Press Ad – 1925

Mr. and Mrs. Carl Bennett opened their restaurant in 1924 in the store formerly occupied by Arthur Long Grocery at 702 E. Third Street (the Hansen Building).

See the
RUSSIAN DIAMONDS
in their original
settings.

Now on display in
our window.

Courtesy of the
White Bear Fire Department

Harry M Peterson Jeweler

Courtesy of the White Bear Press

White Bear Press Ad – 1933

Harry M. Peterson moved into the Hansen Building in 1931.

White Bear Press Ad – 1937

Robert Martin opened White Bear Wine & Liquor Shop in the Martin Building, the Hansen Building of yore, in February of 1937, taking over the space that Harry M. Peterson Jeweler had occupied.

WHITE BEAR WINE & LIQUOR SHOP
700 Third Street, 2 doors east of P. O.
Tel. 77   Free Delivering

Come in tomorrow and save tremendouly on our
"SATURDAY ONLY SPECIALS"
Don't fail to take advantage of these reductions.

☞ **"FEATURING CITY PRICES"** ☜
on all nationally advertised brands of Scotches
Bourbons, Cognacs, Gins, Wines Cordials, Beers

(White Bear's Only Exclusive Liquor Store)

WHEN LOW IN SPIRITS—CALL 77   FREE DELIVERING
ROBERT (BOB) MARTIN, ProP.

Courtesy of the White Bear Press

Courtesy of Cynthia Vadnais

Evans Music Store and the Waterlily – Summer 2003

The old Burkard blacksmith building is still in great shape after all these years. In the late 1970s it was the home of the Quirk of Fate before it moved to the White Bear Theatre building. It has been Evans Music for a number of years. The Waterlily is located in the old Brachvogel Barbershop building just west of Evans Music store.

Courtesy of Cynthia Vadnais

The Gathering – Head of Washington Avenue on Third Street – Summer 2003

What had once been three separate stores now is the location of one, The Gathering. Earlier, the buildings housed a variety of stores, including William Goesch's Dry Goods, Flandrick's Meat Market, Bazille's Grocery, Theodore Hansen's Restaurant, A. R. Long's Grocery, and King & Company, to name a few.

Joe Miller's Sample Room and Boarding House

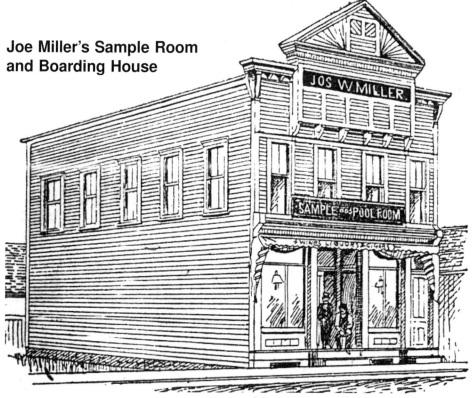

Courtesy of the White Bear Lake Area Historical Society

Joe Miller was born in 1850 in Ohio. The *White Bear Press* reported that as a professional baseball player, "He was with the Keokuks in 1874-75, with the old Chicagos in 1876, with Indianapolis in 1877, and with the Davenports in 1878, when he left the diamond to go into the saloon business in White Bear. Joe was the famous second baseman in the series of 1874-75 between the Empires and St. Louis Reds, when the rivalry was so strong that Joe's nine were in danger of their lives from a mob of friends of the other nine." He settled in Minnesota, working at the store at Fort Snelling. In 1880 he moved to White Bear, and by 1881 he had opened a saloon, pool room, and large boarding house located across from the railroad depot on Third Street, just east of the Getty Building.

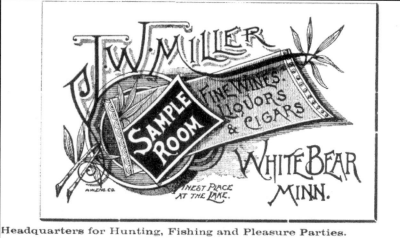

1890 Ad

Courtesy of the White Bear Lake Area Historical Society

Lake Breeze Ad – 1892

By 1892 Robert Anderson was the proprietor of Joe Miller's establishment. It was renamed the White Front Saloon.

Courtesy of the White Bear Lake Area Historical Society

The White Front Saloon,
ROB'T ANDERSON, Prop.

The Most Pleasant Resort for Visitors to the Lake.

Constantly on hand the popular brands of Beers, Wines and liquors for family use.

Orders delivered at any part of the lake.

Third Street, Opposite Railroad Park.

WHITE BEAR, : : : : : MINNESOTA.

White Front Saloon Interior – Proprietor August Holzheid behind the Bar

Courtesy of Bob Thein

From the mid-1890s into the early 1900s August Holzheid was the owner of the White Front Saloon, also referred to as Gus' Place. James Bazille was the next owner, with Joseph H. Weinand buying it from Bazille in 1911. R. J. Coats owned the establishment in the 1920s, selling to Jim Palmer in 1928.

Courtesy of the White Bear Press
August Holzheid – 1902

Hollihan's Pub – Summer 2003

Joe Miller's Sample Room and Boarding House has changed quite a bit, except for the fact that the building still houses a bar, Hollihan's Pub.

Courtesy of Cynthia Vadnais

Courtesy of the White Bear Lake Area Historical Society

North Side of Third Street, Looking East toward Railroad Park – 1917

On August 27, 1914 Sam Slone opened a clothing store at 116 Third Street. That same year Slone took on T. Garber, a businessman from North St. Paul, as a partner and the store was renamed Garber & Slone. In 1916 M. Greenstein of Minneapolis bought the business.

D. A. Coates Store – North Side of Third Street between Railroad and Banning Avenues – Circa 1900

Shown are Margaret and Corine Macey, Mrs. Coates, the two Coates boys, and Byrd and Forest Henkel.

D. A. Coates opened for business on May 10, 1900, selling carpets, household furnishings, mattresses, and stoves.

Courtesy of the White Bear Lake Area Historical Society

The Old Getty Home on Birch Lake Avenue – Early 1870s

From left to right: Ida Keller, George W. Getty, Mrs. Mary Getty, Robert W. Getty, Daniel Getty, Adam K. Getty, Aunt Hannah E. Keller, and Grandma Keller.

Courtesy of the White Bear Lake Area Historical Society

Daniel Getty was born February 16, 1826 in Northern Ireland. He was trained as a cabinetmaker. In 1855 he brought his family to Minnesota moving to White Bear in the early 1860s. Getty's first wife, Mary Keller, died on May 3, 1883, and he married again in 1884 to Hannah Elizabeth Keller, the sister of his first wife. Daniel Getty died on November 13, 1903 and his second wife Hannah died in 1922.

The children born to Daniel and Mary Getty were John Adam, Alice, Henry (Harry) Keller, George Walter, Adam Keller, and Robert Wilson. John Adam lived from 1853 to 1926, Alice died as a baby in 1855, Harry lived from 1856 to 1928, and George from 1861 to 1884. George Walter died single at age twenty-three. Robert, the youngest, was born in 1868 and died in 1945. He graduated from the University of Pennsylvania Medical School in 1891 and spent most of his life practicing medicine in Montana.

Daniel Getty Home – First Street – 1890

Courtesy of the White Bear Lake Area Historical Society

Courtesy of the White Bear Lake Area Historical Society

Daniel Getty & Co. Store – 1875 to 1890

Daniel Getty had the distinction of opening the first general store in White Bear in 1870. The eighteen-by-twenty-foot establishment offered a line of general merchandise. The next year Getty took over as postmaster and, for the first time, the post office in White Bear was located in a public store. In 1875 he erected a twenty-by-sixty-foot, two-story wood building, shown in the above picture, on the corner of Third Street and Clark Avenue, facing Clark Avenue. The upstairs area served as a public hall. Four of his sons, John Adam, Harry Keller, Adam Keller, and George Walter, shared in the business.

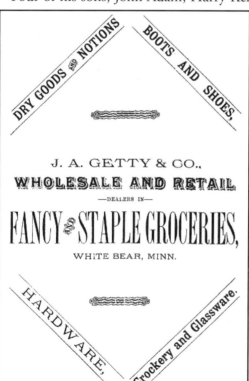

J. A. Getty & Company Ad – 1888

By 1888 the business name was J. A. Getty & Company. The Getty brothers had a complete line of merchandise, including dry goods, notions, boots and shoes, hardware, crockery, glassware, and fancy and staple groceries. Daniel Getty's business interests had changed to real estate and insurance.

Courtesy of the White Bear Lake Area Historical Society

Getty Block – Early 1900s

Courtesy of the Lawrence R. Whitaker Family

A larger building was conceived that would leave a lasting legacy. In 1889, David Hanna began the work on the new $18,000 brick building, called the Getty Block. The two-story wood Getty Building was relocated to the southeast corner of Third Street and Banning Avenue.

Lake Breeze Ad – 1894

Andrew Schoch and Company leased the Getty Building in the mid-1890s, selling the business in 1895 to the White Bear Mercantile run by John H. Spink, who would later purchase the building. Spink sold off the feed department to T. E. Fellows & Company in 1897, and by 1919 all departments except the hardware department had been sold off. Spink died suddenly in 1922.

During the time that Spink ran the White Bear Mercantile Company, the building housed a variety of businesses and professional people, including the post office, the telephone exchange, E. F. Soule's Barbershop, G. H. Lemon Hardware store, White Bear Electric Company, Mary P. Hopkins M.D., William Bull Photo Gallery, Earl F. Jackson (a lawyer), S. O. Francis M.D., J. H McClanahan M.D., J. A. Alrick (dentist), Arch L. LeRue (lawyer), F. L. Shapler (dentist), Gericke Drug Store, and the White Bear Candy Company, to name a few.

Courtesy of the White Bear Lake Area Historical Society

White Bear Mercantile Company Workforce
Notice the reflection of the fire hall in the window behind the man with the white apron.

Cassavant Dry Goods – Mercantile Block
Shown in the photograph are J. A. Cassavant and his oldest daughter, Lessie.

In 1919 J. A. Cassavant purchased the Mercantile Dry Goods stock from J. H. Spink, changing the name to Cassavant Dry Goods. The business remained in the same location. By this time the building was referred to as the Mercantile Block.

Courtesy of the White Bear Press

White Bear Press Ad – 1919

Courtesy of the White Bear Press

White Bear Life Ad – 1912

Northwestern Telephone Exchange Office – Second Floor of the Getty Building – Circa 1916

Shown standing are chief operator, Dora Goesch, and wire chief, C. O. Banhorn.

Courtesy of the White Bear Lake Area Historical Society

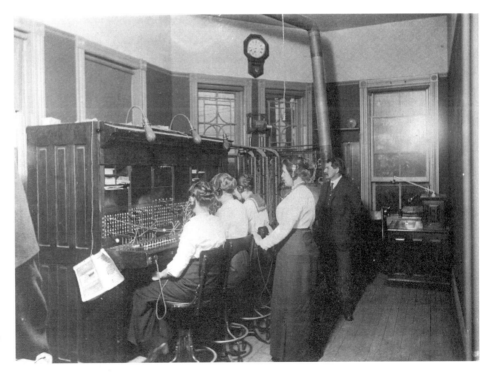

    John H. Spink, George Reif, J. S. Chisholm, and Phillip Gilbert organized the local telephone service in White Bear in 1901. In 1904 it was sold to the Northwestern Telephone Exchange Company, and by 1918 Tri-State Telephone Exchange had all the phone services in White Bear. Northwestern Bell Phone Company was given a franchise in 1933, merging with Tri-State in 1942. In 1954, the year switchboards disappeared in White Bear, Northwestern Bell built a new office on the south side of Fourth Street between Murray and Miller Avenues.

Courtesy of the Richard Vadnais Family

I.O.O.F. Members – Early 1900s

Members shown (from left to right): Williams, F. Reif, L. Knipps, J. Lamdeat (or David Hanna), C. Strom, A. Dupre, J. Pogoant, Underlighter, J. McGrath, O. Taylor, J. Gordy, J. Lonergan, R. Long, B. Bacon, F. Long, Flynn, J. May, N. Eak, L. Bacon, George Torinus, B. Lock, O. Luzerke, J. Forcier, J. Long, J. Peltier, G. Clewett, L. Getter, D. Ivett. (The names were handwritten, so some of the spellings may not be correct.)

The Odd Fellows organization started in 1889 in Wyoming with sixteen charter members, and in 1891 moved to White Bear, where the first president was O. M. Tombler. The first meeting in White Bear was held in the old wooden Getty Building. Subsequently, they met in the Cobb Block until it burned in 1894. After that meetings were held in the new brick Getty Building.

The purpose of the organization was to attend to the sick, bury the dead, educate orphans, and provide a home for those members who were aged and indigent. Three interconnected chain links symbolize the organization's motto: "Friendship, Love, and Truth."

Courtesy of Cynthia Vadnais

Third Street from Highway 61 – Circa 1948

Courtesy of Cynthia Vadnais

Mercantile Grocery Company – Circa 1948

In 1927 there were several businesses located in the Getty Building. George E. Farnen (groceries) and Ted L. Schweitzer (meat) owned the Mercantile Grocery & Meat Company. Other businesses on the street level included the White Bear Variety Store started by Mr. R. H. Wickersham, who first came to White Bear as a summer visitor, and Uppgren's Hardware, owned by R. M. Uppgren, which specialized in electric appliances, sporting goods, and Crosley radios in addition to a general line of hardware. The post office, the telephone exchange, the *White Bear Press*, Marguerite Therrin's Beauty Parlor, and dentists Frank Gardner and E. W. Swenson were all located in the second story of the building.

Blooms Department Store Display Window

In 1929 R. J. (Bob) Bloom moved his store, Blooms Department Store, to the Getty Building, taking the space that had held the White Bear Variety Store.

Courtesy of the White Bear Lake Area Historical Society

The 1936 *White Bear Press* reported, "Nash, proprietor of the Getty Block is making some more improvements in that building. Every square foot of housing space in the block now is occupied. Of these tenants are four public service concerns – the post office, the central telephone, the Federal Land Loan office and the newspaper office – which together with nine other business concerns, make it the concentrated business center of the city." Percy Nash passed away in 1946.

In September 1941, when the cyclonic storm hit White Bear, one of the ornamental brick points was torn off the Getty Building and smashed into the roof.

Ted Schweitzer retired from the meat market business in 1949, dying eight years later in 1957. His successor was John Bucher. James Adamson ran the Mercantile Grocery. The grocery closed in 1951. John Bucher continued with his meat market and Anne L. Ciresi opened Ciresi's Liquor Store.

In February 1952 Anne L. Ciresi opened Ciresi's Liquor Store, which has been continuously in business at this location for more than fifty years. Avalon Arts and Uptown Images are in the same building to the east along Third Street.

Courtesy of Cynthia Vadnais

Ciresi's Liquor Store – Summer 2003

Courtesy of the Lawrence R. Whitaker Family

Hardy's Grocery and Feed Store – Circa 1900

Shown from left to right: Prosper LeVasseur, Billie Schuhr, Joe Forcier, Fred Whitaker, Lorenzo Markoe, Joe Hardy, Lucy Francis, ——, ——, Frances Flandrick, Martin Schuhr, Henry Pondesul, and Oscar Nelson.

Born in Canada in 1857, Joseph Hardy came to White Bear around 1893. He started in the grocery business in the mid-1890s. Shortly after that, Prosper J. LeVasseur, who lived with the Hardy family, went to work for Mr. Hardy. The store, located in what would become known as the Hardy Building, was situated on the southeast corner of Third Street and Banning Avenue.

Hardy's eighteen-by-twenty-foot feed store building, adjacent to his grocery business on the east side, was moved to this location from the southwest side of Railroad Park. The small building had originally housed the first general store in White Bear, where Daniel Getty was the proprietor. When the brick Getty Building was erected in 1890, the two-story wood frame Getty Building was moved to this corner, becoming Hardy's Store.

Courtesy of the Lawrence R. Whitaker Family

Hardy – Whitaker Home

The home shown to the far left in the previous photograph was the Joseph and Jane Hardy home, conveniently located near Hardy's place of business.

Frederick E. Whitaker married Louise Hardy May 3, 1904, and they eventually made this their home, raising their six children here while renting the second floor rooms to teachers.

Courtesy of the Richard Vadnais Family

Hardy's Store Interior – Early 1900s

Joseph Hardy is fourth from the left, Edna Olson is at the counter, and Prosper LeVasseur is second from the right.

Courtesy of the Lawrence R. Whitaker Family

Bernier and Company Groceries

    Esdras Bernier, who had previously run a grocery store in Mendota, rented the Hardy Building in 1907. Bernier died on January 24, 1911 and the grocery went out of business in 1912.

Courtesy of the Lawrence R. Whitaker Family

Harry K. Getty's Dry Goods Store and Hardy's Grocery – Circa 1917

    In 1908 Hardy opened a sewing machine shop, the business he had been in before taking up selling groceries. In April 1910 he opened a grocery business on Railroad Avenue but was back at his old location on Third Street and Banning Avenue on January 1, 1913. In 1915 the small feed store was torn down, and Hardy added a forty-four-by-sixty-foot addition that he used as a feed store and storeroom. In 1917 he sold his dry goods business to H. K. Getty, one of Daniel Getty's sons, and the feed business to Delphis Picard, a former assistant. Getty located in the addition next to Hardy and Picard opened Picard's Feed Store at 204 East Third Street in 1918.

Harry K. Getty's store at 804 East Third Street occupied the addition Hardy built in 1915. Getty was one of the pioneer volunteer firemen and was the treasurer of White Bear for forty-two years. He relinquished the job of treasurer in 1923 in order to devote his full attention to his business.

Getty, who was married to Charlotte Murray, the daughter of James C. Murray, the first postmaster in White Bear, was the sole proprietor of the business until late 1927 when he took Robert J. Bloom as a partner. Getty ran the men's clothing and shoe department, while the dry goods end of the business was run by Bloom. Upon Getty's death on October 25, 1928 at age seventy-one, the store became R. J. Bloom's. Bloom moved his business to the Getty Block, at Third Street and Clark Avenue, in 1929.

Courtesy of the White Bear Press

White Bear Press Ad – 1926

Portion of the back of a White Bear Lake Postcard

Hardy sold the grocery business to Mr. A. A. Perkins in 1919 and retired. Hardy was struck and killed by a truck on March 23, 1922 in Deland, Florida. In October of 1920 Prosper LeVasseur took over the grocery store. Perkins died in 1924.

Courtesy of the Lawrence R. Whitaker Family

Mr. Arthur A. Perkins

Courtesy of the White Bear Press

Courtesy of the Richard Vadnais Family

H. K. Getty's Dry Goods Store and LeVasseur's Grocery Store – Early 1920s

Having bought out A. A. Perkins in 1920, Prosper LeVasseur's grocery store was located at Third Street and Banning Avenue from 1920 until 1922. A fire broke out in LeVasseur's store in 1921, causing only slight smoke damage to Getty's stock, while LeVasseur's stock and fixtures were destroyed and the building damaged. Until LeVasseur could get things repaired, Getty graciously shared his space with LeVasseur.

Courtesy of Cynthia Vadnais

Hardy Building – Third Street and Banning Avenue – Summer 2003

The American Legion and Edward Jones Investments are located in the former Hardy Building.

LeVasseur's Grocery at Bald Eagle and Birch Lake Avenues – Circa 1915
Courtesy of Bill Dillon

Shown from left to right: Prosper LeVasseur, Constance LaMotte, ——, and Lawrence LeVasseur.

Prosper LeVasseur went into the grocery business for himself in 1912, a few years after getting married to Rose Schuhr. He was not a wealthy man, which necessitated his going to Mr. Warner, the manager of the First State Bank, and asking for a loan to get started in business. In exchange for a $500 loan, Prosper offered the only collateral he had, his "honest face."

J. P. Perrault built the twenty-four-by-fifty-foot building in 1912 on the northwest corner of Bald Eagle and Birch Lake Avenues. Prosper LeVasseur ran his business from this location until 1920, at which time he sold to Charles P. Conway, who had worked for the Mercantile Grocery Company. In 1928 Conway purchased a portion of the Gerken Block, 611 Fourth Street, and moved his business. Near the end of 1928 LeVasseur was once again back in this location, opening the Big-Little Store, with his son Lawrence managing the operation. By 1929 he decided to rent the building out again and consolidated his stock to his store at Third Street and Banning Avenue. Mrs. Howard Bloom's Grocery was located in the building from 1929 to 1937. On July 1, 1937 Mrs. Bloom's son-in-law, Walter Berg, purchased the business and renamed it Berg's Grocery.

Courtesy of Bob Thein

LeVasseur's First Delivery Vehicle

Prosper was the first grocer in White Bear to use an automobile to deliver groceries. The 1915 Studebaker served a dual purpose as it was often leased, for $5, by the local mortuary to use as a hearse.

Interior of LeVasseur's Grocery at Third Street and Banning Avenue

Shown from left to right are: Prosper LeVasseur, Desire Parenteau, and Frank LaBore

Courtesy of Bob Thein

White Bear Press Ad – 1921

Courtesy of the White Bear Press

Interior of LeVasseur's Grocery at Third Street and Banning Avenue – July 1927

Shown from left to right are: Flossier, Prosper LeVasseur, Lawrence LeVasseur, and ——.

Courtesy of Bob Thein

Courtesy of the White Bear Lake Area Historical Society

LeVasseur's Grocery Store – Washington Avenue – Circa 1939
LeVasseur's Grocery is the second building from the right and has a white front.

    In 1932 LeVasseur exchanged locations with the Sanford and Shaffer R. C. U. Store, taking up residence in the building just to the north of Greengard's at 314 Washington Avenue. Prosper had by this time taken his son Lawrence as a partner.

    In 1940 LeVasseur began erecting a modern building at the other end of the block, where Lemon's Hardware store had been located earlier in the century. The store was barely finished when Prosper retired and sold the business to C. Thomas Stores in 1941, and then to the National Tea Company in 1943. In 1945, after Prosper's sons had returned from the war, LeVasseur's Food Shop was opened by William (Bill) LeVasseur at the original location on Bald Eagle and Birch Lake Avenues. Bill remained in business until his retirement in 1967.

White Bear Press Ad – 1927

    Sometime around 1920 Marshall Washington opened the White Bear Furniture Exchange, also known as Ye Antique Shoppe, on the east side of Harry Getty's Dry Goods store. By 1927, with a high demand for new and used furniture, Washington had expanded to two locations. In 1933 he purchased the Auditorium on Fourth Street and moved.

Ye Antique Shoppe

M. Washington, Prop.

TWO STORES:
714 E. Third St.   806 E. Third St.

The largest stock of Genuine Antique
Furniture in the Northwest

EVERY ARTICLE GUARANTEED
AS AUTHENTIC.

NEW AND USED FURNITURE.

Packing   -   Crating   -   Transfer

Courtesy of the White Bear Press

U. S. Post Office

In November of 1858, James C. Murray became the first postmaster in White Bear. Running the post office from his home, he would make the trip to St. Paul to pick up the mail for the area twice a week. He gave up his position in December of 1870 when Daniel Getty was appointed postmaster.

Getty moved the post office to his general store where it had the distinction of being the first post office in White Bear in a public place. The job was a bit easier for Getty, since the mail was delivered by rail. In 1871 Getty put in a pigeonhole cabinet with twenty spaces that increased by eighty spaces in 1875 and another eighty in 1880. The post office was made a money order office in 1885.

Courtesy of the White Bear Lake Area Historical Society
James C. Murray House – Lake Avenue – 1890

T. B. Murray was appointed postmaster in 1889, resigning in 1891, with J. M. King serving out Murray's unexpired term. King moved the post office to the Cobb Block located between Fourth and Fifth Streets on Railroad Avenue. There the post office shared quarters with the *Lake Breeze* run by A. H. S. Perkins.

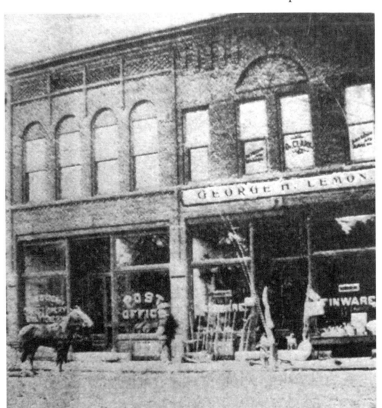

Post Office – Getty Block on Third Street

Lorenzo J. Markoe was appointed postmaster in 1893. Markoe relocated the post office to the east store of the Getty Building on Third Street after the Cobb Block burned down July 11, 1894. All the furniture and mail also burned.

In 1897 J. M. King became postmaster again, at which time he moved the post office upstairs in the Getty Building at 200 W. Third Street.

Courtesy of the White Bear Press

Postmaster Fred Campbell

Courtesy of the Richard Vadnais Family

By 1913 Markoe was once again postmaster, with his assistant being Miss Boody and Delia Cardinal as clerk. An important change occurred in 1916, when an experimental free delivery route was established with one carrier. Markoe resigned in 1918 because of poor health, at which time Fred F. Campbell, an assistant under King for one and a half years, and for some four and a half years a railroad mail clerk, became postmaster with Lucy Francis as postmistress.

John Fournelle Delivering Mail by Horse and Sleigh – 1924

Courtesy of Bill Dillon

The way the mail was delivered would once again change in 1930 when the Northern Pacific Railway removed two mail trains resulting in street car service used to get the mail out to White Bear.

U. S. Post Office White Bear Lake – Getty Building from 1905-1937

The White Bear Post Office made state history on July 1, 1920 when it became a second-class post office faster than any other town in Minnesota history. This placed it on the same footing as the St. Paul Post Office.

Courtesy of the White Bear Lake Area Historical Society

In 1922 J. M. King was assistant to Fred Campbell. By the late 1920s the post office was serving Bald Eagle, Manitou Island, White Bear Beach, Dellwood, Mahtomedi, East Shore Park, Forest Heights, Delmar, Wildwood, Wildwood Manor, Willernie, Birchwood, Bellaire, Cottage Park, Chester, and Lakeshore.

Courtesy of the White Bear Lake Area Historical Society

Lorenzo J. Markoe and Delia Cardinal – 1913

Courtesy of the White Bear Lake Area Historical Society

Interior of the Post Office in the Getty Building – Summer 1930

The post office staff (from left to right): C. Fournelle, E. Mailloux, A. Sandahl, Postmaster Campbell, Al Kindsten, Gladys Long, Floyd Trunnell.

Laying the Cornerstone for the New Post Office – August 2, 1937

Courtesy of the White Bear Lake Area Historical Society

A most significant change occurred, since the inception of a post office in White Bear, when on August 2, 1937, on the south side of Washington Park facing Third Street, ground was broken for a post office building on land purchased from the Northern Pacific Railway for $7,000. The fifty-nine-by-sixty-foot, one-story building would provide the White Bear Post Office with its first permanent home.

Courtesy of Cynthia Vadnais

New Post Office Building on Third Street

The government building, constructed of brick, was finished in 1940 for a cost slightly more than $42,000. Postmaster Campbell occupied the building in early 1938 even though it was not finished. C. E. Davies was the first person to rent a box in the new building.

The post office was remodeled in 1963 to add more floor space, more dock space, and a larger parking area for the postal trucks.

Fred E. Campbell retired as postmaster in August 1949. He had served in the position for thirty-five years. Campbell died in 1951.

Voyageur Mural Painted by Miss Nellie Best

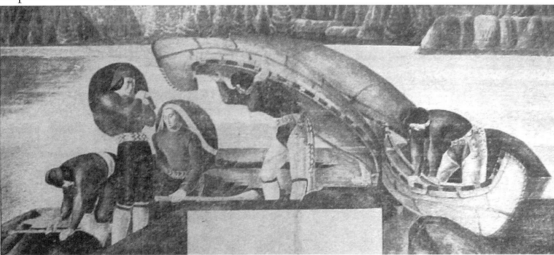

Courtesy of the White Bear Press

In 1939 Nellie Best, an artist from Minneapolis and California, won a Works Project Administration job that paid her 1 percent of the cost of the new post office building. She was hired to paint a twelve-by-four-foot mural inside the post office. According to the March 17, 1939 *White Bear Press*, her winning entry featured "a lake with Indians carrying canoes to be loaded with supplies. In the background running down to the water's edge the forests of Minnesota are depicted." Miss Best arrived in White Bear in February 1940 and was finished with the mural by April 1940. The mural was restored in 1969 because time had faded the colors of the water-based paints, called casein. Sadly, today the mural no longer exists.

Courtesy of Cynthia Vadnais

Current U. S. Post Office at White Bear Lake

By the early 1970s it was necessary for the post office to find a new location. The northeast corner of Fifth Street and Banning Avenue was secured, and in 1976 the new post office was being constructed.

Courtesy of Cynthia Vadnais

Premier Bank – Summer 2003

In the late 1970s and early 1980s the old post office building was a popular restaurant and bar called Bobbies in the Park. Premier Bank bought the building in the late 1980s, renovating both the interior and exterior. The most prominent change to the exterior was the addition of a columned entrance with a clock tower.

Looking Down Fourth Street

Courtesy of Ruth Mattlin

White Bear Armory – Southwest Corner of Fourth Street and Cook Avenue

In 1922, upon the removal of the J. E. Extrand home from the southwest corner of Fourth Street and Cook Avenue, the White Bear Armory was built, sharing a wall with the Auditorium building to the west of it. The Extrand house was moved to a new location on Cook Avenue in its entirety, scarcely inconveniencing the occupants. The Armory formally opened on February 27, 1923 as the home of the Headquarters Company, Second Battalion, Sixth Infantry, Minnesota National Guard.

When the large building, designed for drilling, was not in use by the National Guard unit, it functioned as a place to hold dances and roller skating sessions, play basketball, practice shooting, and for Boy Scout, American Legion, and GAR to meet, among other activities.

On December 7, 1928 the front portion of the Armory burned, due to what was thought to be faulty wiring. When the Auditorium next door burned six days later on December 13, 1928, it also caused damage to the Armory. Adding to the catastrophes, on September 4, 1941 a tornado struck White Bear tearing a section of the roof off the Armory, besides damaging the cornice on the front of the building.

For a number of years, the city has owned the building. It is home to the White Bear Center for the Arts and the Lions Club.

White Bear Press Ad – 1926

```
ROLLER SKATING
WHITE BEAR ARMORY
Every Sunday Afternoon    From 2 to 5
Sunday and Thursday Nights, 7:30 to 10:30
Spectators only, 10c   Admission, Skating and Checking, 40c
Saturday afternoon for Children, 20c
```

Courtesy of the White Bear Press

White Bear Unit of the Minnesota National Guard – January 6, 1941

This photograph was taken the day the men left for Riverside, California.

Courtesy of Bob Thein

The men of the 101st White Bear unit of the Minnesota National Guard enlisted with the intention of serving their country for a year. After approximately two weeks at the Armory they were shipped to Riverside, California to serve their time. On December 7, 1941 the Japanese bombed Pearl Harbor and the one-year tour of duty turned into five years. Some of the men were sent overseas, while most provided antiaircraft protection in San Francisco. Only two men out of ninety-eight in the unit were lost during the war.

Courtesy of the Lawrence R. Whitaker Family

Y.M.C.A. and Auditorium Association Building – Circa 1912

The Y.M.C.A. Building, erected by C. E. Davies in 1907 at a cost of $12,500, was dedicated in 1908 and became the White Bear Auditorium Association in 1912. It was located on the south side of Fourth Street just west of the Armory. The building was transferred into the city's possession in 1921.

"The Cubs"

Ella LaMotte, Mildred Bacon, Grace Hogan, Marqueritte Bazille, and Delphia – Late 1920s outside the Auditorium Building

Courtesy of Lorraine Billingsley

The Auditorium was a center for both social and athletic gatherings. In addition, it provided a place for organizations such as the Eagles, the Odd Fellows, and the American Legion to hold their meetings. Over the years, besides providing meeting areas, the building housed the municipal bowling alleys, billiard tables, public restrooms, a municipal dining room and kitchen, a sizable theater, and police court. Numerous dances were also held there.

White Bear Press Ad – 1927

The Auditorium Theatre opened around 1916 under the management of A. M. Campbell. From 1919 to 1923 E. A. Jackson operated the theater, after which Mrs. Jessie Jensen took it over and ran it until she built the Avalon Theater in 1928.

In 1923 the building was damaged by fire and restored. However, in November 1928, another fire virtually destroyed the building, rendering it all but useless for several years. The only serviceable part was at the rear of the building, where in 1929 the White Bear Knitting Mills opened for business.

AUDITORIUM THEATRE

MRS. E. W. JENSEN, Prop.

None but the Latest High-Class Pictures Shown, and these often before they are shown in the Twin Cities.

We endeavor to co-operate with every organization and individual in the City of White Bear Lake.

Average Picture Prices, 10c and 25c
Extra Big Pictures, 15c and 35c
Could anyone ask them for less?

This is a 400-seat Theatre. We expect to give you a 700-seat theatre before long.

Courtesy of the White Bear Press

Auditorium Building – Summer 2003

Courtesy of Cynthia Vadnais

Courtesy of Cynthia Vadnais

Courtesy of the White Bear Press

White Bear Press Ad – 1928

South Side of Fourth Street between Cook and Banning Avenues – Circa 1938

In 1933 Marshall Washington purchased the Auditorium building from the city. Washington had been in business in White Bear for a number of years at two locations on Third Street. The Auditorium building provided the perfect location for his furniture factory that had been located near the southeast corner of Third Street and Banning Avenue (Whitaker Block). Washington remodeled the building, creating living quarters for himself, a display area for the furniture, an antique shop, and a furniture manufacturing area. In 1941 Washington closed out his stock but continued to manufacture reproductions. In 1943 Louis J. Marsh opened White Bear Frigid Lockers in the building formerly occupied by Washington.

In 1895 Sewall C. Smith, a self-proclaimed veterinarian, and his family moved to White Bear from Stillwater, opening a livery stable on the north side of Fourth Street between Banning and Cook Avenues. As of 1899 his was the only livery and boarding stable in White Bear, where he housed twenty-two horses and five Shetland ponies, along with every kind of rig from a pony cart to a four-horse tally-ho.

Smith's love of horses led to his building a race track on White Bear Lake in January of 1896, and in 1900, he built a half-mile race track with a baseball diamond in the center (this was probably the baseball field that was located on the northwest corner of Bald Eagle Avenue and Fourth Street).

Smith sold his business to George A. Beckstead in 1907, after which Smith became justice of the peace, a position he held for a number of years. He died September 17, 1934.

Courtesy of Bob Thein

Sewall C. Smith

Courtesy of Cynthia Vadnais

White Bear Auto Livery Vehicle Photographed on Clark Avenue about Third Street – Circa 1915

George A. Beckstead was the successor to Sewall C. Smith in 1907 and was in business until the early part of 1916. Over the years he remodeled the barns by putting in concrete floors and expanded other areas, equipping them with city water, electricity and phones. The remodeling of the horse barn allowed for the sheltering of up to twenty horses. In 1913 he installed a "gasoline filler station" that was open day and night. The livery and boarding stable changed to an auto livery in 1914. Upon quitting the livery business Beckstead went into the ice business, retiring from it in 1939. Beckstead died in 1942 at the age of seventy-nine.

Courtesy of the White Bear Lake Area Historical Society

George A. Beckstead's Livery and Boarding Stable

With automobiles and horse drawn buggies having to share the roads, it was impossible to avoid problems. The 1916 *White Bear Press* stated that George Beckstead has had two illustrations of late of the fact that the automobiles are knocking the buggies out of the livery business. Within the past two weeks two of his livery buggies have been run into by fool drivers of automobiles and demolished. In the last "accident" the horse was badly injured. The occupants of the buggy were thrown out and the young lady, we understand, was thrown under the rig, and had it not been for the extreme gentleness of the horse, she would probably have been severely injured, if not killed... How long must these accidents occur before a clause, insuring carefulness and the use of common sense, will be incorporated into the examination papers of those who would engage in driving autos?

GEO. A. BECKSTED
FIRST CLASS
Auto Livery and Garage

SERVICE
Day and Night

Fourth Street near Banning Avenue
WHITE BEAR

Courtesy of the White Bear Press
White Bear Press Ad – 1914

White Bear Life Ad – 1901

ANTON BARTH, MAKER OF AND DEALER IN
Boots and Shoes.
Harness Repairing, Etc.
East Fourth Street, White Bear

White Bear Life Ad – 1906

Horse Shoeing Prices
No. 1, 2, 3 and 4 shoes, 40c each
" 5 " 45c "
" 6 and 7 " 50c "
Hand Turned " 50c "
Re-setting " 25c "

GEO. W. ANDERSON
Successor to N. W. LECLAIR

C. L. CLARK
Blacksmithing Horse Shoeing
Auto Body Building
Acetylene Welding
Saddle-Horse Shoeing a Specialty.

White Bear Life Ad – 1907

White Bear Press Ad – 1927

Courtesy of the White Bear Press

Conveniently located across Fourth Street from Smith's (and later Beckstead's) Livery Stable was a blacksmith shop that, over the years, had a number of different owners. Anton Barth was in the location in the early 1900s, followed by N. W. LeClair around 1906. George W. Anderson was the successor to LeClair in 1907, followed by Joseph S. Garceau. C. L. Clark, who went to work for Garceau in 1913, bought out Garceau in March of 1923. Clark eventually moved his shop to his home on the northwest corner of Fourth Street and Murray Avenue.

Courtesy of the White Bear Lake Area Historical Society

Fourth Street, Looking West from between Banning and Cook Avenues

In the foreground on the right is Arcand's Garage (Bert Arcand Ford), built in 1920 by Bert Arcand. On the left, in the foreground, is a large horseshoe sign for the Joseph Garceau blacksmith shop. His residence was just west of his shop on the southeast corner of Fourth Street and Banning Avenue. Beyond Garceau's is W. W. Vincent's Grocery on the southwest corner of Fourth Street and Banning Avenue, and across the street from Vincent's Grocery is Gerken's Hardware.

The *White Bear Press* reported, "The completion of Bert Arcand's new garage gives White Bear the finest appearing building of its kind in this section. The considerable frontage is largely of glass with copper casings, the entire floor space is of cement and the side and rear walls are of pressed stone. The garage and work shop is equipped with every modern device necessary, giving us a Ford agency such as most towns do not possess. The brick work in the front is of art brick."

White Bear Press Ad – 1916

In 1915 Bert Arcand was located on Banning Avenue, just behind Vincent's Grocery, in the Haussner Building, where he sold farm implements. By 1916 he had moved to Beckstead's White Bear Auto Livery, where he sold Chalmers and Ford automobiles. Arcand was in partnership with John E. Collins until 1919, when the partnership was dissolved and Collins opened his own garage and filling station.

Bert Arcand sold the business in 1923 to A. C. Podvin and F. A. Biernes. They continued to sell Ford vehicles but changed the name of the business to White Bear Motor Sales.

In 1931 Bert Arcand was back in the Haussner Building, once again selling farm implements and running a feed store with his son. Arcand died in 1943 at age seventy.

```
FORD
THE UNIVERSAL CAR
New Prices August 1, 1916
The following prices for Ford cars will be
effective on and after August 1st, 1916
Chassis    . . . $325.00
Runabout   . .    345.00
Touring Car .    360.00
Coupelet   . . .  505.00
Town Car   . .    595.00
Sedan      . . . .645.00
         f. o. b. Detroit
BERT ARCAND & CO.
These prices are positively guaranteed against any
reduction before August 1st, 1917, but there is no
guarantee against an advance in price at any time.
```

Courtesy of the White Bear Press

Bert Arcand Ford – Pre-1920 – The Old White Bear Auto Livery Location

Courtesy of Bob Thein

Courtesy of the White Bear Press

White Bear Motor Sales – 1928

In the mid-to late-1920s White Bear Motor Sales had an orchestra with fourteen members called Mel and his Harmony Bears. One of the places they played in 1927 was the White Bear Castle.

Charles Breen sold his interest in the company in 1940, buying Elgin Miller's gas station, then located at Lake Avenue and Highway 61.

Podvin moved White Bear Motor Sales to Peter Fournelle's garage at 215 Clark Avenue in 1945. In 1956 Herb Tousley purchased the Clark Avenue business from Podvin and renamed it Herb Tousley Ford, with Tousley leasing the building from Podvin.

In 1964 the White Bear Motor Sales building on Fourth Street, along with the house to the west on the corner, would be demolished and in part occupied by a Goodyear Tire and Rubber Company store.

Courtesy of Bob Thein

White Bear Motor Sales – Fighter Fred Lenhart in Back Seat

Fred Lenhart became a professional boxer at eighteen years of age. From 1927 to 1937 he competed in 176 fights, having only fourteen losses, eight of those to decisions. He was the Minnesota heavyweight champion boxer in 1937 and a contender for the light heavyweight boxing crown.

Courtesy of Dick Hanson

White Bear Body and Fender Shop – 1940

In March 1938 White Bear Motor Sales leased Charlie Clark's blacksmith shop just west of Washington's on Fourth Street. Eric Hanson, a Swedish immigrant, became the proprietor. Hanson, an experienced automobile repairman, had learned the trade by working in shops in Omaha and Chicago before coming to White Bear in 1936. The building underwent major remodeling in 1946 and again in 1955. In 1962 Eric's son, Dick, bought the business. Dick was the owner until December 31, 2003, when he sold to longtime employee Dennis Graves.

Dick Hanson's White Bear Body Shop – Summer 2003

Courtesy of Cynthia Vadnais

Vincent's Grocery – West Fourth Street near Division Avenue – Circa 1911

On March 13, 1911 William W. Vincent opened his grocery store on the north side of Fourth Street, just west of the corner of Division Avenue. He conducted his business from here until 1914, when he relocated to the southwest corner of Fourth Street and Banning Avenue.

Courtesy of the White Bear Lake Area Historical Society

White Bear Press Ad – 1927

Courtesy of the White Bear Press

"Vincent's of Course"
The Pioneer Grocery Man

WE HAVE watched White Bear grow and have the utmost faith in its future.

For the new and greater White Bear we will give the same reliable service and will continue to carry a complete stock of standard groceries. . . . .

W. W. VINCENT

Vincent's Grocery – August 1932 – Flooding after a Heavy Rainstorm

Courtesy of the Richard Vadnais Family

Vincent constructed a foundation for his new store on Fourth Street and Banning Avenue; the upper stories were a portion of the Ramaley home on Bald Eagle Avenue that he had purchased and moved to the location. In 1923 he added a three-car garage to the rear of the store.

Vincent, who had only one arm, kept his pet bulldog in the store. It is said that the dog spent much of its time in the window and that the children passing by loved to tease it until it caused quite an uproar. The store was owned by Vincent until his death on March 23, 1959. He had been a resident of White Bear for fifty-six years.

In March 1960 Chris Engen and his son Art moved their store, Engen Color Center, from the Hardy Building to Vincent's corner. Engen's sold the business in the early 1990s.

Courtesy of Cynthia Vadnais

Joel Sherburne Jewelers – Summer 2003

The original Vincent's Grocery building currently houses Joel Sherburne Jewelers. They have occupied the building since 1994.

WHITE BEAR BAKERY

L. A. Thauwald, Prop.

FIRST CLASS BAKERY GOODS

Telephone 342-M

718 E. 4th St.

Courtesy of the White Bear Press

White Bear Press Ad – 1927

In June of 1920 Louis A. Thauwald purchased the White Bear Bakery located on the south side of Fourth Street just west of Vincent's Grocery. Over the next seventeen years he not only renovated, but also remodeled by adding a waterproof basement, a brick face, and a two-story addition that had a garage below and a sunroom above. In 1937 his son Gordon took over the business and ran it until 1960, when he sold to Mr. and Mrs. Herman Sax. They renamed the bakery Sax's White Bear Bakery. Sax sold the bakery to Don Eden in 1972, when it became Eden's Bakery.

Chico's Clothing – Summer 2003 – the Former White Bear Bakery Building

Courtesy of Cynthia Vadnais

Fourth Street – A Heavy Rainstorm Caused Flooding in August 1932

Courtesy of Bob Thein

Fourth Street, looking east. The truck driving down the road is just about at Banning Avenue. Shown on the left is Gerken's Hardware and to the right Vincent's Grocery. Beyond Banning Avenue on the left is White Bear Motor Sales.

Gerken's Hardware – Northwest Corner of Fourth Street and Banning Avenue – Circa 1910

Courtesy of Bob Thein

Henry Gerken, one of the pioneer businessmen in White Bear, started in business in 1896, when he rented the blacksmith shop of Joe Burkard on Third Street. Early in 1898 Gerken erected a new building for his blacksmith shop at Fourth Street and Banning Avenue. *White Bear Life* wrote that the new building was "to be large enough to accommodate all branches of horseshoeing, blacksmith and wagon work on a larger scale." The Gerken Block covered a quarter of a city block. He rented out the other stores that were a part of his building.

Gerken's business consisted of a hardware store, department store, blacksmith services, tin shop, and for a brief time around 1910, Mr. Gerken was an authorized director for C. E. Hawkins and Company funeral directors and embalmers.

White Bear Life Ad – 1913

Courtesy of the White Bear Press

Upon Gerken's death in 1935, his wife became the owner and his son Harry C. the manager. In January 1938 the Gerkens closed out the business. Harry joined Raymer Hardware Company in St. Paul and the building was sold to Mitch Parenteau.

Courtesy of the White Bear Press

White Bear Press Ad – 1937

M. H. "Mitch" Parenteau went into the meat business in 1927. After the Gerkens closed their store in 1939, Parenteau bought it and opened a meat and grocery business. That year he had a brick veneer put on the front of the building. During WWII he had five trucks that drove two routes per day, delivering grocery orders. Soon after the war Parenteau sold the grocery business to pursue a new line of business, clothing.

Parenteau's Clothing Store – 1949

In April 1949, Parenteau bought the Home Trade Store at 626 Fourth Street from Sam Kaufman. In 1950 he moved his business, Parenteau's Clothing, to 618 Fourth Street, the storefront just east of the old Coast to Coast Store. Dick, Mitch's oldest son, joined the business full-time in 1958. The next year they moved back into the Gerken Building. Mitch died an untimely death on July 6, 1962 at the age of fifty-eight. The family carried on in the clothing business, remodeling the exterior of the store in 1964. Youngest son, Mike, joined the family business in 1969, and that same year the interior of the store was remodeled and enlarged by a third. Parenteau's Clothing was in business until 1997, when Bear Patch Quilting Company took over the storefront.

Bear Patch Quilting Company – Summer 2003

Courtesy of Cynthia Vadnais

Bob Velin's Super Value Food Market – Early 1950s

Courtesy of Bob Thein

In April 1947, soon after Parenteau quit the meat and grocery business, Ed Chapple opened Chapple's Food Market in the old Gerken Building. In March 1951 Chapple handed the reins over to Bob Velin, who had run the C. Thomas Food Store on Washington Avenue after LeVasseur sold out in 1941. Velin remodeled the building, opening a Super Value Food Market. Just before Parenteau moved back to the location in 1959, it was Bazille's Big Ten Store.

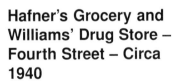

Hafner's Grocery and Williams' Drug Store – Fourth Street – Circa 1940

Courtesy of Bob Thein

In 1928 Charles P. Conway moved his grocery store from the corner of Bald Eagle and Birch Lake Avenues to 611 Fourth Street, on the north side of the street, about halfway between Washington and Banning Avenues. Near the end of 1936, Conway sold his grocery store to M. Hafner, who renamed it Hafner's Food Market. In October 1942 Arnquist and Drummond opened the Daylight Food Market at this location, and in 1969 Dave Uppgren and Bob Schletty moved Uppgren's Hardware from Third Street to this location. The White Bear Variety Store, which closed in 2003, was the last business to occupy the building.

C. G. Nickel opened Nickel's Drug Store at 607 Fourth Street in 1931. After several months in business, he sold the operation to Harry Williams, who changed the name to Williams' Drug Store.

Hall Drug Store Pharmacy Area – Harold Hall

Harold Hall bought out Williams' Drug Store in 1951 and renamed it Hall Pharmacy. Hall remodeled the store from 1957-1958. The business was sold to Harvey Lillestol in 1969.

Courtesy of the White Bear Lake Area Historical Society

In 1889 electric street lights were installed in White Bear, and by 1891 a local stock company called White Bear Electric Company was organized. The Acme Company had been granted the franchise in 1889 but had not lived up to their end of the bargain and had to remove their equipment and poles. The town boasted more than one-thousand-five-hundred lights in stores, halls and private homes by 1899. Also in 1899 service had been extended to Manitou Island. Consumer Power, a privately owned company, was the next owner of the franchise. They were bought by Northern States Power Company in 1916. The Northern States Power building was just east of the 617.

Courtesy of the White Bear Press

Northern States Power Company (NSP) – Fourth Street – 1930

Demolishing the NSP Building – 1973

Just before it was razed, the NSP building had housed the Youth Resource Bureau.

Courtesy of the Richard Vadnais Family

Medicine Chest – May 2004

Lillestol built the Medicine Chest in 1973 at 615 Fourth Street. It occupies the old Northern States Power building site and the alley that had been just to the east of it. The Medicine Chest, owned by Dick Sundt since 1977, looks much the same today as when it was built.

Courtesy of Cynthia Vadnais

Avalon Theater – Circa 1929

Courtesy of Bob Thein

Mrs. Jessie L. Jensen, a widow, moved to White Bear with her children in 1920 and took over the ownership of the Auditorium Theatre from Mr. Jackson in 1923. With help from her two children she ran the theatre three nights a week. However, she had much bigger plans for moviegoers in White Bear, and in 1928 she constructed the Avalon Theater Building for about $50,000. The theater, designed by St. Paul architect Kenneth B. Worthen, was 66-feet by 135-feet and could seat six-hundred people. It was to be English with Norman influences in style both inside and outside. The interior gave the effect of being in an English garden, complete with garden walls and plants. A unique feature of the theater was the sky dome above the seating area, with its starlight effects and shifting clouds. In 1928 the *White Bear Press* described it this way: "The exterior with its old-time gables and latticed windows. The foyer with its Spanish tile floor, rough-finish walls in gold and the ceiling in panels of dull red with black trimmings, while a stairway with black iron railing in English effect leads from the main floor. Quaint lanterns hang from the ceiling while on the walls are massive light-brackets of candle effect… the seats being upholstered in Spanish leather."

On May 21, 1929 the first talking picture shown in the theater was *The Donivan Affair,* starring Jack Holt, William Collier Junior, and Dorothy River.

THE AVALON,

White Bear's Beautiful, New Movie Theatre Opens

Sunday Evening, Dec. 30

With Alice White in "The Show Girl." Also Monday Night.

Tuesday and Wednesday, Jan. 1 and 2, "White Shadows of the South Sea."

Thursday, Friday and Saturday, Jan. 3, 4, 5, Joan Crawford in "Dream of Love."

Admission   -   15c and 35c.

Courtesy of the White Bear Press

At the front of the building flanking each side of the theater were storefronts that Mrs. Jensen rented out. The first two businesses to occupy these spaces were Minnehaha Cleaners and the Park Sweet Shop owned by Melvon Kirkby.

Albrecht remodeled the Kirkby space and opened the 617 on March 9, 1934. His was one of the first liquor licenses issued in White Bear after Prohibition. He owned the bar for thirty-four years, selling it in 1968 to Rod Olson, an employee since 1951. Mary Montpetit bought the business in 2003. The 617 has been in continuous operation since opening in 1934.

White Bear Press Ad – 1928

Upon graduating from college, Mrs. Jensen's son, Paul Albrecht, became a partner in his mother's business. She retired in 1940 and was ill for about fifteen years before dying on October 24, 1961. Paul continued in the business, purchasing the competing White Bear Theatre, on the northeast corner of Third Street and Banning Avenue, in the mid-1950s. He closed that theater until 1968 when he remodeled it, opening it under the name Cine Capri.

ANNOUNCING the Grand Opening of 617

Friday Evening, March 9

On and Off Sale of the Finest Domestic and Imported Beverages.

Truly the most beautiful store of its kind in the North West.

617 4th St., Avalon Theatre Bldg.

We Deliver   Phone 617

Courtesy of the White Bear Press

White Bear Press Ad – 1934

Removing the Avalon Theatre Sign – 1973

Shown (from left to right): Phil Bonin, Carroll Mattlin, and Mike Parenteau.

In 1973 the Avalon Theater became the White Bear Cinema. The White Bear Cinema closed in the early 1980s but the building still remains, housing a number of retail stores and offices.

Courtesy of the White Bear Press

Avalon Building and Medicine Chest (to the right) – Summer 2003

Courtesy of Cynthia Vadnais

White Bear Press Ad – 1931

Charles Breen opened up White Bear Miniature Golf Course in 1931 just across the street from the Avalon Theater. The south side of Fourth Street between the Home Trade Store and Thauwald's Bakery was then a large vacant lot.

Courtesy of the White Bear Press

White Bear MINIATURE GOLF COURSE
Charles Breen, Proprietor
Fourth Street, Opposite Avalon Theatre

NOTHING IN TWIN CITIES TO COMPARE TO IT
ELECTRIC HAZZARDS ---- 18 HOLES
FOURTEEN 500-WATT SPOT LIGHTS

TO OPEN SATURDAY EVENING, MAY 2

Rounds: 25c Daytime -:- 35c Nightime

Miss Frances McHugh in charge.

Courtesy of Bob Thein

Ben Franklin Store – Circa 1940

Fred A. Brass opened the White Bear Variety Store in 1937 in the west compartment of the Avalon Theater. A portion of the vacant land across the street from the theater was developed in 1939, with Brass moving into the largest storefront that same year. From then on this was a Ben Franklin Store, which was later run by his son Bob. The other spaces built to the east of the store were intended as offices for dentists or physicians. In 1939 Spark's Beauty Shop moved into the storefront just west of the Ben Franklin Store, adding Spark's Dress Shop in 1944. Mitch Parenteau had his clothing store at the Spark's location from 1950 to 1959. The vacant land on Fourth Street to the west of these stores was developed in 1949 when a Coast to Coast store was built.

Courtesy of Cynthia Vadnais

Goodthings, Wuollet's Bakery, Sentry Systems and Lake Country Booksellers – Summer 2003

Goodthings occupies the old Ben Franklin Store and Wuollet's Bakery occupies what was once Parenteau's Clothing. Coast to Coast used to be in the Sentry Systems location, and on the corner, Lake Country Booksellers is located in what was once part of the White Bear House.

Ernst Jahn Blacksmith Shop – Northwest Corner of Fourth Street and Division Avenue – Circa 1912

Courtesy of Bob Thein

Ernst Jahn is the second person from the right in the photograph. A close-up view of Ernst Jahn from the photograph above is shown on the next page.

From around 1880 until 1920 the corner of Fourth Street and Division Avenue was home to a blacksmith shop. Known blacksmiths at this location include Leopold Auger, Frank Cormier, Peter Denoyer, Ernst Jahn, and Carl A. Schmidt. Carl Schmidt succeeded Ernst Jahn in 1914.

ERNST JAHN,
HORSE SHOEING,
GENERAL BLACKSMITHING
AND WHEELWRIGHT.
Repairing Promptly Done.
West Fourth St., - White Bear.

Courtesy of the White Bear Press

White Bear Life Ad – 1901

Courtesy of Bob Thein

Ernst Jahn – Circa 1912

C. A. Schmidt
HORESHOEING
and
General Blacksmithing
Repairing Promptly Done
204 West Fourth Street

Courtesy of the White Bear Press

White Bear Press Ad – 1917

Courtesy of the White Bear Lake Area Historical Society

Storefronts Facing Fourth Street at the Corner of Division Avenue

The building on the right was, for years, the storefront for Parcells Brothers. The building on the left had housed Vincent's Grocery from 1911-1914.

In the later part of 1919 Parcells and Bonham opened a store "for the farmer and his mechanical needs" in the Flatiron Building on the southwest corner of Third Street and Clark Avenue. Less than half a year later, on March 13, 1920, Frank L. Gerten and Arthur L. Parcells opened Gerten and Parcells, a hardware store, at the corner of Fourth Street and Division Avenue. A storefront was built and the blacksmith shop was used as a storage area. By the end of 1920 Wesley and Arthur Parcells were running the business under the name Parcells Brothers Hardware. The business closed in 1934.

In 1928 J. W. Gatten operated a two-table pool and billiard hall at the Vincent's Grocery location just west of Parcells. Edwin Long's Hamburger Shop was run from here in the early 1930s, with Bill Jantzen Jr. leasing from Long in the later part of 1936. In 1937, A. P. Zwolenski leased from Long, opening his jewelry store called Empire Jewelry Company.

In May 1935 Earl B. McGill and Kuckler leased the Parcells' Building, becoming distributors for Yoerg Brewing Company. By July 1935 Freddie Chase was running the distributorship that supplied Engesser and Gluek Breweries' products. McGill had converted Parcells' storehouse, which was, in part, the old blacksmith shop, into a bar and tavern called The Shingle Shanty. The *White Bear Press* commented, "Mr. McGill has equipped it with old-time relics, old-time tables and other quaint articles and it instantly became popular with scores of his St. Paul and White Bear friends who enjoy cold lunches, pretzels, and 3.2 beer."

McGill and Fred Lenhart formed a partnership in 1936, purchasing the Shingle Shanty property. The bar became known as Lenhart and McGill's. By the later part of 1937 it was Lenhart's Shingle Shanty when McGill left with the intention of opening a gas station. Lenhart continued running the business, and by 1945 it was the Fred Lenhart Tavern and eventually just Lenhart's Bar.

Lenhart sold to W. Ratler and Julius Matlinsky of St. Paul in August 1952. They renamed it the Sportsmen's Bar. Their ownership was short-lived since by April of 1954 it was once again Lenhart's Bar.

Courtesy of the White Bear Press
White Bear Press Ad – 1926

White Bear Press Ad – 1935

Courtesy of the White Bear Press
White Bear Press Ad – 1937

In 1957 the bar was called Lenhart and Hanke's, but by the early 1960s it was once again just Lenhart's Bar. Lenhart sold the bar to Fred and Helen Thiede in 1965.

Courtesy of the White Bear Press

Courtesy of Lorraine Billingsley

LaCroix Cafe – Early 1950s

Shown are Lorraine Hogan and her father, Julius Hogan. The service station shown behind the car was built in 1927 by J. R. Palmer.

Fred Lenhart built the LaCroix Cafe in 1946. The name changed to the Bamboo Inn in 1954. Later the building housed Carbone's Pizza, and most recently, Ursula's Wine Bar and Cafe.

James R. Palmer established the West Side Cement Block Company in 1917, selling the business to Carl J. Mattlin in 1927. He then built a service station on the south side of Fourth Street at Division Avenue. It opened September 1927. Others also ran the station, including Julius Hogan. A more unusual occupant was George Goulette, who ran his barber shop out of the building. In 1973 Glen and Craig Johnstone opened the Cup and Cone at the location. The Cup and Cone still occupies the building.

White Bear Bar and Ursula's Wine Bar and Cafe – Summer 2003

The front of the White Bear Bar building was redone from 1974-1975. Today the bar is known as the White Bear Bar and the city of White Bear Lake owns the building.

Courtesy of Cynthia Vadnais

White Bear Press Ad – 1937

The Gordons opened Gordon's Cash and Carry in 1920. The store was located on the south side of Fourth Street just west of Division Avenue. Booths were added to the store in 1927, which served light lunches, refreshments and ice cream.

Courtesy of the White Bear Press

Courtesy of Lorraine Billingsley

Gordon's Cash and Carry Interior – Late 1920s

The Gordons had their store for about fifteen years, during which time they lived in the house attached at the rear of the building. When they sold the business to Julius Hogan, the dining room at the back of the store was closed off and incorporated into the house.

Courtesy of the White Bear Lake Area Historical Society

Gordon's Cash and Carry Grocery – West Fourth Street

Hogan's Grocery 1935-1955

Courtesy of Lorraine Billingsley

Gertrude and Julius Hogan moved to White Bear from Wisconsin in 1921. Mr. Hogan worked at Peter Fournelle's garage before opening his own automobile repair service in the garage behind the family home on the northwest corner of Fourth Street and Miller Avenue. The Hogans took over Gordon's Grocery on January 23, 1935. It was all in the family, as Mrs. Gordon and Mrs. Hogan were sisters. Having bought the business, Hogan purchased the building in 1938 from Henry Molitor. Joe Moore took over for a few months in 1955 before it became Dolfay's Grocery. The Dolfays had the store until around 1960, when Glen Johnstone purchased it. The Johnstones continued in the grocery business until about 1980.

C. J. Mattlin Company – Division Avenue just South of Fourth Street – 1949

Courtesy of the White Bear Press

Courtesy of the White Bear Press

Carroll and C. J. Mattlin Standing in Front of the New Store Sign – 1952

Mattlin's Appliance City – 1992

Courtesy of Lorraine Billingsley

Carl J. Mattlin was a tower man at the Bald Eagle Railroad Depot when he decided that he would take on a second job. He went into the plumbing and heating contracting business in 1913, later becoming a general contractor. He purchased J. R. Palmer's cement plant in 1927 and developed the location into a home base and retail center for his business. Carl's son Carroll was born on December 25, 1913 in the second-floor apartment at the Bald Eagle Railroad Depot across from the tower where his father worked. Carroll went into the contracting business with his father. Over the years, besides building hundreds of homes, the company built the brick fire station at Clark Avenue and Second Street in 1930, a service garage for A. J. Vadnais at Fourth Street and Bald Eagle Avenue in 1932, the White Bear Yacht Club in 1939, and the Sunset Bowling Center in 1940. Mattlin's business had great success, expanding by five-thousand square feet in 1950 and another 3,500 square feet in 1966. In 1979, at sixty-six years old, Carroll sold the business. The building was torn down in 1997 to make way for a development the city had planned.

White Bear Press Ad – 1927

William Vadnais started drilling wells in 1907, running his business out of his home on Miller Avenue just north of Fourth Street. Over time he expanded to include all facets of the plumbing business.

Wm. Vadnais
Well Drilling

Water Connections
and
Sewer Connections

Conscientious Work
Satisfaction Assured
Phone 114-M
114 Miller Avenue
White Bear Lake - - Minn.

Courtesy of the White Bear Press

William Vadnais Well Drilling

Shown with circa-1920s well drilling equipment are Earl Martineau (left) and William Vadnais.

Courtesy of the Robert Vadnais Family

William and Robert Vadnais – 414 Miller Avenue

William's son Robert W. took over the business in the early 1940s, running the business from the same location, now 4786 Miller Avenue, until he retired in the late 1970s. A third generation has continued in the business, with both of Robert's sons, Roger and Paul, owning plumbing companies.

Courtesy of the Robert Vadnais Family

White Bear Press Ad – 1925

AUGER BROTHERS
4th and Bald Eagle Ave.
White Bear Lake, Minn.
PHONE 587-M

Courtesy of the White Bear Press

Auger Brothers Garage – Circa 1925

Courtesy of the Richard Vadnais Family

Henry L. and M. S. Auger opened Auger Brothers in 1921. Henry had been doing general automobile repair in White Bear since 1917 in the Harris Perron Building on Railroad Avenue.

Courtesy of the Richard Vadnais Family

Auger Brothers Garage Interior – Henry and Steve Auger – Circa 1930

Auger Brothers were successful from the start, and by 1924 they expanded their business, located on the southeast corner of Bald Eagle Avenue and Fourth Street, to include selling and servicing Dodge Brothers Motor Cars. By 1937 they were selling and servicing Plymouth and DeSoto vehicles.

A modern building was constructed in 1927 to accommodate the growing sales and service of Dodge Cars. The practically fireproof building was fifty-five-by-ninety-feet in size, built of steel, cement and brick. It was constructed around the shell of the old building.

Courtesy of Cynthia Vadnais

Auger's Garage – Summer 2003

Paul Auger is the third generation of the family to own Auger's Garage. He has worked in the business for about thirty-four years. Auger's Garage is the oldest continuously owned family business in White Bear.

Norman Bibeau's Home and Store

Norman Bibeau's home and small grocery store were located on the northeast corner of Bald Eagle Avenue and Fourth Street. Robert Vadnais said that in the winter, Norman would allow one to buy on credit but during the summer one was expected to pay one's debt. He carried a very small variety of groceries.

Courtesy of the Richard Vadnais Family

In 1929 Bibeau opened the White Bear Laundry on Tenth Street near Stewart Avenue. By 1931 the laundry was under other management. In 1932 the Bibeau brothers, Norman, James, and Thomas, were affiliated with Model Laundry.

In the early 1940s, Norman Bibeau's store, which by now housed the White Bear Oil Company offices, was moved to the west side of Campbell Avenue just south of Third Street and converted into a residence. A new brick building for Berg's Grocery would soon be constructed on the vacant lot.

Courtesy of the Richard Vadnais Family
Relocating Norman Bibeau's Home

Northeast Corner Fourth Street and Bald Eagle Avenue

Walter Berg purchased Mrs. Howard Bloom's Grocery on Bald Eagle and Birch Lake Avenues in July 1937. Besides being in the grocery business, Berg was a member of the White Bear Fire Department for thirty-one years, from 1941 to 1972.

Courtesy of Cynthia Vadnais

In 1945 Archie LeMire built the new Berg's Grocery on the northeast corner of Bald Eagle Avenue and Fourth Street. A. J. Vadnais owned the thirty-by-sixty-foot building. Because it was built during war time, the structure was not totally finished until later. On November 19, 1945 Berg opened the grocery store. Along with his wife, Gladys, and brother-in-law, Bud Bloom, he ran the business from this location for twenty-two years, closing the store in 1967.

The White Bear Oil Company offices were located in the building from 1967 to 1989, when the building was sold. It is currently the home of Pathway Health Services.

Louis Crawford Home – Fifth Street Between Division and Bloom Avenues

Courtesy of the Richard Vadnais Family

In 1917 Adlore J. Vadnais, while still working for the Northern Pacific Railroad at night, went to work for Standard Oil, delivering oil using a horse drawn five-hundred-gallon tank wagon and later a Model T Ford truck. Standard Oil owned the trucks and carried the accounts, but around 1920, when they changed their policies, Vadnais, along with his partner, Louis Crawford, decided to go into business for themselves. Using an old car as a trade-in, they bought a 1923 Ford truck for $422.58, reduced to $272.58 with the trade-in. The partners purchased bulk oil tanks, and a gas pump was installed at the Crawford residence on Fifth Street between Division and Bloom Avenues. White Bear Oil Company, the first fuel oil delivery company in White Bear, had opened.

White Bear Oil Co.
L. J. Crawford, Mgr.

Gasoline, Kerosene, Greases and Oils

We Deliver anywhere---Everywhere

Phones 409 and 153=M

White Bear Lake, Minn.

Courtesy of the White Bear Press
White Bear Press Ad – 1926

White Bear Oil Company – Early 1920s

Courtesy of the Richard Vadnais Family

Louis Crawford, his three children, and A. J. Vadnais (from left to right) are shown in this early 1920s photograph of White Bear Oil Company, then located on Division Avenue north of Fourth Street.

Jack Vadnais and Pete Bacon – Station Number 1 – Circa 1945

A lifelong White Bear resident, Pete Bacon was the mechanic for the company until he retired in the early 1970s.

Courtesy of Jack Vadnais

Crawford and Vadnais dissolved their partnership in 1928 and Vadnais continued in the company. The gas pump located at Crawford's house was moved to the Vadnais home at 1309 Fourth Street, where Mrs. Vadnais pumped gas for customers. In 1930 Vadnais decided to retire from the railroad, devoting himself full-time to the oil company. Crawford died in 1932.

Station Number 1, was located on the northwest corner of Bald Eagle Avenue and Fourth Street. Carl Mattlin built it in 1932. That same year the White Bear Oil Company installed the first electric gasoline pumps in White Bear. In 1933 the company was also the first in the area to use metered fuel oil service. A grease room was added to the north side of the station in 1938, and around 1939, Station Number 2 was purchased on the northeast corner of Washington Avenue and Third Street.

Courtesy of the Richard Vadnais Family

Adlore Vadnais and his Sons

Shown from left to right: (top row) George, Gordon, and Charles; (bottom row) Adlore, Richard, and Jack.

The White Bear Oil Company was run by Adlore and eventually included his sons, George, Charles, Dick, Jack, and Gordy. George ran Station Number 2 while Adlore and Charles ran Station Number 1. Dick, Jack, and Gordy ran the fuel oil end of the business; later each ran other parts of the company.

White Bear Oil Company – Ready to Serve – Circa 1946

Courtesy of the Richard Vadnais Family

Out front of the station on Bald Eagle Avenue are (from left to right): Charles Vadnais, Dick Vadnais, Adlore Vadnais, Jack Vadnais, and George Vadnais.

Adlore Vadnais with First Gasoline Hand Pump Used by the Company – Circa 1970

Courtesy of the Richard Vadnais Family

Early White Bear Oil Delivery Truck at Vadnais Home on Bald Eagle Avenue

Courtesy of Bob Thein

Courtesy of Bob Thein

White Bear Oil Bulk Oil Tanks and Railroad Stockyards

Around 1930 the White Bear Oil Company bulk oil tanks were located on the west side of the railroad tracks, just south of Second Street at about Highway 61.

Courtesy of Jack Vadnais

White Bear Oil Company – Fourth Street and Bald Eagle Avenue

Around 1947 Station Number 1 was rebuilt. Over the years the business expanded to include other station locations, Hudson car sales, International Harvester products, Bombardier snowmobiles, commercial grade oils, tires, batteries, and accessories.

Adlore died on May 4, 1973. George retired in 1974 after having run Station Number 2 for twenty-two years. He died on May 1, 1994. Charles retired from the company and died on June 11, 1989. In 1989 the surviving brothers, who had carried on the business, retired and began selling off the various parts of the company.

Looking Down Banning Avenue

Courtesy of the White Bear Lake Area Historical Society

1888 Lumberyard Ad

M. J. Mackenhausen and Rudolph F. Fritschie were in the lumberyard business in White Bear on the corner of Banning Avenue and Fifth Street. The general area of Banning Avenue between Fourth and Fifth Streets would not be without a lumberyard until the end of 1964.

Consolidated Lumber was managed for a short time by Tisdale E. Fellows, who had previously owned the business. Consolidated Lumber Company of Stillwater named the local operation White Bear Lumber and Coal Company. After a fire in May 1929 a 163-foot long by 80-foot deep store was erected of brick and tile on Banning Avenue between Fourth and Fifth Streets. The *White Bear Press* stated, "The lumber yard has given place to the lumber store," and later said of the completed building, "It is two full stories in height, with a storage attic. At the north and south sections of the front are spacious display windows, while the middle section of the front is devoted to office space and store. In this store are shelves and counters, and here are carried the stocks of builder's hardware, paints, ..."

```
CONSOLIDATED LUMBER CO.
SUCCESSORS TO
T. E. FELLOWS & CO.
TELEPHONE 40.
LUMBER. FUEL. FEED.
T. E. FELLOWS,
Manager White Bear Yard.
```

Courtesy of the White Bear Press

White Bear Life Ad – 1904

Courtesy of Bob Thein

Lumberyard Crew – Early 1900s

This lumberyard crew, with French men wearing dark shirts and Swedish men wearing light shirts, includes Prosper LeVasseur standing at the right in front of the white horse. The different colors of shirts probably helped with communication, since many of the men may not have been fluent in English.

Courtesy of the Richard Vadnais Family

Adlore Vadnais Working in the Lumber Yard – Circa 1904

White Bear Lumber Company – Early Delivery Truck

Courtesy of Bob Thein

Courtesy of the White Bear Lake Area Historical Society

October 3, 1964 – White Bear Lumber Company Fire

In late afternoon on October 3, 1964 a fire was reported in a lumber storage shed at the White Bear Lumber Company. The lumber company fire was not going to be controlled since it was fueled by strong winds and doomed by two unfortunate events: one, the paint and roofing shed exploded, and two, an employee strengthened the fire when he tried to remove company vehicles from the windward side of the building. The lumberyard was destroyed and closed permanently December 31, 1964. An investigation of the fire determined the cause was accidental: sparks from an incinerator at Del Farm Foods, just east of the lumberyard, had started it.

W. H. Jackson Home and Shop – Northwest Corner of Banning Avenue and Fifth Street – 1890

Courtesy of the White Bear Lake Area Historical Society

William Jackson came to White Bear in 1883 where, for the next fifty-four years, he was actively involved in contributing to and improving the community. He built the first fire house in White Bear in 1888, Zion Evangelical Lutheran Church in 1891, St. Mary's School in 1914, and Beach School in 1922. Jackson was one of the principal organizers of the First State Bank in 1902, serving as the vice-president of the institution. In 1907 and 1908 Jackson served as mayor and he was an active councilman for several terms.

He was married to Maria Taylor, who, interestingly, was one of seven Catholic children who in 1871 were taking Catechism instruction in a most unusual place, a wigwam, located at Lake Avenue and Shady Lane.

Having retired in 1929, Jackson died in 1937, leaving a lasting mark.

Courtesy of the White Bear Lake Area Historical Society

1890 Ad for Jackson's Business

Courtesy of the White Bear Lake Area Historical Society

White Bear Steam Laundry Company – Circa 1911

The White Bear Steam Laundry building was constructed in 1910-1911 by J. C. Fulton, who sold it to his future brother-in-law and then-mayor, F. H. Murray, who sold it to the Garnet Lodge, No. 166, A. F. and A. M.

The Masonic Building was dedicated on August 24, 1911. The lodge held a parade from its old home in the Getty Building to its new location on the west side of Banning Avenue behind the Gerken Building. The newspaper reported that the lodge members were "All in aprons many of them in various lines of human endeavor but all placed on the same level by the simple white apron that constituted their regalia."

By 1912 the steam laundry, which occupied the first floor, was closed. Billy Wells had all the laundry equipment removed to make way for the Doric Family Theater. His intention was to renovate the interior by installing a stage, scenery, and seating for four-hundred. Whether this was ever done is doubtful, since Matt Mackenhausen Jr. opened a garage and general automobile supply store in the building in 1913. By 1936 the Masons were holding meetings at St. John in the Wilderness Church. On May 3, 1957, ground was broken for the current Masonic Temple at Ninth Street and Stewart Avenue. In 1940 Henry Kohler remodeled the building for his growing Kohler Ice Cream Mix Company, which he sold in 1953.

The White Bear Steam Laundry building no longer exists. In 1974 a parking lot was constructed, covering the southwest corner of Banning Avenue and Fifth Street, along with most of the interior of the block.

Courtesy of the White Bear Lake Area Historical Society
White Bear Steam Laundry Interior – Circa 1911

In 1928 White Bear Knitting Mills moved into a garage on Banning Avenue just south of the White Bear Lumber Company. Not long after, in May 1929, a fire destroyed the White Bear Lumber Company, the White Bear Motor Sales shed, and the White Bear Knitting Mill location. The back of the Auditorium building on Fourth Street was renovated and the company made its new headquarters there.

50 WOMEN WANTED

To sew pockets and collars on sweaters.

Work at home. 50c each garment.

Garments delivered at your home and called for.

White Bear Knitting Mills
Opposite Masonic Temple

White Bear Lake,   Minnesota

Courtesy of the White Bear Press
White Bear Press Ad – 1928

White Bear Press Ad – 1916

The feed store on Banning Avenue was located on the west side of the street directly behind Vincent's Grocery.

NEW Feed Store
110 Banning Avenue
E. P. STEIGLEDER, Prop.
Flour, Feed, Hay, Grain, Cream Separator and Gas Engine and do Feed Grinding
Prompt Delivery
T. S. Phone 53   N. W. Phone 38

Courtesy of the White Bear Press

Bert Arcand & Company Feed Store – Circa 1915

Courtesy of the Robert Vadnais Family

In 1916 Arcand sold the business to E. P. Steigleder. It was known as Long and Alford's by 1921 and later sold to H. J. Hilbert in 1922. The business would become known as the White Bear Feed and Seed. Hubert Bring was the owner of the business in 1963 and had been the owner since about 1935, when it was decided that a 164-car parking lot be created. Part of the land to be used for the parking lot included most of the lots along the west side of Banning Avenue between Third and Fourth Streets, including the feed store property.

In June 1956 Elaine and Bill Ross took over Mabel's Eat Shop, formerly owned by Mabel Bohrer, located in the building adjoining the feed store on the south side. The business was renamed Little Bear Cafe. They moved their business to 314 Washington Avenue in 1959.

The Little Bear Cafe building was also leveled in 1964 to make way for the parking lot.

In the early part of the 1900s the building had been the location of the office of contractor C. E. Davies.

Courtesy of Bob Thein

Little Bear Cafe Building and White Bear Feed and Seed – Circa 1963

David Hanna Home – 1890

Courtesy of the White Bear Lake Area Historical Society

David Hanna – Builder of Webster School and Washington School

Courtesy of the White Bear Lake Area Historical Society

David Hanna was born in New Brunswick in 1846. He came to White Bear in 1883, where he continued to live until his death on June 10, 1920 at the age of seventy-four.

Hanna, whose home was located on the northwest corner of Fourth Street and Johnson Avenue, built both Webster and Washington Schools. Hanna also built the Getty Block and the Cottage Park Clubhouse, which he managed.

Active politically, Hanna was elected mayor in 1889, reelected in 1890 and again in 1899. In an official act as mayor, Hanna had the saloon owners put on notice that they were not to have minors either drinking or playing in their place of business.

Courtesy of the White Bear Press

West Side of Banning Avenue Between Third and Fourth Streets – 1964

All of the buildings in this photograph were removed to make way for the parking lot that is still in use today behind the stores on the east side of Washington Avenue north of Third Street and south of Fourth Street. The White Bear Appliance building on the west side of Third Street just east of the White Bear Oil Company station was also bulldozed to make way for the lot. The lot, which was built in 1964, created 164 more parking spaces in the downtown area.

Courtesy of Bob Thein

Independent Meat Market – Banning Avenue – Late 1910s

William Hartzell came to White Bear in 1916 and opened the Independent Meat Market on the east side of Banning Avenue. In 1920 Hamilton's Hardware was located in a building on Railroad Avenue that was owned by the Hamm's Brewing Company. Hartzell purchased that building and moved into his new location in May 1920. The store was named the People's Market. Hartzell sold the business to L. A. Markeson in October 1936 and retired. He died in 1944.

Sew What! – Summer 2003

The Sew What store has for a number of years occupied the old Independent Meat Market location on Banning Avenue. The building looks much the way it did in the early 1900s.

Courtesy of Cynthia Vadnais

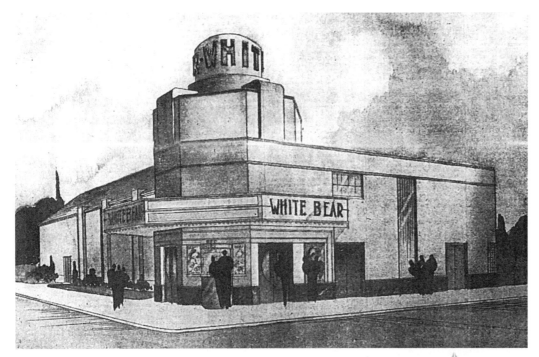

White Bear Theatre – Artist's Drawing – 1939

Courtesy of the White Bear Press

Sun Bear Spa and Salon – Old White Bear Theatre

Courtesy of Cynthia Vadnais

In 1939 Mr. Rattner built the white stucco White Bear Theatre on the northeast corner of Third Street and Banning Avenue. The thoroughly modern theater opened on August 4, 1939, boasting seating for over six-hundred people, including "loveseats" built for two. The *White Bear Press* reported that there were "Smoking loges for your comfort. Ventilated and acoustically treated for your enjoyment." They also reported that the building had "Healthenized Air – conditioned for summer and winter. No draft. No wind. Automatically regulated."

Around 1949 Rattner sold the theater to Howard Goldman, who ran it for another eight or nine years before selling it to Paul Albrecht, the owner of the only other theater in town, the Avalon. Albrecht closed the theater. After standing vacant for a number of years, the theater was remodeled and opened in 1968 as the Cine Capri. By 1973 it had closed for good.

In November 1980 Pat and Dorothy Quirk purchased the building, remodeling it to suit their needs, and moved their popular gift shop, the Quirk of Fate, to the location. They closed the store in the late 1980s. Today the main portion of the building is occupied by Sun Bear Spa and Salon.

White Bear Press Ad – 1919

Courtesy of the White Bear Press

White Bear Press Ad – 1922

"The Chicken Shop," as Curry's White Bear Tavern was often called, was located in the old Cobb house on the northwest corner of Banning Avenue and First Street. The establishment was owned by C. C. Curry and was in business from about 1912 to 1923.

Courtesy of the White Bear Press

Looking Down Clark Avenue

Courtesy of the Lawrence R. Whitaker Family

Clark Avenue, Looking South from Second Street – Circa 1915

Gates A. Johnson, the surveyor for the Lake Superior and Mississippi Railroad, named Clark Avenue after Frank H. Clark, the president of the railroad in 1871.

Clark Avenue and its parkway have long been considered one of the loveliest streets in White Bear. In the early days passengers would disembark from the trains and, looking to the south down Clark Avenue, they would get a glimpse of the lake. For anyone traveling the avenue, whether coming to or leaving White Bear, it left a lasting impression of the beauty of the White Bear Lake area.

Daniel Getty's general store, the first fire hall, St. John in the Wilderness Church, and Milner's Meat Market were among the early establishments along the avenue. Additionally, both permanent and summer residents built many fine homes on the southern end.

Clark Avenue was the road that led to the center of the business area of White Bear. In the early 1910s, the town landscaped and lighted Clark Avenue and Railroad Park. Holm and Olson put in the shrubbery and other plants, and J. S. Chisholm and his crew installed the "White Way" of lights. The only thing lacking was a paved surface.

In 1925 the *White Bear Press* reported that Clark Avenue was featured on the cover of a magazine with a large circulation. The magazine labeled Clark Avenue as "The Most Beautiful Street in the World."

The street was paved in 1920 and new single-globe light poles were installed in 1934.

Courtesy of Cynthia Vadnais

Clark Avenue, Looking North from Lake Avenue – Late 1930s

Civil War Monument – Erected in 1913

In 1912 E. B. Gibbs Post, No. 76, Grand Army of the Republic (G. A. R.) decided to erect a monument to the men of Minnesota and White Bear who had defended the Union during the Civil War. The Soldiers' Monument Association of White Bear was formed and funds were raised, in part by the G. A. R. and from private subscriptions, with the balance from a county appropriation. The white bronze monument erected is an exact copy of one in Marion, Ohio. The monument stands twenty-one-feet-two-inches tall including the six-foot Union soldier.

The association wanted it to be located in the middle of the first oval on Clark Avenue between First and Second Streets, but not everyone was happy with the proposition. T. L. Bourquin, a property owner along Clark Avenue, wrote in a letter to the newspaper that he "did not dream at the time that a project would be set on foot to spoil all our plans for beautifying the street by placing a Soldier's [sic] Monument in the center of the boulevard thereby, interfering with the view of the lake from the depot and giving the large traveling public an impression of a graveyard to gaze at while waiting for their respective trains." Regardless of the opposition, the monument was unveiled on May 30, 1913. The monument, landscaping, and walkways cost a total of $1,600.

Courtesy of the Richard Vadnais Family

Members of the E. B. Gibbs Post, No. 76, Grand Army of the Republic – Decoration Day 1883

Courtesy of the Lawrence R. Whitaker Family

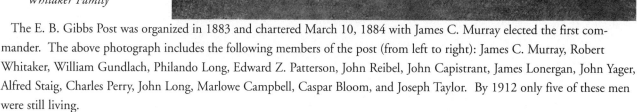

The E. B. Gibbs Post was organized in 1883 and chartered March 10, 1884 with James C. Murray elected the first commander. The above photograph includes the following members of the post (from left to right): James C. Murray, Robert Whitaker, William Gundlach, Philando Long, Edward Z. Patterson, John Reibel, John Capistrant, James Lonergan, John Yager, Alfred Staig, Charles Perry, John Long, Marlowe Campbell, Caspar Bloom, and Joseph Taylor. By 1912 only five of these men were still living.

The post's namesake, Eugene B. Gibbs, was a captain in the Second Regiment, California Infantry, Company "E," from 1862 to 1866. He served those years in California, mostly safeguarding the settlers from the Indians. E. B. Gibbs was living in White Bear by the late 1870s.

Sewall C. Smith and his Dog "Jackie" – 1932

As of 1932, Smith, at ninety-four years of age, was White Bear's last surviving member of the Grand Army of the Republic (G. A. R.). Smith had fought in twenty-six battles during the Civil War. Smith died on September 17, 1934.

Courtesy of the White Bear Press

Clark Avenue Toboggan Slide – Circa 1920

Courtesy of Bob Thein

Clark Avenue Looking North – Circa 1933

Notice the train depot at the far end of the street.

Courtesy of the Lawrence R. Whitaker Family

Courtesy of the White Bear Press
Albert H. S. Perkins

Courtesy of the White Bear Lake Area Historical Society
A. H. S. Perkins Home – Fifth Street – 1888

Albert Perkins moved to White Bear in 1887 from Belvidere, Illinois and started the *Lake Breeze*. His first offices were located above King & Company on Third Street. Soon after he moved his offices to a small building on Third Street, just east of the corner of Clark Avenue. By 1890 the newspaper had relocated to the rear of the post office in the Cobb Block on the north end of Railroad (Washington) Avenue. The paper was published every Saturday, with a subscription costing $1.50 per year in advance.

In 1888, a wonderfully humorous piece was published in the *Lake Breeze* in regard to a delinquent subscriber. It quipped, "One of our subscribers who is considerably in arrears said he would call by January 1 and settle, if he were alive. He still appears on the streets but he did not call. It is natural to suppose he is dead and is simply walking around to save funeral expenses."

A. E. Ball from Rushford, Minnesota bought the business from Perkins in the summer of 1891, at which time Perkins went to Bluffton, Alabama to start a newspaper there. Ball sold to R. H. Luenberg in the spring of 1892; Perkins returned to White Bear that summer. On July 20, 1892 Perkins published one issue of *The Wave*, a competing paper, and by July 27, 1892 the *Lake Breeze* was once again his paper. Luenberg was no competition for the witty newspaperman whom the people of White Bear had taken to so quickly just a few years previously. Perkins bid farewell for good on December 6, 1893 because of failing health. The paper was sold to A. E. Quinn, the publisher of the *Cloquet Pine Knot and Sentinel*. Thereafter, other publishers owned it until, in 1895, it was published in St. Paul and distributed in White Bear. A new newspaper, *White Bear Life*, began publishing in White Bear in 1896. The *Lake Breeze* would "blow no more."

Lake Breeze Ad – 1888

Courtesy of the White Bear Lake Area Historical Society

The first meat market in White Bear, run by Thomas Milner, was housed in a small wood-frame storefront just behind the Getty Building on Clark Avenue. Milner, who came to White Bear in 1851, built and opened the sixteen-by-twenty-four-foot meat market. In the late 1870s he built a forty-by-thirty-five-foot addition on the south side as a residence. By the late 1880s Milner had been associated with a few different partners, including Nick M. Henkel (1885-1887), and a man from St. Paul named Hopkins (1887-1888). By the spring of 1887 Henkel was located on Third Street, operating a meat market with John Flandrick, under the name N. M. Henkel and Company. Milner's Meat Market building was torn down in 1925 to make way for a driveway behind the Getty Building.

Courtesy of the White Bear Lake Area Historical Society

Getty Building and Milner's Meat Market

The *White Bear Life,* later to be known as the *White Bear Press,* started on April 17, 1896 with A. S. Dimond as publisher. Subscription rates were $1 per year, with the paper published each Thursday. The newspaper offices were located just east of N. M. Henkel's Meat Market on Third Street. Dimond once commented, "It is a modest and unpretentious building, but large enough for our present needs and has the advantage of having a big tree in its front yard to shade the porch."

White Bear Press Front Page Banner – 1934

On August 12, 1899 Dimond sold the business to Edward Lippitt Fales. Fales sold to Herbert J. Keeler from Prescott, Wisconsin on January 24, 1914. Finally, on April 9, 1914, Keeler published the first issue of the renamed newspaper, the *White Bear Press*, formerly the *White Bear Life*.

White Bear Press Ad – 1915

Keeler was not only a publisher but also an undertaker. He used a portion of the newspaper building as a funeral home while maintaining the paper in the space it had occupied since 1913, 214 Clark Avenue. This location was the old Milner home on the east side of Clark Avenue, just south of the Milner Meat Market building. The *White Bear Press* offices would remain in this location until 1920. An active member of the community, Keeler was instrumental in forming the White Bear School Band, which provided concerts in the park during the summer months.

Walker G. Miller purchased the newspaper business from Keeler in 1920, while Keeler continued with his undertaking (and floral) business until his death in 1923. Adeline M. Keeler took over the business, but shortly thereafter she sold it. In 1920 Miller moved the newspaper business to the second floor of the Getty Building, where it would remain until 1958. Ross R. Miller, W. G. Miller's former partner in business, took over the newspaper in 1922.

On December 30, 1922 Warren A. Stickley, who was born in Ainsworth, Iowa on February 1, 1878, moved to White Bear, along with his wife, Helen, daughter, Doris, and son, Armand. Captain W. A. Stickley purchased the *White Bear Press* from Ross R. Miller, taking over publishing on January 4, 1923. It was a family affair for a few years since Armand worked as a linotype operator at the newspaper until taking a job at 3M in 1926. In 1935 Stickley was the first person, designated Citizen No. 1, elected to the White Bear Hall of Fame. Just the previous year he had helped to organize the White Bear Lake Historical Society.

Captain Warren A. Stickley

The newspaper made it through good and bad times with Stickley at the helm. In 1937 he wrote, "It has been a rocky road,... ill health, slim patronage, financial reverses over which we had no control, several years of depression... However, while things are better, though not rosy, we are pegging along."

Stickley sold the paper to Vernon S. Tegland in November 1946, dying shortly after in the summer of 1947. In June 1947 Tegland sold the paper to Aaron M. Litman and Herschel Johnson. A new building was constructed on the west side of Bloom Avenue between Fourth and Fifth Streets in the early part of 1958. In August of that same year the paper moved from its home of thirty-eight years in the Getty Building. Upon Litman's death on February 21, 1969, his widow took over, only to sell the operation the next year to White Bear native Eugene (Gene) D. Johnson, the present owner.

Courtesy of Cynthia Vadnais

White Bear Press Office – 4779 Bloom Avenue – Summer 2003

Odd Fellows – Circa 1900

Courtesy of Ruth Mattlin

The Mercantile Company Barn, a branch of the White Bear Mercantile Company, was located on the west side of Clark Avenue between Second and Third Streets. The Methodist Episcopal Church, which was bought in 1918 by the First Church of Christ Scientist, was located just south of the barn.

The barn was demolished in 1925, which led to a query in the newspaper about the depression that was left behind. It asked, "Since the old Mercantile barn across Clark avenue from the Getty block has been razed, it is found that there is a depression in the earth of two or three feet and inasmuch as there is high ground all round it, several parties have asked if the barn was built over a 'pot-hole..' We don't know. Is there any old-timer who does?" The pothole question never seemed to be answered. By 1927 Joe Boppre began to build Boppre Chevrolet Company on the site of the old barn, putting the pothole question to rest forever.

White Bear Ice Company Delivery Wagon – Circa 1915

This photograph was taken on Clark Avenue near the Mercantile Company Barn. On the left is Norman Taylor and to the right Bill Koch.

Courtesy of Bob Thein

In 1912 Reuben N. Clewett bought Norman Taylor's "Home Ice Market" business. Clewett sold the business and his residence in 1919 to O. M. Cherrier. Cherrier ran the business into the early 1940s. February 1941 the *White Bear Press* reported, "Cherrier fills his ice houses [423 Seventh Street] with 14,000 cakes (3,500 tons)."

The White Bear Ice Company sold its ice by the month. In 1918 the schedule to householders, based upon a flat delivery per month, was as follows: "350 pounds per month, 3 deliveries per week: $1.75, 650 pounds per month, daily deliveries except Sundays: $2.95, 1,300 pounds per month, daily deliveries except Sundays: $5.85, 2,000 pounds per month, daily deliveries except Sundays: $9.00."

In 1927 Joe Boppre built a forty-one-by-eighty-foot garage with fourteen-foot ceilings on the west side of Clark Avenue, where the Mercantile Company Barn had been located. The building had a full basement with a reinforced floor that was the only one of its type in White Bear at that time.

Prior to building the new Chevrolet garage, Boppre had owned and managed the White Bear Battery and Tire Station along with being the "keeper" of the bowling alley, a job that paid $125 a month in 1923. In 1932 he opened the Auto Club Pure Oil Station on the west side of Resthaven Sanitorium. By 1935 Boppre Chevrolet was gone and Smith Chevrolet Company took its place.

> **When in Need of**
> # ICE
> Call White 128
> **WHITE BEAR ICE CO.**
> All orders receive prompt, courteous attention.
> O. M. CHERRIER, Prop.

Courtesy of the White Bear Press

White Bear Press Ad – 1921

Courtesy of the White Bear Press

White Bear Press Ad – 1927

Kosman Chevrolet Company – Clark Avenue – October 1956

Lou Kosman, owner of Kosman Chevrolet, is shown feeding a doughnut to a bear. The attraction was brought in to help promote the new line of 1957 Chevrolets he had just received.

After the White Bear Hotel was bulldozed in 1938, Cleo Smith added a garage to the north end of his Chevrolet dealership. Lou Kosman was the owner of the business after Smith.

Fournelle Auto Company – Circa 1926

Peter Fournelle, a resident of White Bear since the 1880s, opened Fournelle's Auto Livery on Banning Avenue in 1913. In 1917 he had a garage built just north of the Methodist Episcopal Church on the west side of Clark Avenue between Second and Third Streets, where he relocated his automobile business. The new building was forty-five-by-ninety-feet with a forty-five-by-twenty-foot repair shop, constructed of tile and brick, that could hold up to thirty cars. Fournelle also owned a station on the northeast corner of Fourth Street and Railroad Avenue, which he sold to J. A. Reed. Two gas pumps were added in front of the business in 1927. By that time Fournelle had been selling Studebaker cars for fourteen years and Overland cars for five years.

Courtesy of the White Bear Lake Area Historical Society

Fournelle Auto Company

Politically active in the community, Peter Fournelle was mayor of the village of White Bear from 1916 to 1922. After a new city charter was submitted to, and approved by, the village council, a special election for mayor was held in March 1922 between Fournelle and Earl Jackson, which resulted in a tie. After a Supreme Court fight, another special election was held, ending with Jackson becoming the first mayor of the city of White Bear Lake.

Fournelle sold his business to Adolph J. LeMire and A. J. Marrier in 1928. Fournelle was to take over Marrier's Shell filling station opposite the depot. LeMire and Marrier sold to Ed Peltier in 1929 and in 1945 White Bear Motor Sales took over the business, with A. C. Podvin moving his already established Ford dealership from Fourth Street to the Clark Avenue location. In 1956 Podvin leased the building to Herb Tousley, who opened Herb Tousley Ford. A fire in March 1964 destroyed the building. Tousley had previously moved to the northwest corner of County Road E and Highway 61. Upon being rebuilt, the building on Clark Avenue was occupied by a Sears store. Fournelle died on May 5, 1959. Herb Tousley died in an airplane crash in Alaska on July 31, 1977.

WHITE BEAR FIRE DEPARTMENT

Previous to the formal organization of a fire department in White Bear, all that was available for fire protection were two dozen buckets and a few ladders.

The White Bear Fire Department was organized on March 5, 1888 with M. J. Mackenhausen as the first fire chief. In May of the same year the department purchased additional equipment, including a side-arm engine, a hose cart, and a hook and ladder truck.

In May of 1888 the department spent $2,000 for a 50-foot by 117-foot lot, situated on the northwest corner of Clark Avenue and Second Street, for the purpose of building a fire house and public meeting hall. W. H. Jackson was awarded the contract to build the hall at a cost of $1,320. A ball was scheduled for Thanksgiving Eve 1888 to celebrate the completion of the building.

Courtesy of the White Bear Lake Area Historical Society
White Bear Fire House – Built in 1888

White Bear Fire Department – 1888

According to Peter R. Reis, in his book *White Bear's Hometown Heroes*, "One of the attractions of belonging to the Fire Department was the uniform that the firemen wore at social occasions. These began under Department sponsorship immediately after it was formed."

Courtesy of the White Bear Lake Area Historical

305

Horse-Drawn Waterous Steam Pumper and Crew – 1895

Courtesy of the White Bear Lake Area Historical Society

Shown in the above photograph are (from left to right) Jack McGrath (driving the team of horses), Bill Junk, Lyle Parker, Jim King, Frank Rief, Judge Winship, Stan Milner, Philando Long, Gus Holzheid, ——, and Dan Ivett.

In 1888 the fire department members erected the bell tower atop the firehouse and a 270-pound bell was installed. The signal system for the bell, according to the local paper, was as follows: "In case of fire, short strokes in rapid succession; for regular meetings, three steady taps at intervals; for special meetings, two steady taps at intervals." A 540-pound bell that could be heard at a greater distance replaced that bell in 1898. The old bell was sold back to the foundry for $27.

As with any volunteer organization, it was difficult to keep members interested over time. The White Bear Fire Department was not immune to this problem. As a result, in 1889 the department was reorganized, complete with rules, regulations and penalties. The new department was named the White Bear Volunteer Fire Department. H. K. Getty was elected as chief.

A fire engine was purchased on May 10, 1895 and delivered by train to White Bear on May 11. In those early days, the first team of horses to the firehouse would get paid for hauling the engine.

Richard G. Brachvogel

Richard Brachvogel joined the White Bear Fire Department on August 6, 1886, serving the community until January 30, 1929, when the State Firemen's Association required that he retire. He had been a fireman for almost forty-three years serving twenty-eight of those years as fire chief.

Courtesy of the White Bear Press

Courtesy of the White Bear Lake Area Historical Society

General J. B. Sanborn Cottage – 1885

The J. B. Sanborn cottage, located on the northwest corner of Lake and Moorhead Avenues, was purchased in 1884 from Wm. R. Merriam, the governor of Minnesota from 1889-1893.

In 1895 Daniel Ivett, a member of the fire department, started keeping a journal of all the fire calls. The first fire call that Ivett recorded was at J. B. Sanborn's playhouse. In answering the call, the fire engine was taken to the shoreline near the foot of Fourth Street. Ivett wrote that the engine sank in quicksand, and an outside party had to be hired to dig it out and bring it back to the firehouse. No mention was made as to whether or not the fire had successfully been extinguished.

In 1916 the left stall in the firehouse was widened in order to accommodate a new fire-fighting truck, a sign that the wooden structure was becoming obsolete.

In 1920 the First Church of Christ Scientist was located just north of the fire hall. Housed in the old Methodist Episcopal Church, the building was turned in a north-south direction in 1938. Fournelle Auto Company was the next business to the north at that time.

Courtesy of Bob Thein

White Bear Fire Department – 1920s

White Bear Volunteer Fire Department in Front of the First Fire House Shortly Before it was Razed

Courtesy of the White Bear Lake Area Historical Society

In 1928 the city-owned Auditorium building on Fourth Street burned. It was later decided that some of the insurance proceeds from the fire would be used toward the erection of a new firehouse, with the Auditorium property to be sold at a later date. It was also decided that some of the radiators, brick, and stone from the Auditorium would be salvaged and used in the construction of the new fire house.

The new combination fire hall-city hall-jail was designed by Allan Fleischbein and built by C. J. Mattlin. The cornerstone was laid on May 10, 1930.

The building was in use as the police and fire department until 1961, when a new building, still in use today, was constructed just west of Highway 61 on Second Street and Miller Avenue.

New Firehouse – 1930 *Courtesy of the White Bear Lake Area Historical Society*

The fire department's 1916 Studebaker and the new 1929 LaFrance fire engine appear in the photograph. Chief Fred Campbell is in the white coat with his hand on his personal Model A Ford coupe, specially equipped with a siren.

White Bear Fire Carnival!!
Proceeds of Which Go Toward Paying for This Fire Truck

This truck cost $15,000. It was presented to the City of White Bear by the business men and citizens of White Bear and surrounding communities. It pumps 1,000 gallons per minute and is the highest type of perfection in fire-fighting apparatus in America.

We still owe over $1,000 on this truck and it MUST be paid by the offerings of these carnivals. Do not consider that you are throwing your money away when you spend it here, but consider it as your patriotic duty to give. In fact, "give till it hurts."

FOUR NIGHTS, JULY 18-19-20-21

White Bear Press Ad – 1934

Courtesy of the White Bear Press

It was evident that the fire department was in dire need of new equipment after the three major fires erupted between 1928-1929 — at the Armory, the Auditorium, and finally the White Bear Lumberyard. To raise money for this purpose, the department decided to hold a fire carnival. In 1929 the first fire carnival was held for the purpose of raising funds to purchase a pumper truck. The carnival was a success and plans were made to continue the event in order to buy other equipment and pay off debt. Carnivals were held in 1930 and 1931. In 1932, in the depths of the Depression, it was decided that no carnival would be held. Even with the continuing Depression, the people of White Bear rallied and had a carnival in 1933 and each year thereafter, with the last fire carnival held in 1937.

A *White Bear Press* ad for the 1934 White Bear Fire Carnival prodded, "This truck costs $15,000. It was presented to the City of White Bear by the business men and citizens of White Bear and surrounding communities. It pumps 1,000 gallons per minute and is the highest type of perfection in fire-fighting apparatus in America. We still owe over $1,000 on this truck and it MUST be paid by the offerings of these carnivals. Do not consider that you are throwing your money away when you spend it here, but consider it as your patriotic duty to give. In fact, 'give till it hurts.'"

The Toonerville Fire Department was a major attraction at the carnivals. Buildings were either donated or built and when "set on fire" the Toonerville Fire Department would amusingly attempt to put out the fire. The White Bear Fire Department would come to the rescue and show how it was done by actually setting the building on fire, demonstrating how their equipment could quickly douse the flames.

Courtesy of the White Bear Lake Area Historical Society
Toonerville Fire Department and Supporting Actors – 1931

Along with the Toonerville Fire Department, some of the other attractions the fire carnivals offered over the years included drawings for cars and diamond rings, aerial acts, amusement rides, trained animal shows, a high dive act, and band concerts.

The Jewelry of a Russian Countess

Martha Yablonski had been a countess in Russia and was rescued after the czar was overthrown by an American soldier named Martinson. They married and eventually settled in the Bald Eagle area, where he worked as a machinist and telephone lineman while she took care of the farm. Falling on hard times, the couple ran short of money and the fire department came to the rescue. The department, at that time, had a surplus of money and took a second mortgage on the farm for $2,500. In 1927 Martinson accepted a railroad job in Oregon, leaving the jewels behind as collateral. The loan was never paid so the department became the owner of the jewels.

The jewels were used, in part, as prizes given to ladies at some of the fire carnivals for top ticket sales as well as door prizes each evening. Florence (Vadnais) Smith was the top ticket sales winner in 1935 and received a diamond as her prize. In the mid-1940s the remaining jewelry was appraised and sold off at a loss of $1,500.

Courtesy of the White Bear Press

White Bear Volunteer Fire Department Members – Early 1930

Courtesy of the White Bear Lake Area Historical Society

This photograph must have been taken right before the old fire hall was razed, as John Fournelle did not join the department until February 10, 1930. Shown standing (from left to right) are: John Fournelle, Frank J. LaBore, Earl Milette, Charles P. Conway, William Holzheid, Dave Bazille, Louis Peltier, William J. Luedke, Les H. Palmer, Sidney E. Henkel, William E. Rose, Frank Swanson, Fred F. Campbell, Elmer Long, Prosper J. LeVasseur, ——, and George Flandrick. The six men in the back row (from left to right) are: Robert J. Bloom, Al Wallin, Howard W. Bloom, Peter Fournelle, Dave Auger, and Miles Nelson. Other firemen not shown here were: William Sandahl, William Bauer, and William Baer.

Courtesy of the White Bear Lake Area Historical Society

Presentation of the 1937 Ford V-8 Combination Police Car – Ambulance

Shown (from left to right): Frank Taylor from the First State Bank (representing the Junior Chamber of Commerce); Walter Berg, grocer and fireman; William Holzheid, city manager; Charles Buckbee, mayor of White Bear; George Lund, manager of Northern States Power Company; and Durward Bahnemann, manager of Inter-State Lumber Company. The police officers (from left to right): A. Long, William Rose, and Frank Swanson.

The Junior Chamber of Commerce presented a combination police car-ambulance to White Bear in 1937. The vehicle was specially equipped and included a folding stretcher with cushions. Three times within the following year doctors credited the use of the specialized vehicle with the saving of lives.

Domino's Pizza – Summer 2003

Courtesy of Cynthia Vadnais

The fire department moved from the corner of Clark Avenue and Second Street to its new home at 4700 Miller Avenue in the fall of 1962. The location has been a good one for a number of businesses, including Domino's Pizza, which has been in the old fire department building since the mid-1980s.

Courtesy of Cynthia Vadnais

White Bear Lake Government Center – Spring 2004

Since 1962 the fire and police departments (above) have been located on the northeast corner of Second Street and Miller Avenue. The City Hall Building (left) was constructed in 1988.

Courtesy of the White Bear Lake Volunteer Fire Department

White Bear Lake Volunteer Fire Department – June, 2003

Shown (from left to right): (front row) Jerry Loberg, Paul Peltier, Mike Machus, Chief Tim Vadnais, Doug Peltier, Mike Turnbull, Ron Hawkins, Steve Engstran; (second row) Jeff Wenzel, Paul Munns, Jon Rasch, Colleen Jefferson, Joy Banning, Derek Cooper, Jeanenne Rausch, Adam Schauls, Maevis Solomon; (third row) Todd Thelen, Steve Lawrence, Brian Bogdonavich, Bob Peterson, Aaron Gross, Ricky Revering, Derek Schauls, Greg Krueger, Del Koenkamp, Mark Wietecki, Mike Clauson. Not pictured: Tom Ballis, Harley Currier, Dick Kindsvater, Jason Gahm, Jeff Kessel, Mark Anderson, Mike Barnard, Suzanne Chase, Bill Counihan, Rob Ehlert, Andy Engen, Ron Gay, Dick Grundtner, Hans Hittner, Greg Kerola, Tim Linder, Leslie Loberg, Brian Loomis, James McCarthy, Terell Nelson, John Paulsen, Adam Senarighi, Chris Wickland, Matt Bouthilet, Chris Garcia, Erica Olson, Chris Voss.

WHITE BEAR LAKE PUBLIC LIBRARY

In the early 1880s, Mr. and Mrs. J. E. Burns started a reading room in their home. It was a place where young people would gather to read and play games. The great success of this early reading room led a Mr. Herbert Hinckley to donate his library for a public reading room called The White Bear Reading Room Association. Mr. and Mrs. Chase provided a room for the collection at the rear of their home.

The success of the reading room led to Daniel Getty's appearance before the city council on November 4, 1889 to request the organization of a public library. The city council was easily moved by the request and appointed a nine-member board, with chairman Dr. S. O. Francis and board of directors James M. King, James Lonergan, Cyrus B. Cobb, Daniel Getty, Abel E. Leaman, Luke H. Bacon, C. J. Gottshall, and John E. Extrand.

The White Bear Reading Room Association was asked to join forces with the Public Library group, resulting in the association turning books and property over to the Public Library. Daniel Getty furthered the cause by donating a bookcase and the use of a small building located at the west side of Railroad (Washington) Park. The building had been the location of the first store in White Bear. It was eventually moved to Third Street, on the south side between Banning Avenue and Cook Avenue (the American Legion location), where it was used by Joseph Hardy as a feed store. With no public money for new purchases, people were asked to donate books and periodicals to help the library grow. The directors catalogued the books and took their turns as librarian. The library remained in this location until May 1891.

The Getty Block – Corner of Third Street and Clark Avenue

Courtesy of the White Bear Lake Area Historical Society

On October 20, 1891 the library opened in room two on the second floor of the Getty Block with a reception for which two-hundred invitations had been sent. Each invitee had been requested to bring any good books that could be donated. With money raised via a tax levy, the library was able to purchase a Standard Dictionary, several subscriptions, and a stove to heat the new area. There was an annual rental fee of $50.

Mr. Frederick E. Whitaker had the distinction of being the first paid librarian. With a dedicated employee, it was decided that the library would be open each evening from seven to nine, with it only being open for two hours on Saturday between April 30 and September 30 in order for patrons to exchange books. The library boasted 656 books and sixty-one borrowers in 1894, and by 1897 there were one-thousand books.

In November 1901, an adjacent room in the Getty Block was rented for an additional $2.50 a month. The wall between the rooms was taken down, more shelves were installed, and the room was painted to match the old room.

An increase in rent caused the library to move, on October 1, 1908, to the two front rooms in the upstairs of the Y.M.C.A. Building, later called the Auditorium, which was just west of the Armory on Fourth Street. Here the rent included both heat and light.

Y.M.C.A. Building – Early 1900s

Courtesy of Cynthia Vadnais

Courtesy of the Lawrence R. Whitaker Family

Librarians Stella Long and Emory Clewett – Circa 1910

Some of the early librarians in White Bear included Frederick E. Whitaker, Harold Robinson, Emily Extrand, Stella Long, Emory Clewett, Nellie Freeman, Lucy Tarte, and Ada Palmer.

The Carnegie Library of White Bear Lake

Courtesy of the Lawrence R. Whitaker Family

In May 1912 the Carnegie Foundation offered to donate $5,000 to build a Public Library in White Bear. The foundation's offer was contingent on the City Council's agreeing to provide a site free of debt, plus $500 for maintenance. The site, located on the southwest corner of Second Street and Clark Avenue, was purchased from T. C. Fulton for $850, with the council providing $500 and the library board the other $350 (part of which was donated by the Soldiers' Monument Association). The current library sits, in part, on this same site.

It is interesting to note how Andrew Carnegie ended up founding and funding libraries across the United States. According to a story in *Youth's Companion*,

> While waiting for an answer to a dispatch to a Mr. Anderson, young Carnegie walked into the library and became immersed in a volume on steel making. When Mr. Anderson finally came down with his answer the boy turned and apologized for having taken the book. Mr. Anderson asked whether he was interested in steel. "Oh Yes, it is fascinating to me," Carnegie replied. "Take the book home and read it and return it when you are through with it, " said Mr. Anderson. Carnegie did so and was told to take another; then Mr. Anderson said he might have access to the library. Carnegie said to me that then and there he made up his mind that if he ever became wealthy he would found libraries and give young men the same opportunity that he was enjoying.

Miss Ada Palmer – Librarian at White Bear Lake from 1915 to 1953

Just after the Carnegie Library opened in White Bear, Miss Palmer joined the staff. For almost four decades she served as a librarian for the people of White Bear Lake.

Courtesy of the White Bear Press

White Bear's Carnegie Library – Southeast Corner of Clark Avenue and Second Street

Courtesy of Bob Thein

    The Carnegie Library of White Bear was built during 1914, with A. S. Devore as the architect, and C. E. Davies as the general contractor. That year Davies had just finished building the St. Paul Automobile Club. Late in October, the newly finished library opened its doors to the public for the first time with Miss Tarte as the librarian. Out in front of the red-brick building, a flag donated by the E. B. Gibbs Post G. A. R. flew.

    The building was used for two separate purposes, with city offices in the basement and the library on the upper floor. The city relocated to offices in the new fire hall in the fall of 1930. Upon their moving, the library quickly occupied the much-needed space. The Women's Club, who had been long-time supporters of the library, furnished the newly acquired basement reading room.

    The Carnegie Library of White Bear proved to be adequate until 1962, when space above the old fire station, on the northwest corner of Second Street and Clark Avenue, was utilized for a children's library.

White Bear Public Library – Summer 2003

Courtesy of Cynthia Vadnais

    The current library is located, in part, on the property once occupied by the old library. On April 30, 1973, the old library was leveled, along with two houses on Second Street and one on Clark Avenue, to make way for the current library. The thirteen-thousand-square-foot building was erected at a cost of about $400,000.

Parks, Players, Pike and Plays: Pleasant Pastimes

Courtesy of Cynthia Vadnais

Railroad Park – Circa 1905

Courtesy of Cynthia Vadnais

Railroad Park – Mid 1920s

In 1914 the trees were thinned out to make more space for ongoing activities held in the park. The park was renamed Washington Park in 1932.

Courtesy of the Lawrence R. Whitaker Family

Washington Park Bandstand – Circa 1936

Music in the park has been a long-standing tradition for the people of White Bear. The bandstand shown was the third one to be built in the park. The first was torn down in 1887 and the second in 1914. This one was removed around 1937 to make way for the new post office on the north side of Third Street in a section of the park.

White Bear School Band – May 30, 1926

This photograph shows the White Bear School Band with director Harry Hauglie at the far left.

Courtesy of Bob Thein

Professor Farrar and H. J. Keeler organized a band March 1, 1914 to play concerts in the park. The first concert was given on June 5, 1914, with H. J. Keeler directing. These events proved to be so popular that one 1923 account marveled, "The concert of Tuesday evening was attended by the largest crowd of the season. There were 258 autos parked around the square. This does not include those on the side streets nor those in circulation. The estimate on the number of people is 1,700."

Torinus Fountain in Railroad Park – Early 1900s

Courtesy of Cynthia Vadnais

The stone beehive-shaped fountain was built and presented to the people of White Bear by the Torinus family. Helen M. Torinus was married to Hiram King, of King & Company; her brother, George E., bought Cyrus Cobb's lumber business in the early 1890s. Louis E. Torinus, the father, was the owner of St. Croix Lumber Company and upon his death left a sizable estate to his family. The fountain was torn down at the same time as the gazebo to make way for the new post office in 1937.

Courtesy of Bob Thein

Queen's Ice Palace – 1935

In 1935 White Bear held a Mid-Winter Fair. As a part of the fair the Leisure Time Labor Program of the Rural Works Administration, in conjunction with the White Bear Association, built an ice palace. The Queen's Ice Palace, facing Third Street, was built around the bandstand and illuminated at night.

Washington Park Flagpole Dedication – November 11, 1939

Courtesy of Bob Thein

When the idea of erecting a flagpole as a monument to those who fought in World War I was proposed to the White Bear American Legion, a movement began to raise the money for the worthy cause. It was estimated that the total project would cost around $350. The flagpole itself was dedicated November 11, 1939, but the stonework around the flagpole was not finished until May 1940. When completed, the monument consisted of a sixteen-foot-diameter circle of stone, with seating centered on the flagpole. The monument still stands near the southwest corner of Washington Park.

Winterfest Ice Castle – 1993

Courtesy of Beverly Vadnais

The center stage of Winterfest '93 in White Bear was the ice castle. Both old and new equipment was used to harvest the ice, which was taken from White Bear Lake near Matoska Park. The process involved a huge circular saw that sliced the ice while a nineteenth-century conveyor lifted the ice out of the lake onto a flatbed truck that hauled it to the castle site, located just to the southwest of the depot. The thirty-four-foot tall structure, designed by Bill Rust, took 1,101 five-hundred-pound blocks of ice to build.

Thomas Erd, builder of Assumption Church in downtown St. Paul, built this Victorian gazebo in 1883 on the Geist property while he was a guest at their cottage. The eighteen-by-eighteen-foot gazebo was a surprise gift for his daughter and her husband.

In 1911, the lower part of the gazebo was enclosed so it could be used as a honeymoon cottage. Upon getting married, each of the Geist brothers, Emil, John and George, along with their brides, used the gazebo as their honeymoon cottage.

The gazebo eventually fell into disrepair. Efforts were made to acquire the gazebo so that it might be restored, but these failed as the property where it sat changed hands several times. It was not until 1973 that the White Bear Lake Women's Club acquired permission to renovate the gazebo under the condition that it be moved from its original location. By the time it was finally moved to Matoska Park February 27, 1974, it was in quite a state of decay.

Courtesy of the White Bear Lake Area Historical Society

Geist Gazebo – Before 1911

Courtesy of the White Bear Press

Geist Gazebo Before Being Moved and Restored – 1973

Courtesy of Cynthia Vadnais

Geist Gazebo – Matoska Park – 1974

Once relocated, the gazebo was renovated and lovingly restored. Another restoration occurred starting in 1997. The work was finished by 2000. The Geist Gazebo is located in Matoska Park on Lake Avenue, near the head of Fourth Street.

Courtesy of Cynthia Vadnais

William West Park – Summer 2003

In 1927 Mr. and Mrs. William West donated their lake home and surrounding property to the town to establish a park and bathing beach. The property consisted of the block bordered by Tenth and Eleventh Streets, and Lake and Johnson Avenues, along with more land continuing to the Northern Pacific Railroad tracks farther to the north. It was not until 1932 that the West home was torn down to make way for the park.

Today the park is a favorite spot for picnickers because it commands a nice view of the lake and conveniently has a swimming beach just on the other side of Lake Avenue. The park and beach area are slated for a complete renovation beginning in 2004.

The all-American game of baseball has been a favorite pastime of the people of White Bear from the resort era onward. Leip's Park, Wildwood, and the Chateaugay Park had baseball diamonds. In 1887, the *Lake Breeze* reported on a game organized between the "Fats" and the "Leans" at the Chateaugay Park. Noted early residents participating in the game were Daniel Getty as the umpire; James Waters, owner of the White Bear House, scoring; and William Leip as the captain of the "Fats." It appears that anyone was welcome to participate, and fun was had by all.

As the sport grew, organized clubs were formed giving the crowds the "fastest playing outside of the big leagues."

Courtesy of the White Bear Lake Area Historical Society

White Bear Baseball Club – 1908
Shown (left to right): (front row) Burt Davies, Elmer Johnson, Maurice Burrows, Ed Jackson, and Pat Collette; (second row) Emory Clewett, George Farnen, George Flandrick, Ike Milner, and Charley Van Avery; (third row) Russel Long, Fred Campbell, and Earl Jackson.

Courtesy of the Richard Vadnais Family

Baseball Field on Northwest Corner of Fourth Street and Bald Eagle Avenue

---

INTER-STATE LEAGUE

BASE BALL

Sunday, August 3, 1919

3:00 P. M.

STILLWATER
AT
WHITE BEAR

Fastest Playing Outside of the Big Leagues

Tolen, of Stillwater, says to have an ambulance on hand as they intend to put us out of commission

Come and help boost the BEST team in the League as we must win Sunday, at White Bear; also following Sunday, at Stillwater, to get in first place

BATTERIES

WHITE BEAR	STILLWATER
Karger or Michaud and Zalusky	Morse or Keinholtz and Berger

THIS WILL BE A GAME FOR BLOOD

White Bear Press – 1919

In 1903 the *White Bear Life* reported on a baseball game played between White Bear and Stillwater. The reporter titled the article "Diamond Robbery" and went on to grouse, "The Bears went over to Stillwater last Sunday and fought nine Wolfs, a hostile umpire and a vicious crowd of rooters for ten innings. The game belonged to the Bears on its merits, but the handicap was too heavy. If the same clubs were to meet on the White Bear grounds the Wolfs would be beaten by a larger score than last Sunday's. Collette outpitched Dollar, striking out 8 men to Dollar's 5, and the Bears outbatted the Wolfs, having 3 earned runs to their 1." The final score was White Bear 3, the Wolfs 4.

Courtesy of the White Bear Press

White Bear Football Team 1914-1915

Courtesy of the White Bear Lake Area Historical Society

Members of the team (left to right) are: (bottom row) S. Herbert, A. Hard, D. Long, and A. Johnson; (middle row) A. Peterson, D. Edgar, Earl Goheen, and H. Stoddart; (top row) H. Stoddart (a repeat), Joe Finn, P. Rogers, A. Wilzbroker, P. Greengard, Frosty Henkel (Captain), R. Davis, and E. A. Herron (Coach).

Lined up for a Scrimmage

Courtesy of the White Bear Lake Area Historical Society

According to the *White Bear Press*, "The practice field for the 1908 football team was the gravel street in front of the post office at Third and Clark. The players were busy with after school jobs so the practicing was done at night under the arc light at that corner. They were know as the 110-pound team and played against teams from St. Paul, Stillwater, Forest Lake and other communities. Games were played on various empty lots... Each youth was responsible for buying his own uniform."

Football Team Party – Circa 1908

Courtesy of the Richard Vadnais Family

Shown seated (from front left): Earl Jackson, Matt Abbott, George Flandrick, Fred Campbell (captain), Denis Michaud, Bert Davies, Ed —, Emory Clewett, A. Long, S. Markoe. Standing (left to right): — Francis, Mrs. A Francis, Stella Long, and Lucy Francis.

Courtesy of Cynthia Vadnais

Hippodrome – Summer 2003

The Exhibition Hall, later renamed the Hippodrome, was built in 1924 as a part of the Ramsey County Fair grounds. Located on Bloom Avenue at Eighth Street, the 100-foot-by-200-foot building, covering half an acre, was erected at a cost of $23,000. Soon after opening it became one of the first indoor ice rinks in Minnesota. The movie *Ice Castles* was filmed at the White Bear Hippodrome in 1978. Although the building was remodeled about 2000, it looks much the same as when it was built.

Hockey has always been a favored sport in White Bear. Before the Hippodrome was erected, the early teams used the rink at the Webster School grounds.

Courtesy of the White Bear Lake Area Historical Society

White Bear Hockey Team – 1912

Shown (from left to right): Goheen, Davis, Markoe, Finn, Clewett, Lennon, Weidenbouer, Henkel, and Canstner.

Courtesy of the White Bear Press

White Bear Hockey Team – 1920s

Managed by Les Palmer (left) this 1920s White Bear hockey team included (from left to right): Clarence Fournelle, Tom Cunningham, Clarence Melhorn, Pat Shea, Elmer Stanke, Dick Voges, Al Melhorn, John O'Halloran, Albert Schweitzer, Ken Guthunz, and Pete (Snap) Fournelle.

Pat Shea went on to play professionally with the Chicago Blackhawks.

The White Bear Flyers were the champions of the Twin City Suburban League in the winter of 1948-1949, beating out fourteen other teams for the title.

White Bear Flyers at the Hippodrome – Circa 1948

Courtesy of Jack Vadnais

Shown standing (from left to right) are: Bob Shearen, George Buchans, "Puff" Furman, Jack Vadnais, Harold Arcand, and Bob Samuelson. In the front row kneeling (from left to right) are: Buck Rooney, Don Rooney, Jim Rungey, ——, Casper Bibeau, and Terry Rooney.

For a number of years the Old Timers would get together and play the White Bear team in a game of hockey. The *Press* enthused, "If you like good hockey, which has earned the rightful name of being the fastest game in the world, you'll be on hand when the Old Timers tangle sticks with the White Bear team." In 1950 more than eight-hundred people turned out to see the local stars of yesteryear battle it out with the White Bear Flyers. The Old Timers won 6 to 5.

Hockey Players of Yesteryear – 1952

Courtesy of the White Bear Press

In 1952 many of those who had played hockey at the Hippodrome during the 1940s gathered for an old timers game and an evening of food and camaraderie.

Courtesy of the White Bear Press

First Ice Fishing Contest on White Bear Lake – 1947

Started in 1947, the World's Original Ice Fishing Contest became one of the most popular winter traditions in White Bear. Initially sponsored by the White Bear Rod & Gun Club, in later years other sponsors included the St. Paul Dispatch & Pioneer Press in conjunction with the St. Paul Winter Carnival. The gun club claimed that the contest was "not only original but also largest and best." James LaBore was the winner of that first contest with a six-pound, two-ounce northern. He received a trophy, a fishing outfit, and a parka.

From the start, the event attracted thousands of people. In 1950 LIFE magazine wrote an article on the contest that resulted in attendance tripling the next year. The magazine bragged, "This is one indication of the tremendous effect LIFE has on the people living in the Twin Cities area, of whom half are LIFE readers."

As a tradition, each year a design was plowed in the snow on the lake surface and hundreds of holes were cut in the ice. The anglers had a portion of a day to catch the winning fish inside the boundaries of the design. The person who caught the largest fish won a nice prize. Other, lesser prizes were awarded in many different categories. In later years, a highlight of the contest was a visit from the St. Paul Winter Carnival Royalty and their entourage.

Aerial View of the World's Original Ice Fishing Contest – 1952

Willard Bibeau, a lifelong resident of White Bear, took this aerial photograph of the 1952 contest. Lake Avenue is running along the bottom and Goose Lake is at the top right corner of the photograph.

Courtesy of Willard Bibeau

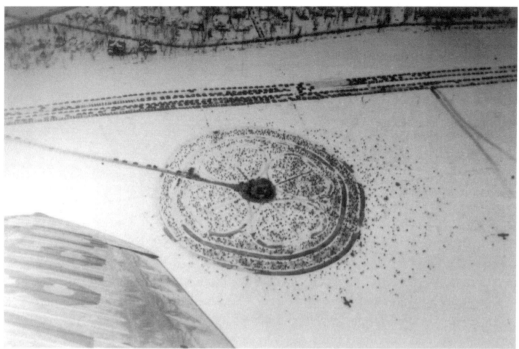

Courtesy of Willard Bibeau

Four-Leaf Clover Design – 1952

This photograph was taken by Willard Bibeau as he flew upside down over the fishing contest site. The four-leaf clover design was used to represent the 4-H organization. Lake Avenue is running along the top of this image.

The Winning Fish – 19th Annual Ice Fishing Contest – 1965

Courtesy of Jack Vadnais

A four-pound seven-ounce northern was the winning fish in 1965. Congratulations are being offered to winner Joe O'Doherty (on the left in the white cap) by Jack Vadnais (right), president of the White Bear Rod & Gun Club, and Chief Justice Oscar R. Knutsen of the Minnesota Supreme Court (middle), who officiated over the contest. O'Doherty's sons are shown sitting in the fourteen-foot Traveler aluminum boat, with a five-horsepower Evinrude outboard motor, that he won.

Courtesy of Jack Vadnais

"H" Design – 1966

The "H" design was created in 1966 as a tribute to then Vice President of the United States Hubert H. Humphrey. That year 4,000 people turned out for the fishing contest, which was held on the lake north of Manitou Island. The winner, Charles Olson of Vadnais Heights, received a fourteen-foot aluminum boat along with a 7 ½-horsepower electric start motor.

Courtesy of Beverly Vadnais

June Caspers Working on Catching the Big One – 1966

Courtesy of Beverly Vadnais

Winter Carnival Clowns Entertaining the Crowds – 1966 Ice Fishing Contest

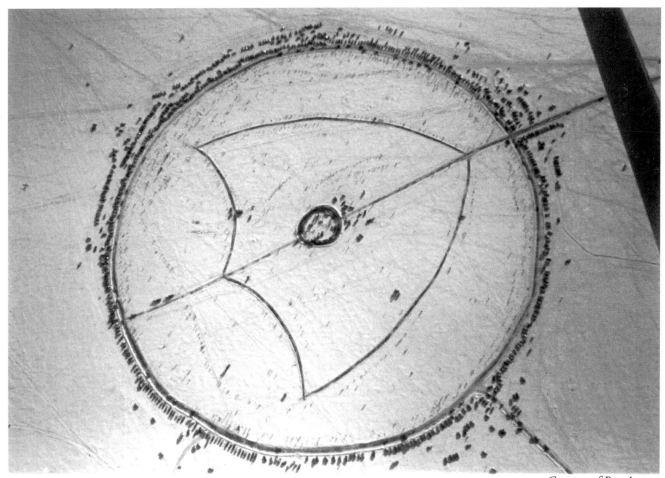

Courtesy of Ray Asmus

Ice Fishing Contest – Arrowhead Design

The last World's Original Ice Fishing Contest, a huge success for thirty-five years, was held in 1982. Thousands of people had participated over those many years, with only thirty-five receiving the "grand" prize for their efforts.

Lakeshore Players Theatre – Summer 2000

Courtesy of Cynthia Vadnais

In 1971 the Lakeshore Players purchased the First Baptist Church on the southeast corner of Stewart Avenue and Sixth Street. It is the oldest surviving church building in White Bear Lake.

In a 1971 newspaper article the *White Bear Press* gave the following history of the group:

> A small group of theatre devotees gathered in the White Bear Lake City Hall on a cold January 5th night in 1953 to organize what was to become one of the oldest continuous amateur theatre groups in Minnesota – Lakeshore Players... Over the next several years Lakeshore Players rehearsed its plays wherever space was available — church rooms, basements, boat works, and the living rooms of its members. Most performances were held in what is now the auditorium of Central Junior High School or Mahtomedi High School... In 1954, realizing the necessity for excellent direction, Lakeshore engaged Mrs. Ebba (Nelson) Kuester, as resident director, the post she held for fourteen years before resigning to move to Seattle... Lakeshore in turn had shown its affection for Ebba by naming its annual awards "Ebbas." A six year Lakeshore dream came true in September, 1959, when Mrs. Sally Irvine and Mr. Robert A. Peters announced the purchase of the old Presbyterian Church by Lakeshore Players... Finally established in its own plant, the group moved immediately into instruction-in-the-arts, and established classes in ballet, tap, baton, and children's theatre in December, 1959, under professional teachers... In the middle of its seventeenth season, disaster struck the Players. The building, a then one-hundred year old landmark was totally devastated by fire on the night of November 22 [1969]... Led by President Joe Tamillo, the Board of Directors immediately arranged to relocate its children's classes... the District #624 School Board... found a way to squeeze the Players into the High School little theater for the remainder of the season...

Six weeks after Truly Latchaw and Laurie Peterson founded the Lakeshore Players, the group put on their first performance, *Ah Wilderness,* written by Eugene O'Neill, at the White Bear High School.

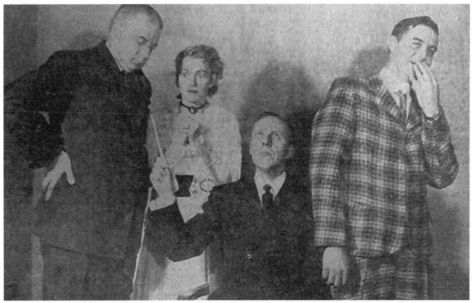

Courtesy of the White Bear Press

Scene from *Ah Wilderness* – 1953

Shown (from left to right) are: Phil Huitkrans as Nat Miller, Dorothy Hargesheimer as Essie Miller, I. V. Johnson as Mr. McComber, and Fred Hargesheimer as Uncle Sid.

Loni Anderson and John Robinson in *Any Wednesday* – 1968

Adele Hofmeister, Loni Anderson and John Robinson in *Any Wednesday* – 1968

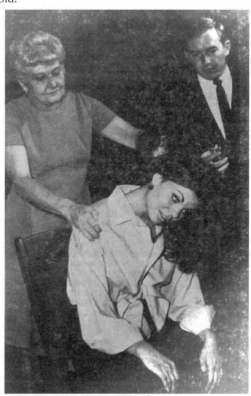

Courtesy of the White Bear Press   *Courtesy of the White Bear Press*

Hollywood actress Loni Anderson was born in Roseville, Minnesota and got her start in acting in the various theaters around the Twin Cities. She was a principal actor in the Lakeshore Players' production of *Any Wednesday*. Anderson is most noted for her character Jennifer Marlowe on the hit TV sitcom *WKRP in Cincinnati* from 1978 to 1982. She was also married to actor Burt Reynolds for a number of years.

Bald Eagle Lake Area

A *White Bear Press* article about Bald Eagle Lake reported, "Bald Eagle is not a city, neither is it an incorporated village... It joins White Bear on the north, and is really a part of this city [White Bear Lake], though not included within the city limits... The lake is said to have derived its name because it was claimed that in the primitive days the island in this lake was thickly inhabited by bald eagles."

Courtesy of the Richard Vadnais Family

Filling the Icehouse – Henry Long's Ice Company

Henry Long went into the ice business on March 17, 1901. That first day out on Bald Eagle lake it was thirty degrees below zero and windy. The ice was thirty-three inches thick. Twenty-six years later on the same date, Long was out enjoying a warm spring day plowing his fields. Those who cut ice were at the mercy of a variable climate. They harvested the ice in the extreme cold and spent the warm months, protecting their harvest from the heat and delivering it.

Long's icehouse stood at the north end of the property now occupied by the White Bear High School. There were four other icehouses in White Bear around the turn of the century.

Long bought George Beckstead's ice business at Bald Eagle in 1908, and in 1921 Long took over the People's Ice Company which had been in business since the 1880s. That same year, the land of the old People's Ice Company icehouses on the northern end of White Bear Lake was donated to White Bear to be made into a bathing beach.

White Bear Press Ad – 1921

Courtesy of the White Bear Press

LONG'S ICE CO.
Formerly The People's Ice Co.

Having satisfied the people of White Bear and Bald Eagle during the past 13 years, we solicit a return of your patronage in the future, with the assurance that the same service will be given as in previous years.

Thanking you in advance for business, we remain,

As B-4

Henry Long's Bald Eagle Ice Company Wagon and Icehouse

Courtesy of the White Bear Lake Area Historical Society

People's Icehouses on the Northwest Shore of White Bear Lake (just to the right of the lower part of the sailboat mast)

Courtesy of the Richard Vadnais Family

Several companies harvested ice out of White Bear Lake including the People's Ice Company, St. Paul Ice Company, West Side Ice Company, White Bear Ice Company, East Side Ice Company, and Citizen's Ice and Fuel Company. In addition, there were many small independent merchants that harvested. Some of the companies contracted to fill their icehouses while others had regular crews

The enormous lake provided ice for the people in the surrounding area and some of St. Paul, as well as other places. Just to give an indication of the amount of ice harvested from the lake, in 1941 the People's Ice Company filled 400 railroad cars each containing thirty-five tons. That's twenty-eight-million pounds of ice!

Henry Long retired from the ice business in 1925. Six years after Long retired, the People's Ice Company icehouses on White Bear Lake were flattened so the bathing beach could be built.

Courtesy of Ruth Mattlin

Bald Eagle Yacht Club – 1900

The Bald Eagle Yacht Club, located at the foot of Buffalo Street on Bald Eagle Boulevard East, started around 1900. The races held each weekend were well attended by the people of the area. A few of the early leaders of the organization were S. H. Thomas and Mahlon Miller's sons. Reputedly, Paul Manship, who would later become a famous sculptor, owned the largest of the yachts to sail from the club. The club faded in popularity soon after WWI, with low lake levels contributing to the decline. It was revived around 1940, only to once again disappear around WWII. Currently the Bald Eagle Yacht Club holds regattas each summer.

Group down by Bald Eagle Lake

Courtesy of Ruth Mattlin

Courtesy of the White Bear Press

Solheim – E. H. Hobe Home at Bald Eagle – 1939

The Engelbrecht H. Hobe home was built in 1897. Hobe, a lumber dealer and Consul to Norway and Sweden, named the 480-acre estate *Solheim*. In 1939 Crown Prince Olav and Crown Princess Martha visited the Consul and Mrs. Hobe at their home to decorate Consul Hobe on behalf of King Haakon.

E. H. Hobe died April 19, 1940 at *Solheim*. His grandson, James Hobe Brodie, and granddaughter, Mrs. R. O. Eckhardt, later sold the land off for development. The main home still stands and has been totally renovated.

Courtesy of the White Bear Press

Dining Room in the Hobe Home where Royalty was Entertained

Bald Eagle Grocery

M. Schuhr, Prop.

Fancy Groceries	Fruits	Vegetables
Candies	Soft Drinks	Ice Cream
Cigars	Cigarettes	Tobbacos

Located at the most logical point for an industrial section with transportation on three railroads, Northern Pacific, Soo, and Milwaukee and State Highways leading to Duluth, St. Paul, Minneapolis and many other points.

For prompt delivery service and personal attention phone 462-J.

Courtesy of the White Bear Press

White Bear Press Ad – 1927

Courtesy of Ruth Mattlin

Interior of Bald Eagle Grocery – Circa 1923

Shown are (right to left): Martin (Mottie) Schuhr, his wife Hattie, and his nephew Bud Bazille.

Mottie Schuhr, a native of White Bear who had worked for the Mercantile Grocery Company, went into business for himself. The experienced grocer opened Bald Eagle Grocery in 1919 on the southwest corner of Long and Park Avenues.

Courtesy of Ruth Mattlin

Bald Eagle Lake and Bald Eagle Island

Until 1904 Bald Eagle Island was owned by the county. That year a group of men organized themselves into the Bald Eagle Island Association and purchased the island. It would remain under their ownership until 1920.

As reported by Virginia Tuttle, "In 1909, the *St. Paul Dispatch*... leased the island for a boy's camp. They called it 'Boy Island City'. Under the direction of Will Stout, who was known for his column on handicraft under the pen name of 'Jack Knife', the boys from under privileged areas of St. Paul organized a perfect community setup. They elected a mayor and councilmen and had their own police and fire departments.... Poison ivy and the thousands of mosquitoes finally caused the closing of the venture..." Boy Island City only lasted for two seasons.

The island is now privately owned and has a beautiful home that was built a number of years ago.

Mahtomedi Area

Courtesy of the White Bear Lake Area Historical Society

Mahtomedi Hotel – 1890

Built about 1883, on what is now Quail Street, the Mahtomedi Hotel provided all the modern amenities. The one-hundred-foot-long rectangular building had forty rooms to accommodate guests. Owned by the Mahtomedi Assembly of the Chautauqua Association, which also platted and owned a large portion of Mahtomedi, the hotel catered to those attending the Chautauqua Association annual summer session, as well as to tourists. During the 1880s the "Literary Summer Resort" was so popular that reservations needed to be made a year in advance.

In 1887 the hotel, as an attraction, brought in an eight-foot alligator from New Orleans and two raccoons. The newspaper referred to the collection of animals as a "menagerie."

By 1912 the hotel had outlived its usefulness. It was dismantled into sections. Some sections were moved to other parts of Mahtomedi. A small portion of the hotel was remodeled and remained on the site of what is now 76 Quail.

Courtesy of the White Bear Lake Area Historical Society

Chautauqua Assembly Building – 1890

    The Chautauqua Assembly building, located near the Mahtomedi Hotel, was quite large, seating up to three-thousand people. A. H. S. Perkins, in his book *All about White Bear Lake,* wrote, "The assembly erected a spacious assembly hall in which they hold interesting annual sessions, which are participated in by many of the most famed literary, musical and religious people of the world. An extremely moral atmosphere, no liquor selling being allowed, and no sports, recreations or any traffic allowed on the Sabbath." The local paper reported, "One summer there were more than 3,000 people staying in tents during the Chautauqua. All for $2.50 per week." The annual sessions appealed to middle-class people. Those who attended wished to expand their intellects and augment their educations while enjoying the surroundings. The annual programs stopped in 1919.

In the early 1900s the Charles and Agnes Whitrock family camped at the end of Fir Street in Mahtomedi. Charles worked for the Northern Pacific Railroad in St. Paul. During the summer the family made their home on the shores of White Bear lake near Wildwood Park. Charles would take the train to work each day while the family stayed at the campsite. Eventually the family built a permanent home in Mahtomedi, as did Charles' son Thomas Whitrock and his wife, Leona.

Courtesy of the Thomas Whitrock Family

**Camping Out in Mahtomedi Near Wildwood Park
– Fourth of July Celebration – Circa 1910**

Charles Whitrock is shown on the right. The picture on the tent is that of William Howard Taft, president of the United States from 1908 to 1912.

Celebrating the Fourth of July by Enjoying an Afternoon Dance

Courtesy of the Thomas Whitrock Family

Whitrock Camp as Seen From the Lake

Courtesy of the Thomas Whitrock Family

A Nice String of Fish for Dinner

Courtesy of the Thomas Whitrock Family

The Sparring Match

Courtesy of the Thomas Whitrock Family

    School District #69 was formed in 1890 by joining two school districts that had been established earlier. For a time, students attended school in a room in Mr. E. T. Warner's store and later at the home of a Mrs. E. J. Demarest.

    Quail School, a red one-room building with green shutters, was constructed on Vincent (Quail) Street in 1891 at a cost of $925. It was described by Sherwood Hough, one of Lincolntown's (Mahtomedi) pioneers, as being located "…on a pretty knoll, surrounded by native oak trees, separated from adjacent woodlands by a 'murmuring brook' which served, not only to soothe the harassed mind of 'teach' but also to provide a handy place for pupils to wade, 'catch cold' and thereby provide a legitimate excuse for absenting [sic] themselves from classes occasionally." When it opened, the school's one teacher, Mary Betaque, was paid $35 a month. Over the approximately seventeen years that the school was in use, there were fourteen different teachers.

Quail School House – 1906

Shown (from left to right) are: (back row) Donald Hough (author of *The Streetcar House*), Luther Harrison, Frances LaRoche, Frank Clewett, Katherine Hough, Jessie Johnson, George Wilzbacher, and teacher Margaret Borrowman; (center row) Allie Wilzbacher, Roland Brunner, Raymond Schifsky, Daisy Hendrickson, Margaret Christ, Mary Bichner, Mildred Jaeger, and Sybill Brunner; (front row) Pearl Warner, Buddy VonVories, John Bichner (holding the sign), May Warner, and Fred Miller.

Courtesy of Independent School District 832

Courtesy of Julie Ahlman

Mahtomedi School – Circa 1925

Mahtomedi School was built about 1908 on land donated by Mr. J. P. Hanson. The architect was Allan Fleischbein. The two-room grade school building was constructed near Neptune and Mahtomedi Avenues across from the present Mahtomedi District Education Center and District Office ISD 832 building. By 1915 wings had been added to both ends of the school. Eventually two more rooms were completed in the basement to help accommodate the ever-increasing enrollment. The need for space led to the leasing of the library building for the first two primary grades.

A Well-Mannered Class of Young Mahtomedi School Students

Courtesy of the Thomas Whitrock Family

Lincolntown Library

Courtesy of Independent School District 832

The Lincolntown Library, on Maple Street near Mahtomedi Avenue, was built in 1922 by Ralph Drake at a cost of $10,000. E. P. Warner had donated the land for the library.

The library also served other purposes for the community. When Mahtomedi School could no longer house all of its students, Lincolntown Library was rented by the school district to house the first and second grades. On Sundays it was used by St. Andrew's English Lutheran Church for church services.

The library was not very successful due to the sparse population of the area. Upon its closing, the building was rented to the school district to be used for classrooms for primary grades. By 1932 a nightclub and restaurant opened in the old library building. Bert Jensen bought the property in 1938, converting the building into apartments that he named Jensen's Apartments. Today, the building is a private residence.

Courtesy of Cynthia Vadnais

Lincolntown Library Building as it Looks Today

Lincolntown High School – 1932

Courtesy of Independent School District 832

To prevent its students from having to go to White Bear or North St. Paul for a high-school education, Lincolntown High School was built in 1930 by the Tell Construction Company on a tract of land across from Mahtomedi School. When the school opened, it housed grades five through ten, while students in grades one through four continued in the old grade school.

Courtesy of Independent School District 832

Lincolntown High School – 1939 Addition

Notice the tracks in the foreground of the picture to the right.

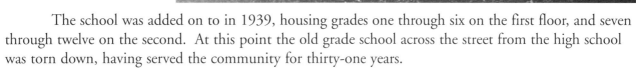

Courtesy of Julie Ahlman

The school was added on to in 1939, housing grades one through six on the first floor, and seven through twelve on the second. At this point the old grade school across the street from the high school was torn down, having served the community for thirty-one years.

The high school building underwent subsequent additions in 1956 and 1964. The building has functioned not only as a high school but also a middle school. The property is the current location of the Mahtomedi District Education Center and District Office ISD 832.

A new high school, Mahtomedi High School, was built in 1972 along Stillwater Road east of Mahtomedi.

Courtesy of Julie Ahlman

St. Andrew's Lutheran Church – "The Little Grey Church"

On January 29, 1922 a Lutheran service was held at the Ark Theatre building in what is now Mahtomedi. The library at Oakleigh Station was used for services starting in August, 1922. St. Andrew's Lutheran Church was built in 1925 on Mahtomedi Avenue, with the cornerstone laid in July of that year. The first service was held in the church on November 3, 1925. The church was appropriately named after St. Andrew, a fisherman of Galilee. The church bell came from the old Mahtomedi School. At first a mission-sustained church, the church became self supporting in 1940. Expansions included an education wing in 1958 and a new parsonage.

In 1966 the old sanctuary came under the wrecking ball, and was replaced by a new church structure that was completed in 1967.

Courtesy of the White Bear Press

St. Andrew's Church being Demolished – 1966

St. Andrew's Lutheran Church – 2003

Located at Hilton Trail and Stillwater Road, the thoroughly modern St. Andrew's Lutheran Church boasts a one-thousand-five-hundred-seat worship center.

Courtesy of Cynthia Vadnais

Mahtomedi Union Chapel

Courtesy of the White Bear Press

Mahtomedi Union Chapel – Now a Private Residence – 2003

Courtesy of Cynthia Vadnais

The nonsectarian chapel, located on Rose Street, was built in 1900 and later moved to Mahtomedi Avenue. Over the years several different groups occupied the building. The structure was added on to at least three times, with the most noticeable addition being a stone front. The last church organization to occupy the building was the Unitarian Church. Officially established on November 18, 1956, the Unitarian Church first held meetings in the Mahtomedi School. In 1959 the Unitarian Church paid $12,500 for what was then the Methodist Church property. Soon after, a Sunday school room was added to the building. The Unitarian Church moved to a site at Centerville Road and County Road H2 in the late 1970s, and later to a location on Maple Street. It is now called the White Bear Unitarian Universalist Church. Currently the Mahtomedi Avenue property is a private residence.

Courtesy of Julie Ahlman

East Side Ice Company – Icehouses

Louis Rohlfing owned the East Side Ice Company from 1902 to 1950. Before he became his own boss, he worked for D. F. Skillman at Echo Lake. Rohlfing located his two-story-plus icehouses on the southwest corner of Oak and Mahtomedi Avenues.

His service was reputed to be second to none. He was so dependable that there were those who were reluctant to buy electric refrigeration when it came in. He also took pride in his work. Rohlfing boasted, "No housewife had to clean house after I put ice in." Stocking a refrigerator with ice was quite messy. Many an iceman, in their trek through the house, would leave a trail of water for which they took no responsibility. There were probably a number of them that also walked right back through the same wet mess making it all that much worse.

On December 1934, one of Rohlfing's icehouses caught on fire and was seriously damaged.

East Side Ice Company – Icehouses

Courtesy of Julie Ahlman

In the Good Old
Summer Time
if White Bear can't
keep you Cool,
Try

THE EAST SIDE ICE CO.

Louis Rohlfing, Prop.

Daily deliveries made to all parts of the Lake.

Phone your order today.

White Bear Press Ad – 1931

Courtesy of the White Bear Press

William E. Spink opened his store in 1905. In 1924 a tragic fire took his store and the life of his meat cutter. He then built a brick building on the southeast corner of Quail Street and Mahtomedi Avenue, where he reopened his Fairway general store, assisted by his wife and his son Ned. The post office was located in his store, with Spink as postmaster. After Spink's death, his son took over the business.

White Bear Press Ad – 1927

W. E. SPINK
Postmaster and Pioneer Merchant of Lincolntown

The Mahtomedi Store

High Class Line Groceries, Meats, Candies, Fruits, Vegetables, Cigars and Tobaccos.

Hardware, Paints, Oils, etc.

MAHTOMEDI, (Lincolntown) - - Minn.

Courtesy of the White Bear Press

Courtesy of Cynthia Vadnais

Spink Grocery Store Building as it Looks Today – Summer 2003
Ramsey and Associates, certified public accountants, are currently located in the building.

When in the White Bear Lake district do not fail to visit Mahtomedi.
We will take pleasure in making your visit a pleasant one.

Chandler's

THE STORE AT MAHTOMEDI

Groceries   Confectionery   Light Lunches
Gas and Oil Station
Cigars   -   Tobaccos
We Specialize in Fresh Fruits and Vegetables
Do not forget we deliver.

Courtesy of the White Bear Press

White Bear Press Ad – 1927

Mrs. Theresa Chandler started Chandler's on the old Wildwood Road. In 1910 her children, Mame and Fred Chandler, built a small store just to the south of Spink's Mahtomedi Store. The *White Bear Press* reported, "They carry a fine stock of groceries, confections, cigars, and tobaccos, and over its popular fountain serves Vander Bies ice cream, and tasty drinks."

In 1929 Frank Guarnera bought the building and had it moved to the southwest corner of Mahtomedi Avenue and Juniper Street, where he opened a dairy store and then Guarnera's, a spaghetti restaurant. His son Vince took over the business after WWII and continued until 1964, when the building was converted into an insurance office.

Brandhorst Building – Summer 2003

Courtesy of Cynthia Vadnais

The Brandhorst Building, also called the Lincolntown Service Building, was built in 1927 in the Tudor style popular during the era, which incorporated stucco and decorative timber. The building, located on the southwest corner of Mahtomedi Avenue and Maple Street, had been designed by architect Allan Fleischbein, who later designed Lincolntown High School.

Among the early businesses to occupy the building were a service station, a taxi service, and a grocery store. When the grocery store failed, the Brandhorsts took it over. Also starting in 1927, a restaurant called Polly's Kettle was opened by Mrs. John L. (Emily T.) Myers and Mrs. Kramer in the basement of the building. That same year A. R. Zimmerman opened a barber shop in the building. About 1929 Mr. Brandhorst opened a tea room that was quite popular with the teachers.

After Prohibition, Jack Andres opened the Jolly Knight Tavern in the basement of the Brandhorst Building. In 1946, just after having moved to Mahtomedi, Ray Rolling operated the Second Base Tavern for six years at the same location.

Ray Rolling was born in Missouri on September 8, 1886. He grew up playing baseball and was most noted for having played with the St. Louis Cardinals. Rolling remained active in baseball his entire life. He established a baseball program for the boys in Mahtomedi, coaching and managing three leagues.

Ted Brandhorst died in 1936, leaving the building to his wife. Over the years, a number of businesses were located there, including Forseen's. The last business to be in the Brandhorst Building was Eddie Antila's Finnish Bakery. Eddie had a strange turn of luck when he became allergic to flour and had to close the business. The building was converted into apartments around WWII, with Mrs. Brandhorst selling it to her daughter and son-in-law in 1960.

Courtesy of the White Bear Press
Ray Rolling at Age 77 – 1963

Appetites
Serviced at
Forseen's
At Oakleigh
(Brandhorst Building)

Home Cooked
Lunches and Dinners

Group Reservations by Appointment.

Phone 73R

Courtesy of the White Bear Press
White Bear Press Ad – 1937

Courtesy of Julie Ahlman

Inter-State Lumber Company – Mahtomedi

The main offices of both the White Bear and Mahtomedi branches of Inter-State Lumber were located in Stillwater. The company was started in 1905 by Mr. H. R. Woerz. The Mahtomedi branch of the business, located just east of Hamline Lake, closed about 1965.

Courtesy of Cynthia Vadnais

Krueger's Fitness Center – Summer 2003

The multipurpose community clubhouse was built in 1921. It opened in March 1922, on the southeast corner of Hickory (View) Street and Mahtomedi Avenue, under the name Lincolntown Community Clubhouse. As recounted in *Mahtomedi Memories* by Alice R. Smith, Sharon F. Wright, and Judy Kaiser, "Dissension developed within the community as to the purpose of the clubhouse. Allegations were made that it was too private, for only a few, too political, and too expensive... At the annual meeting of the clubhouse, the decision was made to drop the word community from the name and be called Lincolntown Clubhouse..." It was destroyed by fire New Year's Eve, 1928.

Once again, Allan Fleischbein was called upon to design a prominent building in the area. The clubhouse opened on March 17, 1930, and the town hall, located at the back of the building, was completed in November 1930. The *White Bear Press* stated that the new building "Has a splendid floor for dancing, a stage, kitchen,..., while in the basement are fine bowling alleys and a refreshment stand," and that "The town hall is located in the second story of the building and is seated for about fifty... The Clerk's office occupies an alcove off the main room. The Town Garage is located in the easterly half of the same building, and is heated. Owing to shortage of funds, only the front part of the garage was completed." One of the functions of the garage was to house the lake fire department.

Lincoln Township's New Town Hall and Garage – 1931

Courtesy of the White Bear Press

    Mr. C. J. Chisholm converted the Lincolntown Clubhouse into a community recreation center in 1933, renaming it The Dells. The place was renovated, and on the east interior wall J. O. Michaud painted a decorative mural of mountains with a stream. The four bowling alleys in the basement were a popular hangout. Mr. and Mrs. Loyd C. Sorenson opened the Dells Food Market at the location in 1944, and in 1945 Ralph Rohrbeck and his cousin, Harvey, bought the business, naming it Harvey's Super Market. Ralph and Harvey parted company in 1960. The business name became Ralph's Super Market. In 1970 Dave Wagner opened a meat market in conjunction with the supermarket. According to *Mahtomedi Memories*, "Other businesses have shared Ralph's building over the years. These have included Hayden Hardware, an ice cream parlor, a beauty shop, an antique shop and a barber shop."

    A well-known tenant of the clubhouse building was August (Gus) Heidbrink. He first visited Mahtomedi in 1929 while still managing several barber shops in St. Paul, one of which was located in the Lowry Building. He moved to Mahtomedi in 1940, opening a shop with Ada Potratz in the building on Mahtomedi Avenue at Juniper Street, where Frank Perrault's store had been located. He later relocated to Ralph's Super Market Building, where he remained until his retirement in 1971. He had been in business in Mahtomedi for thirty years.

Courtesy of the White Bear Press

Gus Heidbrink by his Barber Pole Outside Ralph's Super Market – 1971

Courtesy of Tom and Winnie Stanek

Mrs. Beulah Johnson's Restaurant

In 1914, Mrs. Beulah Johnson built a restaurant and bar bearing her name. It would later become known as The Picadilly (at some later point another "c" was added to the name). The establishment was located on the south side of Stillwater Road just east of Mahtomedi Avenue. The Piccadilly was a favorite watering hole for people visiting Wildwood Park. Joe and May Doupe bought the business in 1922, selling to Rudy Leiner in the mid-1930s. Art and Alice Cheasick took over in 1940, and in 1952 they rebuilt right off Highway 244 just west of the old location.

Tom and Winnie Stanek bought the restaurant from the Cheasicks in 1969. The building was renovated in 1972, with the Staneks selling it to Bob Nemeth and Rich Bohaty in 1980. The Stanek's son, Joe, acquired Rich Bohaty's share of the business in 1989 and Bob Nemeth's share in 2002.

The Piccadilly – 1952

Courtesy of the White Bear Press

Courtesy of the White Bear Press

White Bear Press Ad – 1935

Courtesy of Tom and Winnie Stanek

The Piccadilly – 1972

Stormy Weather

The White Bear Lake area has been fortunate to have had few natural disasters. Damage that has occurred has been caused by wind, water, hail, and a cyclone (what we would now call a tornado). The only remnants of destruction are in newspaper articles and photographs. If one were looking at White Bear today, one would be hard put to imagine, or to remember, the aftermath of the natural disasters, especially the cyclone in 1941. The following are the major events the newspaper reported.

On August 1, 1904, a cyclone struck St. Paul, causing high winds to hit the east shore of the lake. It blew down the wires for the streetcar and sent Louis Heckel's steamboat onto the shore.

In 1929 a storm lifted a long storage shed at Amundson Boat Works. The newspaper reported that "The entire shed was lifted into the air, turned wrong side out and crashed into the street, blocking traffic completely for a distance of 200 feet or more, the wreckage being piled several feet high across the street."

During August 1932, a heavy rainstorm passed through White Bear. No damage was caused by the wind but the streets were flooded. The newspaper stated, "Boating was good."

A cyclone struck White Bear on September 4, 1941. It was the most devastating disaster the people of White Bear had to deal with up to that point.

The most recent natural disaster to strike White Bear happened July 7, 2000, when straight-line winds, along with hail and rain, swept through White Bear in just fifteen minutes. The impact was extensive: the wind, the rain and the hail damaged many homes; vehicles not sheltered had extensive hail damage; trees were uprooted; numerous broken branches littered roads and yards; and power lines were down.

Courtesy of the Richard Vadnais Family

August 1932 Flood

This photograph shows Pete Bacon, a local man, paddling his duck boat south down Bloom Avenue near Eighth Street. The Hippodrome and Ramsey County Fair buildings are shown in the background. The fair was open at the time of the storm.

The next five amateur photographs show the destruction the cyclone wreaked on White Bear Lake on September 4, 1941. The next day the *White Bear Press* told of the storm and the destruction:

White Bear is a mess and a wreck. Wednesday at the noon hour a storm of cyclonic nature and a cloud-burst struck. The rain fell in such torrents vision out a few feet was impossible.

A howling, roaring wind as of a gigantic monster accompanied it. The air was filled with debris, great trees by the hundreds were uprooted or split, twisted and thrown in every direction, covering the path of the storm with debris and wreckage. Signs were blown down, windows blown in and business houses and homes flooded… No one was killed…

Fully 25 residences were practically demolished, more than 100 damaged. Trees smashed some, roofs were blown off, chimneys sent sprawling…

Several parties claim there was a twister in the storm as they saw the funnel shaped giant. Judging from some of the freaks it is evident that such was the case… Lake Avenue shore line… is piled high with trees which had fallen by the score across the avenue. Great beautiful oaks and elms were uprooted tearing craters ten feet deep…

At the southwest approach to town… Wm. Jantzen's eight tourist cabins were hard hit, most of them torn to shreds while three stood on their heads. Ten tourist cabins… located on the former Auto Club property, and facing the highway were smashed to kindling wood and strewn in all directions.

The cornice of the armory and a strip of roof about 10x25 were ripped off.

One of the ornamental brick points on the Getty block was torn off…

Automobiles were blown against others on the street.

A large tier of brick was torn from one side of the White Bear Drug Store…

Every brick on the chimney of the Presbyterian Church was separated but laid over on the roof as if done by hand…

One of the phenomenal freaks of such storms was that in which a row-boat was picked up at the Amundson boat works, split in halves and laid down at the front door of the R. J. Davidson residence, Clark and Lake Avenues, a distance of several blocks across a corner of the lake…

The big electric sign and two windows of the White Bear Theatre were smashed, while across the street a large paine [sic] of the display window of the Huss Jewelry store was blown in…

The velocity of the wind at the government station in St. Paul was so high at times it was impossible to read the instrument.

Courtesy of Jack Vadnais

Home Damaged by the September 4, 1941 Cyclone

Aftermath of the September 4, 1941 Cyclone

Courtesy of the Richard Vadnais Family

Getting Ready to Chop up the Felled Tree – September 4, 1941

Courtesy of the Richard Vadnais Family

Property Destroyed by the September 4, 1941 Cyclone

Courtesy of the Richard Vadnais Family

Debris from Tree Damage – September 4, 1941

Courtesy of Jack Vadnais

Friday, July 7, 2000 started out as a beautiful summer morning. Little did people know that by 11 a.m., the summer sky would turn black and unleash its fury. In less than fifteen minutes, straight-line winds, hail, and rain caused a great amount of damage across the White Bear Lake area. Dozens of trees were downed, some landing on cars and houses, while others blocked streets and took down power lines. Streets were temporarily flooded because drains clogged up with hail and debris. The fast-moving storm caused a lot of damage to property, but thankfully no one was injured.

Courtesy of the White Bear Press

Gene and Kathy Johnson Home – 4753 Lake Avenue

The lovely old Johnson home on Lake Avenue was damaged during the July 7, 2000 storm when a tree limb crashed through an enclosed porch on the front of the home.

Intersection of Fourth Street and Highway 61 Around 11 a.m. – July 7, 2000

Courtesy of the White Bear Press

BIBLIOGRAPHY

Allen, Frederick Lewis. *The Big Change America Transforms Itself 1900-1950.* New York, New York: Harper & Row, 1952. 7, 15-17.

Brey, William. *John Carbutt On The Frontiers of Photography.* Cherry Hill, New Jersey: Willowdale Press, 1984.

Castle, Henry. *St. Paul and Vicinity.*

Chisholm, Nancy LeVasseur. "Les Le Vasseur Du Minnesota."

Cummins, D. Duane and William Gee White. *Contrasting Decades: The 1920's and 1930's.* Consulting editors Dr. Herbert J. Bass and Mr. Anthony J. Petrillo. New York: Benziger, Inc., 1972.

Drake, Carl B. *History of the White Bear Yacht Club.*

Drake, Carl B. *Recollections of Manitou Island, White Bear Lake, Minnesota.* December 1957.

Folsom, W. H. C. *Fifty Years In The Northwest.* Pioneer Press Co., 1888.

Griffin, Otto B. "Bald Eagle Union Church." April 10, 1936.

Haas, Claudia. "Lakeshore Players." *Town Life,* Vol 3, Issue 1, January/February 2001, 24-26.

Haugh, Oscar M. "A Century of Progress, The History of the White Bear Public Schools."

Heilbron, Bertha L. *The Thirty-Second State, A Pictorial History of Minnesota.* Edited by Russell W. Fridley and June Drenning Holmquist. St. Paul: Minnesota Historical Society, 1958.

Holmes, Frank R. *Minnesota in Three Centuries, 1655-1908.* Vol IV. New York: The Publishing Society of Minnesota, 1908.

Johnson, John W. *From Norway to White Bear Lake.* 4th ed. Decorah, Iowa: Anundsen Publishing Co., 2000.

Johnson, John W. *History of St. John in the Wilderness Episcopal Church, Minnesota 1861-2001.*

Johnston, Patricia Condon. *Reflections, The White Bear Yacht Club, 1889-1989.* Minneapolis: Bolger Publications, Inc., 1989.

Johnston, Patricia Condon, "Truman Ingersoll: St. Paul Photographer Pictured the World." *Minnesota History,* 47/4 Winter 1980. 122-132.

Klechefski, Diane. "A History of St. Mary's of the Lake or Tales None Will Admit to Telling." November 27, 1976.

Larson, Paul Clifford. *A Place At the Lake.* Afton, Minnesota: Afton Historical Society Press, 1998.

Leuchtenburg, William E. *The Perils of Prosperity 1914-1932.* Chicago: The University of Chicago Press, 1958

Maccabee, Paul. *John Dillinger Slept Here, A Crooks' Tour of Crime and Corruption in St. Paul, 1920-1936.* St. Paul, Minnesota: Historical Society Press, 1995.

Markoe, William F. "White Bear's Indian Mound."

Mattlin, Ruth C. "A Dream Come True for Carroll R. Mattlin, Preserving and Restoring the White Bear Lake Railroad Depot." March 1999.

Mattlin, Ruth C. "Spring Park Villa Resort on Bald Eagle Lake."

McMillan, Molly Bigelow & Susan S. Wolsfeld. *The History of Manitou Island White Bear Lake, Minnesota.*

Meath, Johanna. "The Legend of Father Goiffon." *Little Canada, A Voyageur's Vision.* Edited by Gareth D. Hiebert. Stillwater, Minnesota: The Croixside Press, Inc. 43-50.

Minnesota Historical Photo Collectors Group. *Joel E. Whitney, Minnesota's Leading Pioneer Photographer, Catalog of Cartes De Visite, Native American & Landscape Views.* 2001.

Minnesota Historical Society (J. Fletcher Williams) to Village of White Bear Council, May 13, 1887. Letter from Minnesota Historical Society to Village of White Bear Council regarding the Indian Mound.

Neill, Edward D. *History of Ramsey County & the City of St. Paul.* Minneapolis: North Star Publishing Co. 1881. 280-288.

Newson, T. M. "Kis-se-me-pa and Kar-go-ka, A Legend of White Bear Lake." *Indian Legends of Minnesota Lakes.* 1881.

Olson, Russell L. *The Electric Railways of Minnesota.* Hopkins: Minnesota Transportation Museum, 1976. 18-23.

Page, Dave & John F. Koblas. *Scott Fitzgerald in Minnesota, Toward the Summit.* St. Cloud, Minnesota: North Star Press of St. Cloud, Inc., 1996.

Perkins, A. H. S. *All About White Bear Lake, The Popular Summer Resort of Minnesota.* White Bear: Lake Breeze Printing House, 1890.

Post Office Time Capsule. White Bear Lake Area Historical Society.

Reis, Peter R. *White Bear's Hometown Heroes, The Story of the White Bear Lake Volunteer Fire Department: 1888-2002.* St. Cloud, Minnesota: Sentinel Printing Co., 2003.

Robinson, H. P. "White Bear Lake, A Glance at St. Paul's Charming Summer Resort." *The Northwest*, Vol. 3, No. 7, July 1885, 18-23.

Schwarck, Don. "W. H. Illingworth: A Biography." In *Exploring with Custer, The 1874 Black Hills Expedition.* 2d ed., Dakota Photographic LLC, November 2002.

Smith, Alice R., Sharon F. Wright, and Judy Kaiser. *Mahtomedi Memories* 1976. Minneapolis, Minnesota: Anderberg-Lund Printing Co.

Snow, Robert F. "Value Judgments." *American Heritage* October 2002: 8.

Stickley, Helen Johnston. "Early History of White Bear Lake, Minnesota." 1933.

Stickley, Helen Johnston. "Legend White Bear." *Indian Legends of Minnesota* by Mrs. Carl T. Thayer. 12-15.

St. Paul Pioneer Press, 1890.

St. Paul Pioneer Press, April 13, 1999.

St. Paul Pioneer Press, August 29, 1920.

St. Paul Pioneer Press, August 4, 1940.

St. Paul Pioneer Press, January 9, 2000.

St. Paul Pioneer Press, June 23, 1941.

St. Paul Pioneer Press, November 23, 2002.

Suburban Life, January 11, 1957.

The Lake Breeze 1887 – 1896.

The Matoskan. White Bear High School Yearbook.

The Sonoma Democrat, Santa Rosa, California. December 9, 1858.

Tuttle, Virginia. "Highlights of Bald Eagle History."

Twain, Mark. *Life on the Mississippi.* Avenel Books, 1986, 395-398.

Vail, Garrett & Renee. Abstract for 2325 6th Street, White Bear Lake, Minnesota.

Westin, Harold. "Reflections on the History of Manitou Island." October 29, 1981.

Whitaker, Francis J. "The Early History of White Bear Lake, Minnesota."

Whitaker, Louise Hardy. Personal Notebook.

White Bear Lake Mahtomedi Telephone Directory, July 1953. Northwestern Bell Telephone Co., 1953.

White Bear Life 1896 – 1914.

White Bear Press 1914 – 2003.

Winchell, Newton H. *Aborigines of Minnesota.* Minnesota Historical Society, St. Paul: Minnesota Historical Society, 1911.

Woolworth, Nancy L., *The White Bear Lake Story*, 1968.

———. "During the 1930s White Bear Lake Faced Many Changes." *The Lake Area Preserver,* Fall 2003. White Bear Lake Area Historical Society.

———. "Kohler's Ice Cream Parlor." *Town Life,* Vol. 2, Issue 4, July/August 2000. 19-21.

———. "Presenting White Bear Lake," League of Women Voters.

———. "Saint Mary's of the Lake School, Dedication October Twenty-First, Nineteen Hundred and Fifty-One."

———. *The American Travellers Journal,* August 1881, Vol 2, #1.

———. *This Fabulous Century.* Edited by Donovan Hedley. Time Inc., 1970.

———. *Tourist & Sportsman,* April 7, 1877.

———. "100 Years of Paper & Ink." White Bear Press Publications.

———. "Wildwood Park on Beautiful White Bear Lake Near the Twin Cities."

INDEX

Symbols

617 197, 264, 266

A

Abbott, Matt 326
Abe 118, 133
Abresch, Arman 205
Acme Company 264
Ada, Palmer 315
Adamson, James 233
Ahren Family 103
Albrecht, Paul 266, 292
Alden Apartments 41
Alden Hotel 41-43, 169, 198
Alden, William L. 41, 190, 198, 199
Alden's Cafe 190
Alexander, Mrs. 67
Allen, Arthur 150
Allen, James P. 15
Alrick, J. A. 229
American Legion 238, 249, 251, 313, 320
Amundson, Adolph 103
Amundson Boat Works 61, 103-105, 150, 357, 358
Amundson, Edwin G. 103, 158
Amundson, Fritjof 104
Amundson, Gustav 101, 103, 104, 106
Anderson, George W. 254
Anderson, Harry 158
Anderson, J. 183
Anderson, Loni 334
Anderson, Mark 312
Anderson, Mrs. H. 158
Anderson, Robert 224
Anderson's Restaurant 198
Andres, Jack 353
Antila's Finnish Bakery 353
Appleton Real Estate Company 201, 213
Arcadia 169
Arcand, Bert 255
Arcand, Harold 328
Ark Theatre 348
Armory 167, 249, 250, 309, 314, 358
Arnquist 263
Arrow, Charles F. & Agnes 69
Artificial Bathing Beach 142
Ashton, Mr. 151
Aubrey, Mr. and Mrs. John 151-154
Aubrey, Mrs. John 171
Auditorium 241, 249, 251, 252, 288, 308, 309. *See also* Y.M.C.A.

Auditorium Theatre 251, 265
Auger 80
Auger, Alfred 188
Auger Brothers Garage 275, 276
Auger, Dave 310
Auger, Eli 50
Auger, Felix 194
Auger, Henry L. 275
Auger, Janette 197
Auger, Leopold 268
Auger, M. S. 275
Auger, Paul 276
Auto Club Pure Oil Station 302
Avalon Arts 234
Avalon Building 197, 265, 267
Avalon Theater 205, 251, 265-267

B

Bacon, B. 232
Bacon Building 188
Bacon, Evelyn 158
Bacon, L. 232
Bacon, Luke H. 313
Bacon, Mildred 251
Bacon, Mrs. T. W. 158
Bacon, Pete 279, 357
Baer Blacksmith Shop 210
Baer, Elmer 210
Baer, William (Billy) 181, 208, 209, 210, 310
Bahnemann, Durward 311
Bald Eagle Avenue 48, 161-163, 180, 184, 239, 241, 252, 259, 263, 274, 276, 277, 279, 280, 281, 324
Bald Eagle Boulevard East 44, 337
Bald Eagle Boulevard West 48
Bald Eagle Depot 274
Bald Eagle Grocery 339
Bald Eagle Hotel 48. *See also* Hotel Benson, Bald Eagle Lake
Bald Eagle Ice Company. *See* Long's Ice Company
Bald Eagle Improvement Association 169
Bald Eagle Island 340
Bald Eagle Island Association 340
Bald Eagle Junction Depot 75, 79
Bald Eagle Lake
    37, 44, 74, 75, 77, 84, 153, 169, 186, 245, 335, 337
Bald Eagle Union Church 169
Bald Eagle Yacht Club 337
Baldwin Cottage 186
Ball, A. E. 298
Ballis, Tom 312
Bamboo Inn 271. *See also* LaCroix Cafe

365

Banhorn, C. O. 231
Banning Avenue
    71, 82, 84, 95, 114, 158, 168, 177, 188, 204, 206, 229, 234, 236, 238, 239, 240, 248, 252, 258, 259, 260, 261, 266, 283, 287-293, 303, 313
Banning, Joy 312
Banning, William L. 71, 72
Barbeau, T. E. 145
Barker-Karpis gang 148
Barnard, Mike 312
Barnum, Emily 154
Barnum House 23. *See also* Leip House
Barnum, Kirby 92
Barnum, Villeroy B. 23, 33, 151
Barnum's Hotel 151. *See also* Barnum House
Barth, Anton 254
Barth, B. 183
Basch, Fran Miller 185
Bauer, William 310
Bazille, Bud 339
Bazille, Dave 310
Bazille, J. A. 168
Bazille, James 225
Bazille, Marqueritte 251
Bazille's Big Ten Store 263
Bazille's Grocery 217, 223
Beach School 186, 286
Beach Tavern 189
Beamis, Jack 62
Bear Patch Quilting Company 262
Becker, D. 183
Becker, H. 183
Beckstead, George A. 252-254, 335
Beckstead's White Bear Auto Livery 254, 255
Behrns, Mr. Williams 183
Bellaire 245
Ben Franklin Store 267, 268
Ben Hur 101
Bennett, Carl 54
Bennett, Charles 54
Bennett, Mr. and Mrs. Carl 222
Benny's Barber Shop 213
Benson, Frederick W. 37-39, 48
Benson, Herman 208
Benson, Margaret 155
Benson, Mrs. 154
Benson, Mrs. Frederick W. 39
Benson, Stella E. 69
Berg, Gladys 277
Berg, Walter 239, 277, 311
Berghammer, Martin 189
Berghammer's Saloon 189
Berg's Grocery 239, 277
Bernier and Company Grocery 236
Bernier, Esdras 236
Bert Arcand & Company Feed Store 289
Bert Arcand Ford 255, 256

Best, Nellie 247
Betaque, Mary 344
Beulke Building 210
Beulke, Gordy 210
Bibeau, C. 183
Bibeau, Casper 328
Bibeau, James 277
Bibeau, Norman 277
Bibeau, Thomas 277
Bibeau, Willard 329, 330
Bichner, John 345
Bichner, Mary 345
Biernes, F. A. 255
Bies, J. N. 199, 205
Big-Little Store 239
Bigelow, Charles H. 16
Binswanger, Mrs. Amy 168
Birch Lake Avenue 161, 227, 239, 241, 263, 277
Birch Lodge 85, 87, 88
Birchwood 245
Blackbird, Shirley 191
Blehart, Nathan W. 81, 190
Bloom Avenue 159, 301, 326, 357
Bloom, Bud 277
Bloom, Caspar 296
Bloom, Casper 20, 21
Bloom, Harriet 156
Bloom, Howard W. 310
Bloom, Mrs. Howard (Vina) 239, 277
Bloom, Robert J. 81, 156, 233, 237, 310
Blooms Department Store 233
Bloom's Grocery 239, 277
Bobbies in the Park 248
Bogdonavich, Brian 312
Bohaty, Rich 356
Bohrer, Mabel 289
Bond Electric 213
Bonham, William 156, 269
Bonin, Phil 266
Boody, Miss 244
Boppre Chevrolet 143, 301, 302
Boppre, Joe 301, 302
Boppre, Mrs. Joe 143
Borrowman, Margaret 345
Borsch 194
Bortie, S. R. 209
Bosse, Reverend Orville K. 164
Boulter, Captain 118
Bourquin, T. L. 296
Bouthilet, Matt 312
Bowen, Naomi 156
Boy Island City. *See* Bald Eagle Island
Boy Scout 249
Brache, C. A. 190
Brachvogel Barbershop 217, 223
Brachvogel farm 186
Brachvogel, Richard G. 39, 188, 217, 306

Bradford, Mr. B. P. 72
Brandhorst Building 353
Brandhorst, Mrs. Ted 353
Brandhorst, Ted 353
Brass, Bob 267
Brass, Fred A. 267
Breen, Charles O. 147, 256, 267
Bring, Hubert 81, 289
Bring's Feed 289
Bristol 118
Brodie, James Hobe 338
Brosious, Burr 156
Brosious, Ruddy 156
Brouwers, Jacques 143
Brown, J. H. 28
Brunner, Roland 345
Brunner, Sybill 345
Buchans, George 328
Bucher, John 233
Buckbee, Charles 148, 311
Buckbee, Mrs. Charles 67
Bucknam, Mrs. 32
Buffalo Lake 85
Buffalo Street 167, 337
Bull, William 221, 229
Bull's Photo Shop 221
Bunghard, John 192
Burgdorf, Mrs. Kenneth 200
Burkard, Joseph 218, 261
Burns, Mr. and Mrs. J. E. 313
Burrows, Al 20, 116
Burrows, Maurice 323
Burrows, Miss Clara 198
Burson Avenue 101
Burson, George 15
Burson, Joann 171
Burson's Island. *See* Manitou Island
Byrne, Reverend James J. 163

C

C. Thomas Food Store 263
C. Thomas Stores 241
Caldwell, Reverend J. C. 157
Calvary Cemetery 161
Campbell, A. M. 251
Campbell Avenue 51, 277
Campbell, Fred F. 163, 244-247, 308, 310, 323, 326
Campbell, Marlowe 296
Canstner 327
Capistrant, John 296
Captain Richards 5
Carbone's Pizza 271
Carbutt, John 5, 6
Carbutt, Mollie 6, 7
Cardinal, David 81
Cardinal, Delia 244, 245
Cardinal, Dolphus 209

Carey, Sylvester M. 16, 18
Carnegie, Andrew 315
Carnegie Library 156, 315, 316.
   See also White Bear Public Library
Carpenter House. *See* Hotel Chateaugay
Carrousel 137
Carver brothers 116
Caspers, June 331
Cassavant Dry Goods 230
Cassavant, J. A. 230
Cassavant, Lessie 230
Cassel's Apparel 213, 214
Catholic Order of Foresters 172
Centerville Road 349
Central Junior High School 333
Chamberlain's Clothing Store 213
Chandler, Fred 352
Chandler, Mame 352
Chandler, Mrs. Theresa 352
Chandler's 352
Chapin, D. 183
Chapman, Mr. Harvey 201
Chapman, Mrs. 62
Chapple, Ed 263
Chapple's Food Market 263
Charpentier, Henry 209
Chase, Freddie 270
Chase, Mr. and Mrs. 313
Chase, Suzanne 312
Chateaugay Park 323
Chautauqua Association 341, 342
Che-Wa 85
Cheasick, Art and Alice 356
Cherrier, O. M. 212, 302
Chester 245
Chico's Clothing 260
Chingachouk 3
Chisholm, J. S. 231, 295
Chisholm, Mr. C. J. 355
Christ, Margaret 345
Christenson, C. H. 158
Christenson, Mrs. C. H. 158
Christian Science Sunday School 168
Chrysler, Hester 171, 174
Church of Christ 43, 169
Churches. *See* Specific Church
Cine Capri 266, 292
Circle Drive 56
Ciresi, Anne L. 233, 234
Ciresi's Liquor Store 233, 234
Citizen's Ice and Fuel Company 336
City Hall Building 312
City of White Bear Lake 304
Clara E. Miller 25, 116
Clark Avenue
    66, 101, 154, 157, 168, 201, 202, 215, 228, 237, 256,
    269, 274, 295-305, 311, 313, 315, 316, 325, 358

Clark, Charlie L. 254, 257
Clark, Dr. C. L. 219
Clark, Frank H. 295
Clark, H. M. 189
Clarke, F. B. 16
Clauson, Mike 312
Clewett 327
Clewett, Albert 12
Clewett, Emory 193, 314, 323, 326
Clewett, Frank 345
Clewett, G. 232
Clewett, Reuben N. 192, 194, 302
Coast to Coast 262, 267, 268
Coates, D. A. 226
Coates, Mrs. 226
Coates Store 226
Coats, R. J. 225
Cobb Block 199, 205, 206, 208, 232, 243, 298
Cobb, Cyrus B. 205, 206, 313, 319
Cobb House 293
Cobb Lumberyard 205, 206
Cobblestone Cafe 191
Cochran, R. 183
Cody, William 217
Coffin, Mr. 190, 191
Collett, Mr. & Mrs. W. B. 55
Collette, Catherine 185
Collette, Pat 323, 324
Colletts' Lake Shore Inn. *See* Lake Shore Inn
Collins, John E. 255
Colony Country Club 144. *See also* St. Paul Automobile Club
Community Club of Bald Eagle 169
Conroy, Mrs. 36
Consolidated Lumber 283
Consumer Power 264
Conway, Charles P. 239, 263, 310
Conway, Mr. 218
Conway, Richard 218
Cook Avenue 168, 175, 176, 249, 313
Cook, George 221, 222
Cook, L. J. 222
Cooke, Jay 73
Cook's Jewelry 221, 222
Cooper, Derek 312
Cormier, Frank 268
Corner Bar 41, 198
Corner Restaurant 198
Cottage Park 33, 51, 109, 245
Cottage Park Association 33, 51
Cottage Park Clubhouse 33, 51, 52, 56, 290
Cottage Park Depot. *See* Lake Shore Depot
Cottage Park Drive 56
Counihan, Bill 312
County Road E 304
County Road F 167
County Road H2 349
Couvillion, Ida E. 176

Craig, Mr. 154
Crane & Ordway Company 87
Crawford, A. 183
Crawford Livingston 25
Crawford, Louis 278, 279
Crever, F. 183
Cunningham, Father P. R. 162
Cunningham, Mrs. E. R. 158
Cunningham, Tom 327
Cup and Cone 271
Currier, Harley 312
Curry, C. C. 293
Curry's White Bear Tavern 293
Cutler, Edward H. 16

D

Darling, Claro 117
Darling, Harry 116, 117
Darling, Timmy 117
Daughters of the American Revolution (DAR) 202
Davidson, R. J. 358
Davies, Burt 323, 326
Davies, Charles E. 44, 81, 139, 140, 156, 247, 289, 316
Davis 327
Davis, R. 325
Daylight Food Market 263
Dean, Addie 171
Dean, William 15, 16, 18
Dean's Ice Cream Parlor 204, 213
Dejong, J. T. W. 27
Del Farm Foods 285
Dells Food Market 355
Dellwood 38, 74, 85, 87, 91, 92, 95, 245
Dellwood Depot 75, 80
Dellwood Short Line Railroad 85
Delmar 245
Demarest, Mrs. E. J. 344
Denoyer, Peter 268
Devore, A. S. 316
Diamon, A. J. 62, 116, 186
Dimond, A. S. 299, 300
Dingle, Joseph 101
Dispatch 25, 116, 133
Division Avenue 258, 268, 269, 271, 273, 278
Dolfay's Grocery 273
Domino's Pizza 311
Don Quixote 25
Donnelly, Ignatius 72
Donohue, E. J. 184
Doric Family Theater 287
Dougherty, Ann 185
Dougherty, Mr. 13
Doupe, Joe and May 356
Dragert, W. L. 147
Drake, Carl B. 16, 91
Drake, Elias F. 16, 18

Drake, Mrs. Mary 40
Drake, Ralph 346
Driscoll, Fletcher 103
Drummond 263
Dungan, Louise 156
Dungan, Virginia 156
Dunn, Lucius C. 33, 158
Dunn, Mary C. 176
Dunn, Mr. and Mrs. Walter 37
Dunn's House. *See* South Shore House
Dupre, A. 232

E

E. B. Gibbs Post, #76, G. A. R. 296, 316
Eagle Brook Church 167
Eagles 251
Eak, N. 232
East Highway 96 167
East Shore Park 245
East Side Ice Company 336, 350, 351
Echo Lake 350
Echo Station 80
Eckhardt, Mrs. R. O. 338
Eden, Don 260
Eden's Bakery 260
Edgar, D. 325
Edward Jones Investments 238
Ehlert, Rob 312
Eighth Street 357
Eleventh Street 322
Elk Laundry 201
Elk Street 169
Elliott, Martha R. 176
Elmer, James P. 91
Empire Jewelry Company 269
Engen, Andy 312
Engen, Art 259
Engen, Chris 259
Engen Color Center 259
Engstran, Steve 312
Episcopal Cemetery 5, 153
Epperly, Fred 81
Erd, Thomas 321
Erie Telegraph and Telephone Company 38
Evans Music 217, 223
Excelsior Amusement Park 130, 138
Exhibition Hall. *See* Hippodrome
Extrand, Emily 314
Extrand, John E. 249, 313

F

Fahey, Father John 162, 163
Faith Lutheran Church 166. *See also* Swedish Evangelical Lutheran Church: First English Evangelical Lutheran Augustana Synod

Fales, Edward Lippitt 300
Fanning, Mrs. 37
Farnen, George E. 233, 323
Farrar, Professor F. F. 178, 318
Fasching, Rollie & Bonnie 20
Federal Land Loan Office 233
Fellows, Tisdale E. 283
Fellows, T. E. & Company 229
Fifth Street 158, 159, 175, 176, 205, 207, 248, 278, 283
Figure-Eight Roller Coaster 124, 129
Fillebrown, Arthur Kingsbury 66, 67
Fillebrown, Harriet Eleanor 66, 67
Fillebrown, Helen Kendrick 66, 67
Fillebrown House 68
Fillebrown, Jonas Walter 66
Finn, Joe 325, 327
Fir Street 343, 344
Fire Carnival 309, 310
Fire Hall 82, 230, 274, 305, 316.
    See also White Bear Volunteer Fire Department
First Baptist Church 167, 333. *See also* Eagle Brook Church
First Church of Christ Scientist 168, 301, 307
First English Evangelical Lutheran Augustana Synod 166
First English Lutheran Church 166
First Evangelical Lutheran Church 167
First Lutheran Church 165, 167
First National Bank 188, 196, 197, 199, 202.
    See also White Bear State Bank
First Presbyterian Church
    33, 157, 158, 159, 160, 333, 358
First State Bank 187, 188, 195, 202, 213, 239, 286, 311
First State Bank Building 214
First Street 154, 184, 206, 227, 293
Fisher, Helen 158
Fitzgerald, F. Scott 98
Fitzgerald, Zelda 98
Flandrick, Carl 218
Flandrick, Frances 234
Flandrick, George 217, 218, 310, 323, 326
Flandrick, John A. 215, 217, 218, 299
Flandrick's Fine Foods 217
Flandrick's Meat Market 217-219, 221, 223
Flatiron Building 201, 269
Fleischbein, Allan 308, 345, 353, 354
Flossier 240
Floyd 118, 133
Flynn 232
Foote, H. 183
Forcier, J. 232
Forcier, Joe 234
Forest Heights 245
Forester Hall 172, 184
Forseen's 353
Foster, Dr. 72
Fournelle and Bloom 200
Fournelle Auto Company 307
Fournelle, C. 246

Fournelle, Clarence 327
Fournelle, John 244, 310
Fournelle, Joseph L. 194
Fournelle, Pete (Snap) 327
Fournelle, Peter 197, 211, 256, 273, 303, 304, 310
Fournelle's Auto Livery 303
Fournelle's White Front Saloon 197
Fourth Street
   36, 51, 74, 77, 80, 84, 114, 162, 163, 168, 177, 188, 190, 201, 205, 206, 211, 222, 231, 239, 241, 249-281, 288, 290, 303, 304, 307, 308, 314, 324, 360
Francis, Lucy 155, 234, 244, 326
Francis M.D., S. O. 229, 313
Francis, Mrs. A 326
Frattallone's Ace Hardware 207
Fred Lenhart Tavern 270. *See also* Lenhart's Bar
Freeborn, William 15
Freeman, Mrs. William 174
Freeman, Nellie 155, 314
Freeman, Robert 81
French Resort 198
Fritschie, Rudolph F. 283
Fulton, James Cooper 154, 195, 196, 287
Fulton, Jane 156
Fulton, Jim 156
Fulton, June M. 196
Fulton, Nellie 156
Fulton, Thomas C. 52, 154, 315
Fun Factory 128
Furman, "Puff" 328

G

Gade, Chris 148
Gahm, Jason 312
Galena Packet Company 5
Garber & Slone 226
Garber, T. 226
Garceau Blacksmith Shop 255
Garceau, Joseph S. 254
Garcia, Chris 312
Gardner, Dr. Frank 233
Garnet Lodge, No. 166, A. F. and A. M. 287
Garvin, Dr. 67
Gatten, J. W. 269
Gay, Ron 312
Geist, Emil 321
Geist Gazebo 321, 322
Geist, George 321
Geist, John 321
Gericke Drug Store 229
Gerken Block 239, 261
Gerken Building 262, 263, 287
Gerken, Harry C. 261
Gerken, Henry 261
Gerken, John G. 183
Gerken's Hardware 168, 255, 260-262

German Lutheran Church 165, 166
Gerten and Parcells 269
Gerten, Frank L. 269
Getter, L. 232
Getty, Adam Keller 227, 228
Getty, Alice 227
Getty Block
   188, 229, 233, 237, 243, 290, 313, 314, 358
Getty Building 224, 229, 232-234, 245, 246, 287, 299, 300
Getty, Daniel 157, 227, 228, 234, 236, 243, 313, 323
Getty, Daniel & Co. 228
Getty, George Walter 227, 228
Getty, Henry (Harry) Keller
   154, 196, 227, 228, 236, 237, 306
Getty, J. A. & Company 228
Getty, John Adam 227, 228
Getty, Mark K. 157
Getty, Mary (Keller) 227
Getty, Mrs. Harry 173
Getty, Robert Wilson 227
Getty's Dry Goods 236, 238, 241
Getty's General Store 295
Gibbs, Captain Eugene B. 155, 296
Gibson, Dora 171
Gilbert, Cass 18, 65
Gilbert, Phillip 231
Glasrud, Ted 179
Glassco, F. L. 209
Glassco, H. D. 209
Goesch, Dora 231
Goesch, William 219
Goesch's Dry Goods 219, 223
Goetz, Fred 148
Goheen, Earl 325, 327
Goiffon, Father Joseph 160-162
Goldman, Howard 292
Goodthings 268
Goodyear Tire and Rubber Company 256
Goose Lake 329
Gordon, Mrs. 273
Gordon's Cash and Carry 271-273
Gordy, J. 232
Gottshall, C. J. 313
Gotzian, Conrad 18
Goulette, George 190, 201, 271
Goulette's Barber Shop 201, 202
Grace, Bishop 161
Graves, Dennis 257
Grayling 103
Great Hope Church of the Nazarene 43, 169
Great Western Railway 116
Greaves, Cyrus 153
Green, Ione 156
Greengard, Jim 200
Greengard, Mrs. Phil 201
Greengard, Phil 201, 325

Greengard Sr., Phil 200, 201
Greengard's Restaurant 194, 199-201, 213, 214, 241
Greenman, Mr. S. P. 33
Greenman's Hotel 33. *See* South Shore House
Greenstein, M. 226
Griffith, H. H. 169
Griffith, Mrs. 168
Griggs, C. Milton 106
Gross, Aaron 312
Grundtner, Dick 312
Guarnera, Frank 352
Guarnera, Vince 352
Guarnera's Restaurant 352
Gundlach, Carrie M. 176
Gundlach, William 296
Gus' Place 225
Guthunz, Ken 327

H

Hafner, M. 263
Hafner's Food Market 263
Hall, Harold 264
Hall Pharmacy 264
Hamilton Hardware 194, 217, 291
Hamilton, Hugh 194, 217
Hamilton, Marie 156
Hamline Lake 354
Hamm's Brewing Company 291
Hanna, David 51, 175, 177, 229, 232, 290
Hansen Building 221, 222
Hansen, Marie 155
Hansen, R. 183
Hansen, Theodore 220
Hansen's Restaurant 220, 221, 223
Hanson, Dick 257, 258
Hanson, Eric 257
Hanson, Mr. J. P. 345
Hard, A. 325
Harding, Charlotte 156
Hardy, Brother Dean 169
Hardy Building 236, 238, 259
Hardy Hall 172, 177
Hardy, Joseph 234, 235, 237, 313
Hardy, Joseph and Jane 235
Hardy, Louise 235
Hardy's 200, 234-236
Hargesheimer, Dorothy 334
Hargesheimer, Fred 334
Harper, F. 183
Harris, Ben 148
Harris Perron Building 208, 209, 275
Harrison, Luther 345
Harry & Joe's Barbershop 217
Hartmann, John 198
Hartzell, William 194, 291
Harvey, Lillestol 265
Harvey's Super Market 355

Hatton, W. B. 32, 39
Hauglie, Harry 158, 183, 318
Haussner Building 255
Haussner, Julius A. 101
Havenor Funeral Home 114
Hawkins, C. E. and Company 261
Hawkins, Ron 312
Hayden Hardware 355
Hazen's Park Liquor Store 213
Hebe 41
Heckel, Louis 115, 357
Heidbrink, August (Gus) 355
Helgeson, R. 183
Helke, M. 183
Hendrickson, Daisy 345
Henkel 327
Henkel & Company Meat Market 215-217, 299
Henkel, Byrd 226
Henkel, Forest 226
Henkel, Frosty 325
Henkel, Lillian 190
Henkel, Nick M. 198, 199, 201, 215, 217, 299
Henkel Saloon 198
Henkel, Sidney E. 81, 310
Herbert, S. 325
Herron, E. A. 325
Hess, Emma 90
Hewitt, Byrd 92
Hickory (View) Street 354
Highway 244 356
Highway 61
    76, 80, 82, 114, 167, 204, 232, 256, 281, 304, 360
Hilbert, H. J. 289
Hill Home 186
Hill, James J. 73, 163
Hillman Insurance Agency 201
Hilton Trail 349
Hinckley Avenue 106
Hinckley, Mr. Herbert 313
Hippodrome 181, 326-328, 357
Hittner, Hans 312
Hoag, S. J. 217
Hobe, Engelbrecht H. 338
Hodskins, Tom 62
Hogan, Gertrude and Julius 273
Hogan, Grace 251
Hogan, Julius 271, 272
Hogan, Lorraine 204, 271
Holden, Tommy 148
Hollihan's Pub 225
Holm and Olson 295
Holtz, Edward 207
Holzheid, August 225, 306
Holzheid, Sophie 155
Holzheid, William 81, 310, 311
Home Trade Store 37, 190, 201, 262, 267
Hoover, J. Edgar 148

Hopkins M.D., Dr. Mary P. 52, 229
Horne, H. 190
Horner, Stirling (Jack) 99
Hotel Benson 37. *See also* Hotel Chateaugay
Hotel Benson, Bald Eagle Lake 48
Hotel Chateaugay 37-39, 48, 166
Hough, Donald 345
Hough, Katherine 345
Houle, E. J. 209
Hoyt, Mrs. 155
Hub Saloon 194, 203
Hubman & Clewett Meat Market 192
Hubman, Julius 193
Huitkrans, Phil 334
Hulse, L. H. 32
Humphrey, Hubert H. 331
Huss Jewelry 358

I

I.O.O.F. 232
I.O.O.F. Hall 168
Ice Boat 63, 64
Ice Castle, Winterfest 320
Ice Fishing Contest 329-332
Ice Palace, Queen's 319
Independent Meat Market 291
Indian Mound 9, 160
Ingersoll, Truman Ward 85-90
Inter-State Lumber Company
    207, 208, 209, 212, 311, 354
Ireland, Archbishop 184
Irvine, Mrs. Sally 333
Ivett, Daniel 232, 306, 307

J

Jackson, E. A. 251
Jackson, Earl F. 229, 304, 323, 326
Jackson, Ed 323
Jackson, Mr. 265
Jackson, William H. 162, 165, 177, 184, 186, 286, 305
Jaeger, Mildred 345
Jahn, Ernst 268, 269
James, Ernest 39
Jameson and Harrison 84
Jameson, Roy 84
Jantzen Jr., Bill 269
Jantzen, Wm. 358
Jefferson, Colleen 312
Jensen, Bert 346
Jensen, Mrs. Jessie L. 251, 265, 266
Jensen's Apartments 346
Jenson, Chris 28
Joe Miller's Sample Room and Boarding House 225
Joel Sherburne Jewelers 259
Johansen, Johan Otto 106
Johansen, O. U. 183
Johnson, A. 325

Johnson, Arthur 197, 198, 201
Johnson Avenue 69, 290, 322
Johnson, Beulah 356
Johnson Boat Works 64, 106-108
Johnson, Conrad 20
Johnson, Elmer 323
Johnson, Eugene (Gene) D. 301
Johnson, Gates A. 72, 295
Johnson, Gene and Kathy 360
Johnson, Herschel 301
Johnson, I. V. 334
Johnson, Iver 106
Johnson, Jessie 345
Johnson, John O. 101, 106
Johnson, John W. 119
Johnson, Larry 147, 189
Johnson, Milton 106
Johnson, Walter 106
Johnston, Maud 24
Johnstone, Craig 271
Johnstone, Glen 271, 273
Johnstone's Grocery 273
Jolly Knight Tavern 353
Jones, Eleanor 156
Jungblut, George 165
Junior Chamber of Commerce 311
Juniper Street 352, 355
Junk, Bill 306

K

Katzenjammer Castle 124, 128
Kaufman, Mr. & Mrs. Sam 190
Kaufman, Sam 262
Kaye, Laura 151. *See also* Aubrey, Mrs. John
Kaye, Sir Lester 151
Keating, Jimmy 148
Keeler, Adeline M. 300
Keeler, Herbert J. 183, 300, 318
Keller, Grandma 227. *See also* Getty
Keller, Hannah Elizabeth 227
Keller, Ida 227
Kelly, Emma L. 171
Kerola, Greg 312
Kessel, Jeff 312
Kidder, Mr. 195
Kilpatrick, William D. 168
Kindsten, Al 246
Kindsvater, Dick 312
King & Company 192, 202, 219-221, 223, 298, 319
King, Hiram T. 219, 319
King, James M. 219, 243-245, 306, 313
King, W. D. 219
Kirby Barnum Hotel 92, 95
Kirkby, Melvon 197, 266
Kirkby's Sweet Shop 197
Kis-se-me-pa and Ka-go-ka 2
Knipps, L. 232

Knutsen, Oscar R. 330
Koch, Bill 302
Koenkamp, Del 312
Kohler, Al 204
Kohler, Aloys 203, 204
Kohler Building 191
Kohler, Clifford 204
Kohler Dairy 203
Kohler, Donald 204
Kohler, Henry 203, 204, 287
Kohler Ice Cream Mix Incorporated 204, 205, 287
Kohler, Reinhard 205
Kohler, Walter 204
Kohler's Romance Parlors 203, 204, 213
Koop, Father 160
Kosman Chevrolet Company 303
Kosman, Lou 303
Kramer, Mrs. 353
Krueger, Greg 312
Krueger's Fitness Center 354
KSTP Radio 148
Kuckler 270
Kuester, Mrs. Ebba (Nelson) 333
Kuhn, Louis 198
Kulkey, E. 183

L

L. P. Ordway (side wheeler) 116
LaBelle, Harry 217
LaBore, Frank 240
LaBore, Frank J. 310
LaBore, James 329
LaCroix Cafe 271
Lafond, Helen 158
Lake Avenue 9, 12, 13, 37, 40, 60, 84, 95, 196, 256, 286, 307, 322, 329, 330, 358, 360
Lake Breeze 206, 208, 219, 243, 298. See also *White Bear Life; White Bear Press*
Lake Country Booksellers 268
Lake Park Depot. *See* Lake Shore Depot
Lake Shore 74, 106, 116, 132
Lake Shore Bowling Alleys 62
Lake Shore Depot 24, 74, 80, 109, 110, 112, 132
Lake Shore Hotel 27. See also Leip House
Lake Shore Inn 54, 55
Lake Shore Sanitarium 53. *See also* White Bear Hospital and Sanatorium
Lake Superior and Mississippi Railroad (LS&MRR) 71-73, 295
Lake Theater 172
Laken, J. C. 209
Lakeshore 245
Lakeshore Players 160, 167, 333, 334
Lakeside Cottage 40
Lakeview Inn 28. *See also* Leip House
Lakewood Park Villa and Inn 28, 62. *See also* Leip House
Lakewood State Junior College 179

Lamb, John 23
Lambert, Joe 217
Lamb's Hotel 23
Lamdeat, J. 232
LaMotte, Constance 239
LaMotte, Ella 251
LaRoche, Frances 345
LaRose Payette Beauty Parlor 201
Larson, William A. 208
Latchaw, Truly 334
Laub, William 217
Laughing Gallery 128
Laventiers, Archie 209
Lawrence, Steve 312
Lawton, A. M. 118
Leaman, Abel E. 39, 101, 119, 313
Leaman, Dean 101
LeClair, N. W. 254
Leiner, Rudy 356
Leip, Agnes 28, 154
Leip House 5, 23, 24, 26, 28, 139
Leip, William 11, 23, 25, 28, 62, 323
Leip's Park 323
Leisure Time Labor Program 319
LeMay, George 209
LeMire, Adolph J. 304
LeMire, Archie 190, 191, 277
Lemon Building 189
Lemon, George H. 187, 188, 208, 229
Lemon Hardware 187, 188, 229, 241
Lenhart and Hanke's 270
Lenhart and McGill's 270
Lenhart, Fred 257, 270, 271
Lenhart's Bar 270
Leninger, Louis 216
Lennon 327
LeRoux, Louie 209
LeRue, Arch L. 229
Letourneau, Bernard 202
LeVasseur, Helen 185
LeVasseur, Lawrence 239-241
LeVasseur, Prosper J. 189, 234, 235, 237-239, 241, 263, 284, 310
LeVasseur, Rose (Schuhr) 37, 239
LeVasseur, William (Bill) 241
LeVasseur's Grocery 238-241
Levine and Swanson 37
Levine, Mrs. Julius 37
Lew's Cafe 216
Lillestol, Harvey 264
Lincoln Avenue 103, 106, 186
Lincoln Township's Town Hall and Garage 355
Lincolntown Community Clubhouse 354, 355
Lincolntown High School 347, 353
Lincolntown Library 346
Lincolntown Mercantile Company 221
Lincolntown Service Building. *See* Brandhorst Building
Linder, Tim 312

373

Lindgren (Frank E.) Company 208
Lindgren, Ella 193
Lindgren, Frank E. 208
Lindquist, E. J. 208
Lions Club 249
Lions Park 145, 150
Litman, Aaron M. 301
Little Bear Cafe 289
Little Canada 1, 72, 160
Loberg, Jerry 312
Loberg, Leslie 312
Lock, B. 232
Log Schoolhouse 151, 153, 157, 160, 171, 172, 174
Lonergan, Frank 171
Lonergan, J. 232
Lonergan, James 296, 313
Long & Smith Grocery 221
Long, A. 311, 326
Long and Alford's Feed Store 289
Long, Art 196
Long, Arthur 221
Long, Arthur R. 201, 217
Long Avenue 339
Long, C. Perry 50
Long, Clifford 81
Long, D. 325
Long, Edward 157
Long, Edwin 269
Long, Elmer 310
Long, Ernestine 157
Long, F. 232
Long, Gladys 246
Long, Henry 335, 336
Long, J. 232
Long, Jacob 157
Long, John 296
Long, Mary 157
Long, Mrs. I. E. 158
Long, Philando 296, 306
Long, R. 183, 232
Long, Russel 323
Long, Stella 314, 326
Long's Grocery 199, 201, 221-223
Long's Hamburger Shop 269
Long's Ice Company 335, 336
Loomis, Brian 312
Lowry, Tom 122
Luedke, William J. 310
Luenberg, R. H. 298
Lund, George 311
Lundgren, John C. 217
Lundy, Mrs. William 198
Luzerke, O. 232

M

Mabel's Eat Shop 289
MacDougal, R. 183
Macey, Corine 226
Macey, John 198
Macey, Joseph 199
Macey, Margaret 226
Machus, Mike 312
Mackay, John F. 176
Mackenhausen Building 188, 200, 209
Mackenhausen, Gladys St. Sauver 197
Mackenhausen Hardware 199
Mackenhausen, John 156
Mackenhausen Jr, Matt 287
Mackenhausen, M. J. 283, 305
Mackenhausen Sr., M. J. 208
Magnuson, Carl 81
Mahtomedi 74, 109, 245, 343, 344, 354
Mahtomedi Avenue 345, 348-355
Mahtomedi Depot 75, 79
Mahtomedi Dist. Educ. Cntr & Dist. Office ISD 832 345, 347
Mahtomedi Fire Department 131, 354
Mahtomedi High School 333
Mahtomedi Hotel 341, 342
Mahtomedi School 345-349
Mahtomedi Store 200
Mahtomedi Union Chapel 349
Mailloux, E. 246
Malt Shoppe 191, 213
Manitoba 109, 112, 116, 133
Manitou Island 1, 4-7, 15-22, 69, 106, 245, 264, 331
Manitou Island Association 15
Manitou Island Association Clubhouse 18
Manitou Island Land and Improvement Company. *See* Manitou Island Association
Mannheimer, Robert 51
Manship, Paul 337
Maple Street 346, 353
Margaux Limitee Restaurant building 214
Marguerite Therrin's Beauty Parlor 233
Marier, J. 183
Markeson & Sons People's Market 194
Markeson, L. A. 194, 291
Markoe, Lorenzo J. 234, 243, 244, 245
Markoe, Stewart 326, 327
Markoe, William 9-12, 160
Markoe, William F. 10, 13, 25, 38, 39
Marrier, A. J. 304
Marrier's Shell Filling Station 304
Marsh, Louis J. 252
Martin Building 222
Martin, Robert 222
Martineau, Earl 275
Martinson, Martha Yablonski 310
Masonic Temple 169, 204, 287
Matlinsky, Julius 270
Matoska Park 320, 321, 322
Mattimore, Mary 69
Mattlin, Carl J. 99, 212, 271, 273, 274, 279, 308

Mattlin, Carroll 266, 273, 274
Mattlin, Carroll & Ruth C. 44, 45
Mattlin, Harold 156
Mattlin, Harold & Mary 45
Mattlin, J. 183
Mattlin's Appliance City 274
Maud 118, 133
May 118, 133
May B 85
May, J. 232
Mayer, George 194
McCarthy, James 312
McClanahan M.D., J. H 229
McConnel, Alice 191
McCulloch, John & Tina 69
McCurdy, William 19
McDonalds 76
McElwain, Bishop 156
McElwain, Rt. Rev. Frank A. 156
McGill, Earl B. 270
McGrath, Jack 232, 306
McGrath Saloon and Boarding House 188
McKusick, Jonathan E. 15
McLaren, Gen. 72
McLaren, Robert N. 16
McMichael and Ellis 39
McMillan, S. J. R. 18
McNair, Zimmerman and Hobe 32
McNeely, Donald and Marjorie 19
Medicine Chest 265, 267
Mel and his Harmony Bears 147, 256
Melges Boat Works 106
Melhorn, Al 327
Melhorn, Clarence 327
Melhorn, F. D. 81
Mendelshon, Mr. 145
Mendenhall, T. J. 103
Mercantile Block 230. *See also* Getty Block
Mercantile Company Barn 301, 302
Mercantile Grocery Company 233, 239, 339
Merches, H. 183
Merriam, John L. 16
Merriam, Mrs. William R. 155
Merriam, William R. 16, 307
Mesabi Big Boy 81
Methodist Church (Mahtomedi) 349
Methodist Episcopal Church 168, 301, 303, 307
Michaud, Denis 326
Michaud, J. O. 355
Mid-Winter Fair 319
Milette, Earl 310
Millard, D. W. 51, 175
Miller Avenue 73, 177, 231, 273-275, 308, 311, 312
Miller, Elgin 256
Miller, Fred 345
Miller, Grace 44
Miller, Joe 224
Miller, Joseph 194

Miller, Mahlon D. 44, 169, 337
Miller, Mrs. Mahlon D. 47
Miller, Ross R. 300
Miller, Ruth 171
Miller, Walker G. 300
Miller's (Joe) Sample Room and Boarding House 224
Milner and Henkel Meat Market 215
Milner, Ike 323
Milner, Stan 306
Milner, Thomas 299
Milner's Meat Market 295, 299
Minneapolis, St. Paul & Sault Sainte Marie ("Soo") 75
Minnehaha Cleaners 266
Minnesota Eye, Ear, Nose and Throat Hospital 53.
    See also White Bear Hospital and Sanatorium
Minnesota Historical Society 12, 13
Minnesota Mining & Manufacturing Company (3M) 87
Minnesota National Guard 249, 250
Minnetonka and White Bear Navigation Company 132
Minnezitka 106
Miss Amy's Nursery School 67
Model Laundry 277
Moffat, Lott 71
Molitor, Henry 273
Montpetit, Mary 266
Moore, Joe 273
Moore, Ross 204
Moorhead Avenue 307
Morissey, J. 183
Morrissey, Mrs. 168
Mound Cottage 9, 160
Munns, Paul 312
Murray, Amelia 157
Murray Avenue 153, 171, 172, 177, 231, 254
Murray, Charlotte 237
Murray, Doctor Jim 174
Murray, Frederick H. 195, 196, 287
Murray House 5, 29. *See also* Williams' House
Murray, James 157
Murray, James C. 29, 72, 153, 196, 237, 243, 296
Murray, James F. 15, 29, 152, 171
Murray, John Bryson 29
Murray, Miss Lottie (Charlotte) 173
Murray, Reverend Bill 167
Murray, T. B. 243
Murray, William P. 72
Myers, Mrs. John L. (Emily T.) 353
Myers, U. S. 162

N

Naphtha Launch 115, 119
Nash, Frank 148
Nash Jr., Louis 156
Nash, Percy 81, 233
National Food Store 213
National Tea Company 241
Natural disasters 357

Naugawese 3
Navis, Henry 216
Nellie 101
Nelson, Miles 310
Nelson, Oscar 234
Nelson, Terell 312
Nemeth, Bob 356
Neptune Avenue 345
New Pershing Inn 145
Newport, Reece M. 15, 16
Newson, T. M. 29, 33, 37
Nickel, C. G. 263
Nickel's Drug Store 263
Nickolaus, F. 183
Ninth Street 287
Northeast Residence 186
Northern Pacific Railroad (NPRR) 45, 54, 73, 77-81, 244, 246, 278, 322, 343
Northern States Power Company (NSP) 264, 265, 311
Northwestern Bell Phone Company 231
Northwestern Telephone Exchange 231
Northwestern Union Packet Company 5
Noyes, Charles P. 16, 18, 65
Nushka 91

O

Oak Avenue 350
Oakleigh Station 348
O'Brien, Christopher. D. 41, 91, 95
Odd Fellows 251, 301
Odd Fellows Building 221
O'Doherty, Joe 330
O'Gorman, W. 183
O'Halloran, John 327
Old Betts 9
O'Leary, Mrs. I. 55
Olson, Charles 331
Olson, Edna 235
Olson, Erica 312
Olson, Rod 266
One-legged Jim 9
Ordway, Lucius P. 87, 88, 91, 95, 98
Oregon Yacht Club 103
Oriental Hotel 39. *See also* Hotel Chateaugay
Otto J. Troseth Groceries 206

P

Palmer, Ada 314
Palmer, James R. 225, 271, 274
Palmer, Judge 18
Palmer, Les H. 310, 327
Parcells, Arthur L. 156, 269
Parcells Brothers Hardware 269
Parcells' Building 270
Parcells, Mrs. Wesley 158
Parcells, Wesley 158, 183, 269

Parenteau, Arthur 190
Parenteau, Desire 240
Parenteau, Dick 262
Parenteau, M. H. (Mitch) 190, 261-263, 267
Parenteau, Mike 262, 266
Parenteau's Clothing 190, 262, 268
Parenteau's Grocery 117
Park Avenue 44, 169, 339
Park Pavilion 109
Park Place Hotel 36, 205
Park Sweet Shop 197-199, 201, 202, 214, 266
Parker, Lyle 306
Parker, Mrs. Emma Guipe 158
Parker, Mrs. F. D. 158
Pathway Health Services 277
Paton, Mr. and Mrs. W. B. 32
Patterson, Edward Z. 296
Paul, Sir Aubrey John 151. *See also* John Aubrey
Paul, Sir John Dean 151
Paulsen, John 312
Pautenberg, S. 183
Peifer, Jack 148
Peltier, Dorathea 158
Peltier, Doug 312
Peltier, Ed 304
Peltier, J. 232
Peltier, Joe E. 217
Peltier, Louis 310
Peltier, Octave 81
Peltier, Paul 312
Peltier, T. 183
Peninsula 62
Peninsula Station 80
People's Ice Company 335, 336
People's Market 194, 213, 291
People's Meat Market 194
Perkins, Albert H. S. 219, 243, 298
Perkins, Arthur A. 237, 238
Perrault, Frank 355
Perrault, J. P. 239
Perron's Tin Shop 212
Perry, Charles 296
Peters, Mr. Robert A. 333
Peterson, A. 325
Peterson, Bob 312
Peterson, Harry M. 222
Peterson, J. S. 194
Peterson Jewelry 222
Peterson, Laurie 334
Peterson, Nicolas 106
Peterson, Thomas 115
Philadelphia Toboggan Company 137
Picard, Delphis 236
Picard's Feed Store 236
Piccadilly 356
Pickle Club 113
Pierce, Harry R. 190
Pippin 130

Plantation 145-150
Plantation Boat Livery & Drive-In 150
Plantation Playhouse 149
Podvin, A. C. 81, 255, 256, 304
Pogoant, J. 232
Police Car – Ambulance 311
Polly's Kettle 353
Pollywog 66. *See* Fillebrown House
Pondesul, Henry 234
Portland Avenue 186
Post Office 206, 208, 228, 233, 243-248, 318, 325
Post Office (Mahtomedi) 351
Postal Photo Gallery Factory 128
Potratz, Ada 355
Premier Bank 248
Price, Charles 156
Price, Col. W. W. 94
Price Field 183
Price, Marian 156
Price, Sterling 156
Priebe, Ed 116
Priebe's Boat Livery 83

Q

Quail School 344, 345
Quail Street 341, 351
Quinn, A. E. 298
Quinn, Jack 205
Quirk of Fate 223, 292
Quirk, Pat and Dorothy 292

R

Railroad Avenue 36, 41, 74, 187-214, 219, 221, 236, 243, 291, 298, 303. *See also* Washington Avenue
Railroad Park 13, 187, 202, 234, 295, 313, 317, 319. *See also* Washington Park
Ralph's Super Market 355
Ramaley, John D. 110, 114
Ramaley Bay 91
Ramaley Boat Company 102, 132. *See also* Ramaley's Boat Works
Ramaley Home 259
Ramaley, J. E. (Gene) 51, 52, 101, 102, 145, 149
Ramaley, John D. 109, 112, 115, 132, 145, 175
Ramaley's Boat Works 115, 145
Ramaley's Pavilion 74, 94, 95, 109-115, 145
Ramaley's White Bear Navigation Company 112
Ramaley's Winter Garden 54, 102, 145, 146
Ramsey, Alexander 72
Ramsey and Associates 352
Ramsey County Agricultural Society 196
Ramsey County Fair 326, 357
Rasch, Jon 312
Ratler, W. 270
Rattner, Mr. 292
Rausch, Jeanenne 312
Rautenberg, R. 183

Red Chalet 65. *See* Fillebrown House
Reed, Harold 211
Reed, Jack 211
Reed, Jacob A. 81, 211, 303
Reed Oil Company 211, 212
Rehbine, William 209
Reibel, Frank 185
Reibel, John 296
Reibel, Rose 216
Reif & Bunghard 37
Reif and Clewett Meat Market 187, 192-194, 214
Reif Brothers Meat Market 192, 215
Reif, Carl 197
Reif, Charles 37, 192, 215
Reif, Frank J. 192, 195, 306
Reif, George 231
Reif, Louis M. 193
Reif, Williams, F. 232
Reihldaffer, Reverend J. G. 157
Resthaven 143, 302
Revering, Ricky 312
Richards, Captain Vic. 24
Rippel, D. 183
Rippel, Kenneth 158
Robert, Father 162
Robertson, B. 183
Robinson, Harold 314
Robinson, John 334
Robinson, Reverend J. C. 158
Roger Vadnais Plumbing 162
Rogers, Charles S. 18
Rogers, P. 325
Rogowski, Joe 49
Rogowski Tavern and Boats 49. *See also* Hotel Benson, Bald Eagle Lake
Rohlfing, Louis 350
Rohrbeck, Harvey 355
Rohrbeck, Ralph 355
Roisner, Morris 148
Rolling, Ray 353
Rooney, Buck 328
Rooney, Don 328
Rooney, Terry 328
Rose Cafe 216
Rose Street 349
Rose, William E. 310, 311
Ross, Duncan 5, 151, 152
Ross, Elaine and Bill 289
Ross, S. 183
Rotary snow plow 106
Roundhouse 73, 79, 80
Ruby 118
Rungey, Jim 328
Rural Works Administration 319
Rust, Bill 320
Ryan Hotel 139

377

S

Sabin, Dwight M. 16
Sailors' Pavilion 92, 100. *See also* White Bear Yacht Club
Samuelson, Bob 328
Sanborn, General J. B. 307
Sandahl, A. 246
Sandahl, William 310
Sanders, Captain 18
Sanford and Shaffer R. C. U. Store 241
Sax, Mr. and Mrs. Herman 260
Sax's White Bear Bakery 260
Schaefer, F. W. 217
Schaefer's Ice Cream Parlor 217
Schafer, B. J. 208
Schauls, Adam 312
Schauls, Derek 312
Schifsky, Raymond 345
Schletty, Bob 263
Schmalzbaurer, Benny 191
Schmidt, Carl A. 268, 269
Schmidt, Emil 37
Schnorr Dairy 203
Schoch (Andrew) and Company 229
Schoch, Andrew 229
School. *See* specific school name
School District #26 186
School District #69 344
Schreiner, Vera and Dean 204
Schuhr, Billie 234
Schuhr, Hattie 339
Schuhr, Martin (Mottie) 234, 339
Schuhr, William & Margaret 37
Schultz, Henry E. 217
Schweitzer, Albert 327
Schweitzer, Ted L. 67, 233
Sears 304
Second Base Tavern 353
Second Street
    37, 73, 82, 153, 157, 160, 168, 172, 184, 202, 274, 305, 308, 311, 312, 315, 316
Sellner Manufacturing Company 128
Senarighi, Adam 312
Sentry Systems 268
Seventh Street 60, 165, 302
Sew What! 291
Shady Lane 9, 286
Shapler, F. L. 229
Shea, Joe 217
Shea, Pat 327
Shearen, Bob 328
Shingle Shanty 270
Shirley, P. D. 81
Shutt, Rev. C. Herbert 155
Sickler, De Wayne 183
Silloway, Mrs. Ga. A. 158
Simms, Mr. P. H. 188
Sister Mary Thomas 184

Sisters of St. Joseph 184, 186
Sixth Street 40, 69, 82, 166, 167, 188, 333
Skally Line (Short Line).
    See Northern Pacific Railroad (NPRR)
Skillman, D. F. 350
Slone, Sam 226
Smith, C. E. 48
Smith Chevrolet 50, 302
Smith, Cleo 50, 221, 303
Smith, Cleo C. 81
Smith, Cleo G. 158
Smith, Florence (Vadnais) 310
Smith, John 117
Smith Jr, James 72
Smith, Mrs. C. G. 158
Smith, Sewall C. 252, 253, 297
Smith's Bald Eagle Air Dome. *See* Bald Eagle Hotel
Soldiers' Monument 296
Soldiers' Monument Association 296, 315
Solheim 338
Solomon, Maevis 312
Sorenson, Mr. and Mrs. Loyd C. 355
Soule, E. F. 229
Soule's Barbershop 229
South Shore House 5, 32-35, 51, 158
Spark's Beauty Shop 267
Spark's Dress Shop 267
Spink, John H. 39, 229-231
Spink, Ned 351
Spink, William E. 351
Spink's Grocery 351, 352
Spirit Island. *See* Manitou Island
Sportsmen's Bar 270
Spring Park Villa 44-47, 169
St. Andrew's English Lutheran Church 346, 348, 349
St. Croix Lumber Company 319
St. John in the Wilderness Church 5, 151, 153-157, 206, 287, 295
St. Mary of the Lake Church 79, 161-164, 184
St. Mary of the Lake Parish Center and School 186
St. Mary of the Lake Parish House 162, 163
St. Mary's School 172, 184, 185, 286
St. Paul 116
St. Paul and Duluth Railroad (St. P & D Ry.) 36, 73-77, 109, 205
St. Paul Athletic Club 61
St. Paul Automobile Club 28, 85, 139-144, 156, 196, 316, 358
St. Paul Automobile Clubhouse 144
St. Paul Dispatch & Pioneer Press 329
St. Paul Elizabethan Drama Club 98
St. Paul Ice Company 336
St. Paul Winter Carnival 329
Staehle, C. W. 74
Staig, Alfred 296
Stancui, Stephen 190
Stanek, Joe 356
Stanek, Tom and Winnie 356

Stanke, Elmer 327
Starkey, Mr. 40
Steamboat. *See* specific name of boat
Steigleder, E. P. 289
Steigleder Feed Store 288
Steinhardt, Robert "Frisco Dutch" 148
Stem, Allen H. 95, 98
Sterner, Dr. E. R. 39
Stevens, Mary 50
Stewart Avenue 37, 41, 158, 165-167, 169, 175, 277, 287, 333
Stewart, Dr. J. H. 72, 157
Stickley, Armand 300
Stickley, Doris 300
Stickley, Helen 300
Stickley, Helen Johnston 3, 13
Stickley, W. A. 81
Stickley, Warren A. 166, 300
Stiles, (Samuel) William 154
Stillwater Headquarters 198
Stillwater Road 347, 349
Stockyards 281
Stoddart, H. 325
Stough, Abigail 178
Stout, Will 340
Stratton, Owen 15
Streetar, Rev. H. S. 155
Streetcar 82, 83, 121, 122, 347, 357
Strom, C. 232
Sullwold, H. A. 140
Sun Bear Spa and Tan 292
Sundt, Dick 265
Sunset Bowling Center 212, 274
Swanson, Frank 310, 311
Swanson's (Jim) Liquor Store 190
Swedish Evangelical Lutheran Church 166
Sweeney, William W. 15
Swenson, Dr. E. W. 233

T

Taft, William Howard 343
Tamillo, Joe 333
Tarte, Lucy 314, 316
Taylor, Albert (Hammer) 173
Taylor, Alton 193, 194
Taylor, Col. 72
Taylor, Frank 311
Taylor, John W. 91
Taylor, Joseph 296
Taylor, Kate C. 171
Taylor, Maria 286
Taylor, Minnie 62
Taylor, Norman 194, 302
Taylor, Oscar 19, 232
Tegland, Vernon S. 301
Tell Construction Company 347
Temple, Rev. William 156

Tenth Street 76, 277, 322
Tenth Street Station 76, 80
Texaco Station 202. *See also* Vadnais Mobil Station
Thauwald, Gordon 260
Thauwald, Louis A. 81, 260
Thauwald's Bakery 267
Thayer, Mrs. Carl T. 3
The Dells 355
The Gathering 223
The Mane Tease 210
The Nest 214
The Wave 298
Thein, Delia 204
Thein, Elizabeth 185
Thelen, Todd 312
Therrin, Marguerite 233
Thiede, Fred and Helen 270
Third Street
    41, 77, 80, 84, 158, 163, 168, 169, 171, 177, 187, 188, 195, 197, 201, 215-226, 228-241, 243, 246, 247, 252, 261, 263, 266, 269, 279, 291, 292, 298, 299, 313, 319, 325
Third Street Bus Depot 84
Thomas, S. H. 337
Tilt-a-Whirl 128
Todd, Captain H. F. 103
Tombler, O. M. 232
Torinus Fountain 319
Torinus, George E. 206, 232, 319
Torinus, Helen M. 319
Torinus, Louis E. 319
Torinus, Ruth 155
Tousley Ford 256, 304
Tousley, Herb 256, 304
Tracy, Jack 174
Trealease, John M. 39
Tri-State Telephone Exchange 231
Trunnell, Floyd 246
Turnbull, Mike 312
Twain, Mark 1
Twin Cities 116
Twin City Lines 82
Twin City Motor Bus Company 84
Twin City Rapid Transit Company 84, 121, 122, 132

U

Underlighter 232
Union Cemetery 13, 152
Union Meat Market 192
Union Sunday School 152
Unitarian Church 349
Uppgren, Dave 263
Uppgren, R. M. 233
Uppgren's Hardware 233, 263
Uptown Images 234
Ursula's Wine Bar and Cafe 271
US Bank 160, 202

V

Vadnais, Adlore J. 274, 277-281, 284
Vadnais, Charles 279, 280, 281
Vadnais, George 185, 202, 203, 279, 280, 281
Vadnais, Gordon 279
Vadnais, Jack 279, 280, 328, 330
Vadnais, Margaret 185
Vadnais Mobil Station 213. *See also* Texaco Station
Vadnais, Mrs. Ellen 279
Vadnais, Paul 275
Vadnais, Richard 279, 280
Vadnais, Robert W. 185, 275, 277
Vadnais, Roger 275
Vadnais, Tim 312
Vadnais, William 174, 274, 275
Vail, David & Joanna 69
Vail, Garrett & Renee 69
Van Avery, Charley 323
Van Avery, Louis 192, 194
Van Ingen, Reverend 153
Van Kirk, C. E. 156, 196
VanGilder, Mr. and Mrs. John 204
VanVoorhis, H. 183
VanVoorhis, Marion 185
Velin, Bob 263
Velin's Super Value Food Market 263
Veterans Memorial Park 114
VFW 115, 116
Victorine 91
Vierig, H. 39
Vincent (Quail) Street 344
Vincent, William W. 258, 259
Vincent's Grocery 255, 258-260, 269, 288
Virginia 103
Vogel's Coffee Shop 190
Voges, Dick 327
Voges, Dr. Adolph E. 53, 219
VonVories, Buddy 345
Voss, Chris 312

W

Wagner, Dave 355
Wagner, Richard & Clara 69
Wahbe Maquah 39. *See also* Hotel Chateaugay
Wahlund, Reverend Gus 166
Wallerick, Ann 135, 136, 137
Wallerick, Frank 137
Wallerick, Frank & Ann 131, 134
Wallin, Al 310
Walter Butler Company 185
Warner, Beth 155
Warner, E. P. 346
Warner, Ellen P. 69
Warner, H. A. 81, 188, 239
Warner, Henry 69
Warner, May 345

Warner, Mr. Allyn 188
Warner, Pearl 345
Warner Sr., Mrs. H. A. 155
Warren, E. A. 169
Washington Avenue
    77, 188, 190, 191, 201, 202, 212, 241, 263,
    279, 289. *See also* Railroad Avenue
Washington, Marshall 241, 252
Washington Park 202, 213, 246, 317, 320.
    See also Railroad Park
Washington Park Bandstand 318, 319
Washington Park Flagpole 320
Washington School 173, 177-179, 181, 290
Washington Square 179
Washington Square Bar and Grill 214
Washington's Antique Shop 252, 257
Water Toboggan Slide 124, 125
Waterlily 223
Waters, James 36, 323
Wayside Cafe 216
Webb, Mr. 156
Webb, Mrs. 156
Webber, Leonard 209
Webber, William 116, 152
Webster Elementary School 176
Webster School 165, 175, 176, 181, 290, 327
Wehr, Nick E. 28
Weidenbouer 327
Weinand, Joseph H. 225
Welch, Dr. 58, 59, 60, 91, 94
Wells, Billy 287
Wentworth, Dorothy 156
Wenzel, Jeff 312
West, Mr. and Mrs. William 322
West Park 322
West Side Cement Block Company 271
West Side Grocery 200
West Side Ice Company 336
West Side School 157, 165, 172, 173, 176, 184
Weyerhaeuser, Fredrick E. 19
Wheelock, Joseph A. 16, 18
Whitaker Block. *See* Hardy Block
Whitaker, Francis 13, 177
Whitaker, Frederick E. 173, 174, 234, 235, 314
Whitaker, Robert 296
Whitaker Sr., Frederick E. 24
White Bear 112, 115, 116, 132, 133
White Bear Appliance Shop 213, 291
White Bear Association 79, 80, 81, 196, 319
White Bear Auto Livery 253, 256
White Bear Bakery 260
White Bear Bar 271
White Bear Baseball Club 323
White Bear Battery and Tire Station 302
White Bear Beach 74, 84, 118, 186, 245
White Bear Beach Station 80
White Bear Boat Works 108
White Bear Body Shop 257, 258

White Bear Bowling Alleys 189
White Bear Cafe 199
White Bear Candy Company 229
White Bear Castle 147, 189, 256
White Bear Center for the Arts 249
White Bear Cinema 266
White Bear Depot 36, 71, 74, 76, 77, 79, 80, 82, 297
White Bear Drug 202, 203, 213, 214, 219, 358
White Bear Electric Company 76, 229, 264
White Bear Elevator Company 196
White Bear Feed and Seed 289
White Bear Fire Department.
    See White Bear Volunteer Fire Department
White Bear Flyers 328
White Bear Frigid Lockers 252
White Bear Furniture Exchange 241
White Bear Hardware 217
White Bear High School 141, 147, 177, 180-184, 333, 334, 335
White Bear Hospital and Sanatorium 52, 53
White Bear Hotel 50, 303
White Bear House 36, 37, 187, 188, 190, 191, 323
White Bear Ice Company 212, 302, 336
White Bear Implement Company 208
White Bear Knitting Mills 251, 288
White Bear Lake Area Historical Society 68, 82
White Bear Lake Boat Yard 103
White Bear Lake City Offices 308
White Bear Lake Government Center 312
White Bear Lake Historical Society 300
White Bear Lake Women's Club 316, 321
White Bear Laundry 277
White Bear Life 298-300.
    See also White Bear Press: Lake Breeze
White Bear Lumber 283, 285, 288, 309
White Bear Marine 103
White Bear Mercantile 103, 229, 230, 301
White Bear Miniature Golf Course 267
White Bear Motor Sales 147, 255-257, 260, 288, 304
White Bear Oil Company 202, 277-281, 291.
    See also Vadnais Mobil Station
White Bear Press 233, 299-301.
    See also Lake Breeze: White Bear Life
White Bear Public Library 313, 314.
    See also Carnegie Library
White Bear Reading Room Association 313
White Bear Rod & Gun Club 329, 330
White Bear School Band 183, 300, 318
White Bear Shopping Center 74, 82, 144
White Bear Stables 143
White Bear State Bank 192, 195, 196, 219.
    See also First National Bank
White Bear Steam Laundry Company 287, 288
White Bear Taxi Company 84
White Bear Theatre 223, 266, 292, 358
White Bear Variety Store 233, 263, 267
White Bear Volunteer Fire Department
    18, 27, 28, 39, 99, 118, 131, 277, 285, 305-311

White Bear Wine & Liquor 222
White Bear Yacht Club 38, 41, 58, 85, 91, 94-100, 106, 148, 274. *See also* White Bear Yachting Association
White Bear Yacht Club Clubhouse 95, 98-100
White Bear Yachting Association 91-94, 101.
    See also White Bear Yacht Club
White Front Saloon 224, 225
White, Reverend Samuel 168
Whitney, Joel 15
Whitrock, Charles and Agnes 343, 344
Whitrock, Thomas and Leona 343
Wiberg 51
Wickersham, Mr. R. H. 233
Wickland, Chris 312
Wietecki, Mark 312
Wilder, Amherst H. 16
Wildwood 82, 84, 91, 245. *See also* Wildwood Park
Wildwood (steamboat) 112, 116, 132, 133
Wildwood Manor 245
Wildwood Park 115, 121-138, 323, 343, 356
Wildwood Park Bathhouse 124, 125, 131, 138
Wildwood Park Boat House 126
Wildwood Park Pavilion 124, 127, 138
Wildwood Park Picnic Pavilion 132
Wildwood Road 352
Wilkinson, Albert & Rosalie E. 69
Wilkinson's Cottage 69, 70
Willernie 245
William Bull Photo Gallery 229
Williams' Drug Store 263, 264
Williams, E. C. 29, 155
Williams, Harry 263
Williams' House 29-32, 37, 39, 101
Williams, J. Fletcher 12
Williams, Mrs. E. C. 30, 154, 155
Wilson, Edward L. 5, 6
Wilson, Mrs. Edward L. 6, 7
Wilzbacher, Allie 345
Wilzbacher, George 345
Wilzbroker, A. 325
Winship, Judge 306
Winter, Reverend A. F. 165
Woerz, Mr. H. R. 354
Wood, O. 183
Works Project Administration 247
Worthen, Kenneth B. 265
WTCN Radio 149
Wuollet's Bakery 268

Y

Y.M.C.A. 156, 250, 314. *See also* Auditorium
Yager, John 296
Ye Antique Shoppe 241. *See also* Washington's Antique Shop
Yoerg Brewing Company 270
Yost, Jack 81
Young, Captain 118
Young, Judge George 65, 66

Youth Resource Bureau 264

Z

Zimmerman, A. R. 353
Zion Evangelical Lutheran Church 164, 165, 286
Zwerenz, Clarence J. 81, 192, 202, 203, 219
Zwolenski, A. P. 269